EARLY MUSIC HISTORY 12

EDITORIAL BOARD

EARLY MUSIC HISTORY 12

STUDIES IN MEDIEVAL
AND
EARLY MODERN MUSIC

Edited by

IAIN FENLON
Fellow of King's College, Cambridge

CAMBRIDGE
UNIVERSITY PRESS

Published by the Press Syndicate of the University of Cambridge
The Pitt Building, Trumpington Street, Cambridge CB2 1RP
40 West 20th Street, New York, NY 10011–4211, USA
10 Stamford Road, Oakleigh, Melbourne 3166, Australia

First published 1993

Phototypeset in Baskerville by Wyvern Typesetting Ltd, Bristol
Printed in Great Britain at the University Press, Cambridge

ISSN 0261–1279

ISBN 0 521 45180 9

SUBSCRIPTIONS The subscription price (excluding VAT) of volume 12, which includes postage, is £45.00 (US $85.00 in USA and Canada) for institutions, £29.00 (US $49.00 in USA and Canada) for individuals ordering direct from the Press and certifying that the annual is for their personal use. Airmail (orders to Cambridge only) £9.00 extra. Copies of the annual for subscribers in the USA and Canada are sent by air to New York to arrive with minimum delay. Orders, which must be accompanied by payment, may be sent to a bookseller, subscription agent or direct to the publishers: Cambridge University Press, The Edinburgh Building, Shaftesbury Road, Cambridge CB2 2RU. Payment may be made by any of the following methods: cheque (payable to Cambridge University Press), UK postal order, bank draft, Post Office Giro (account no. 571 6055 GB Bootle – advise CUP of payment), international money order, UNESCO coupons, or any credit card bearing the Interbank symbol. EC subscribers (outside the UK) who are not registered for VAT should add VAT at their country's rate. VAT registered subscribers should provide their VAT registration number. Japanese prices for institutions (including ASP delivery) are available from Kinokuniya Company Ltd, P.O. Box 55, Chitose, Tokyo. Orders from the USA and Canada should be sent to Cambridge University Press, 40 West 20th Street, New York, NY 10011–4211, USA.

BACK VOLUMES Volumes 1–11 are available from the publisher at £45.00 ($85.00 in USA and Canada).

NOTE Each volume of *Early Music History* is now published in the year in which it is subscribed. Volume 12 is therefore published in 1993. Readers should be aware, however, that some earlier volumes have been subscribed in the year *after* the copyright and publication date given on this imprints page. Thus volume 8, the volume received by 1989 subscribers, is dated 1988 on the imprints page.

CONTENTS

REVIEWS

NOTES FOR CONTRIBUTORS

PRESENTATION

Contributors should write in English, or be willing to have their articles translated. All typescripts must be double spaced *throughout*, including footnotes, bibliographies, annotated lists of manuscripts, appendixes, tables and displayed quotations. Margins should be at least 2.5 cm (1″). The 'top' (ribbon) copy of the typescript must be supplied. Scripts submitted for consideration will not normally be returned unless specifically requested.

Artwork for graphs, diagrams and music examples should be, wherever possible, submitted in a form suitable for direct reproduction, bearing in mind the maximum dimensions of the printed version: 17.5×11 cm ($7″ \times 4.5″$). Photographs should be in the form of glossy black and white prints, measuring about 20.3×15.2 cm ($8″ \times 6″$).

All illustrations should be on separate sheets from the text of the article and should be clearly identified with the contributor's name and the figure/example number. Their approximate position in the text should be indicated by a marginal note in the typescript. Captions should be separately typed, double spaced.

Tables should also be supplied on separate sheets, with the title typed above the body of the table.

SPELLING

English spelling, idiom and terminology should be used, e.g. bar (not measure), note (not tone), quaver (not eighth note). Where there is an option, '-ise' endings should be preferred to '-ize'.

PUNCTUATION

English punctuation practice should be followed: (1) single quotation marks, except for 'a "quote" within a quote'; (2) punctuation outside quotation marks, unless a complete sentence is quoted; (3) no comma before 'and' in a series; (4) footnote indicators follow punctuation; (5) square brackets [ ] only for interpolation in quoted matter; (6) no stop after contractions that include the last letter of a word, e.g. Dr, St, edn (but vol. and vols.).

BIBLIOGRAPHICAL REFERENCES

Authors' and editors' forenames should not be given, only initials; where possible, editors should be given for Festschriften, conference proceedings, symposia, etc. In titles, all important words in English should be capitalised; all other languages should follow prose-style capitalisation, except for journal and series titles which should follow English capitalisation. Titles of series should be included, in roman, where relevant. Journal and series volume numbers should be given in arabic, volumes of a set in roman ('vol.' will not be used). Places and dates of publication should be included but not publishers' names. Dissertation titles should be given in roman and enclosed in quotation marks. Page numbers should be preceded by 'p.' or 'pp.' in all contexts. The first citation of a bibliographical reference should include full details; subsequent citations may use the author's surname, short title and relevant page numbers only. *Ibid.* may be used, but not *op. cit.* or *loc. cit.*

ABBREVIATIONS

Abbreviations for manuscript citations, libraries, periodicals, series, etc. should not be used without explanation; after the first full citation an abbreviation may be used throughout text and notes. Standard abbreviations may be used without explanation. In the text, 'Example', 'Figure' and 'bars' should be used (not 'Ex.', 'Fig.', 'bb.'). In references to manuscripts, 'fols.' should be used (not 'ff.') and 'v' (verso) and 'r' (recto) should be typed superscript. The word for 'saint' should be spelled out or abbreviated according to language, e.g. San Andrea, S. Maria, SS. Pietro e Paolo, St Paul, St Agnes, St Denis, Ste Clothilde.

NOTE NAMES

Flats, sharps and naturals should be indicated by the conventional signs, not words. Note names should be roman and capitalised where general, e.g. C major, but should be italic and follow the Helmholtz code where specific ($C_{,,}$ C, $C\,c\,c'$ c'' c'''; c' = middle C). A simpler system may be used in discussions of repertories (e.g. chant) where different conventions are followed.

QUOTATIONS

A quotation of no more than 60 words of prose or one line of verse should be continuous within the text and enclosed in single quotation marks. Longer quotations should be displayed and quotation marks should not be used. For quotations from foreign languages, an English translation must be given in addition to the foreign-language original.

NUMBERS

Numbers below 100 should be spelled out, except page, bar, folio numbers etc., sums of money and specific quantities, e.g. 20 ducats, 45 mm. Pairs of numbers should be elided as follows: 190–1, 198–9, 198–201, 212–13. Dates should be given in the following forms: 10 January 1983, the 1980s, sixteenth century (16th century in tables and lists), sixteenth-century polyphony.

CAPITALISATION

Incipits in all language (motets, songs, etc.), and titles except in English, should be capitalised as in running prose; titles in English should have all important words capitalised, e.g. *The Pavin of Delight*. Most offices should have a lower-case initial except in official titles, e.g. 'the Lord Chancellor entered the cathedral', 'the Bishop of Salford entered the cathedral' (but 'the bishop entered the cathedral'). Names of institutions should have full (not prose-style) capitalisation, e.g. Liceo Musicale.

ITALICS

Titles and incipits of musical works in italic, but not genre titles or sections of the Mass/English Service, e.g. Kyrie, Magnificat. Italics for foreign words should be kept to a minimum; in general they should be used only for unusual words or if a word might be mistaken for English if not italicised. Titles of manuscripts should be roman in quotes, e.g. 'Rules How to Compose'. Names of institutions should be roman.

AUTHORS' CORRECTIONS

It is assumed that typescripts received for publication are in their final form. There may be an opportunity to make minor emendations at the copy-editing stage, but corrections in proof *must* be restricted to printer's and publisher's errors. Any departure from this practice will be at the discretion of the editor and the publisher, and authors may be subject to charge.

Early Music History (1993) Volume 12

CHARLES BURNETT

EUROPEAN KNOWLEDGE OF ARABIC TEXTS REFERRING TO MUSIC: SOME NEW MATERIAL*

The literature on the problem of Arabic influence on the music and poetry of western Europe in the Middle Ages is vast.[1] The aim of this article is modest. It seeks to draw together some passages on music and musical instruments in Arabic texts that were translated into Latin in the Middle Ages. These texts were not specifically on music, and may have escaped the notice of musicologists for that reason. However, they are interesting in their own right, for they show the role of music in other contexts, such as medicine, astrology and philosophy, and exemplify the modifications that took place when texts were transferred from one culture to another.

*The material in this article relevant to Sicily was first presented in a paper entitled 'Teoria e pratica musicali arabe in Sicilia e nell'Italia meridionale in età normanna e sveva' given in Erice, Sicily, in August 1989 and published in *Nuove Effemeridi*, 3 (1990), pp. 79–89. This article adds much new material and revises and updates the sections included in the Italian article. I am very grateful to Paolo Emilio Carapezza, Christopher Page, Johannes Thomann, Ruth Webb, Owen Wright and Fritz Zimmermann for helpful advice. Eckhard Neubauer has been especially kind in providing me with valuable bibliographical references and criticising an earlier draft of this article.
[1] For guides to this literature see E. R. Perkuhn, *Die Theorien zum arabischen Einfluss auf die europäische Musik des Mittelalters* (Walldorf-Hessen, 1976); Ali Yahya Mansoor, *Die arabische Theorie: Studien zur Entwicklungsgeschichte des abendländischen Minnesangs* (inaugural dissertation, Heidelberg, 1966); the articles in *Basler Jahrbuch für historische Musikpraxis*, 1 (1977); G. Schoeler, 'Die hispano-arabische Strophendichtung: Entstehung und Beziehung zur Troubadour-Lyrik', in *Actes du 8me congrès de l'Union européenne des arabisants et islamisants* (Aix-en-Provence, 1976), pp. 243–66; Eckhard Neubauer, 'Zur Rolle der Araber in der Musikgeschichte des europäischen Mittelalters', *Islam und Abendland*, ed. A. Mercier (Bern and Frankfurt, 1976), pp. 111–29; and Eckhard and Elsbeth Neubauer, 'Henry George Farmer on Oriental Music: an Annotated Bibliography', *Zeitschrift für Geschichte der arabisch-islamischen Wissenschaften*, 4 (1987–8), pp. 219–66. The most important papers of Farmer have been usefully collected together in H. G. Farmer, *Studies in Oriental Music*, ed. Eckhard Neubauer, Institut für Geschichte der arabisch-islamischen Wissenschaften, series B (Frankfurt, 1986).

I

The earliest of these texts are translations of Arabic works on medicine, made by Constantine the African (d. after 1087) who, having emigrated from 'Carthage' (i.e. Tunis) to Salerno, settled in the Benedictine monastery of Montecassino. Constantine translated the *Zād al-musāfir* or 'Provisions for the traveller' of Abū Jaʿfar ibn al-Jazzār (d. 979).[2] Ibn al-Jazzār was a doctor in Qairawān, not far from Tunis, and his work was translated into Greek soon after its composition, apparently by a doctor or scribe in Reggio Calabria also called Constantine.[3] The Latin translation, known as the *Viaticum*, was made directly from the Arabic, but Constantine scrupulously omits to mention both the Arabic author and the name of every Arabic authority cited in the text. The work includes at least two references to music in the context of music therapy:[4]

I. The first excerpt occurs within a series of chapters devoted to psychological illness:

Viaticum, I.16: De stupore mentis.

... Medicetur hec[1] infirmitas itidem ut litargia[2] sed tamen in litargia puppis,[3] in hoc vero[4] morbo prora curetur cerebri.[5] Si ex defeccione et dissolucione sit[6] virtutis, cum camomilla, viola,[7] rosa in aqua coctis[8] ungatur[9] prora capitis,[10] cum sandalis quoque et oleo rosarum et aqua rosarum.[11] Ante infirmum dulcis sonitus[12] fiat de[13] musicorum generibus, sicut campanula,[14] viola,[15] et similibus. His enim[16] anima delectatur[17] et ex delectatione excitatur[18] natura.

---

[2] See F. Sezgin, *Geschichte des arabischen Schrifttums*, III (Leiden, 1970), pp. 304–6, and M. Ullmann, *Die Medizin im Islam* (Leiden, 1970), pp. 147–8. See also W. F. Kümmel, *Musik und Medizin* (Munich, 1977), pp. 336–7.

[3] C. Daremberg, 'Recherches sur un ouvrage qui a pour titre *Zad el-mouçafir*, en arabe, *Éphodes*, en grec, et *Viatique*, en latin, et qui est attribué, dans les textes arabes et grecs, à Abou Djafar, et, dans le texte latin, à Constantin', *Archives des Missions Scientifiques et Littéraires, Choix des Rapports et Instructions*, 2 (1851), pp. 490–527.

[4] The first excerpt is included by Daremberg, who in 'Recherches', pp. 522 and 526, gives the Arabic text from MS Dresden 209, the Greek text from Paris, Bibliothèque Nationale, gr. 2239, and the Latin text from *Opera omnia Isaac* (Lyons, 1515). The second excerpt is given in a translation from the Arabic text in G. Dugat, 'Études sur le traité de médecine d'Abou Djàfar ah'mad, intitulé ZAD AL-MOÇAFIR, "La provision du voyageur"', *Journal Asiatique*, sér. v, 1 (1853), pp. 289–353, see section IV, pp. 307–11. For the Latin text I have used MSS London, British Library, Egerton 2900 (12th century; = E, fols. 12ᵛ–13ʳ, 15ᵛ–16ʳ); ibid., Royal 12.D.IX (late 13th century; = R, fols. 6ʳ⁻ᵛ, 7ᵛ–8ʳ); London, Wellcome Institute for the History of Medicine, 207 (mid-14th century = V, fols. 9ᵛ, 12ʳ⁻ᵛ), and ibid., 208 (mid-14th century = W, fols. 5ᵛ, 7ʳ), and the printed edition in *Opera omnia Isaac* (Lyons, 1515) (= Isaac, fols. 146ᵛ, 147ʳ). I include all variants from the MSS except changes in word order and insignificant variations in orthography.

Concerning mental stupor.

. . . This illness should be treated in the same way as lethargy. However, in lethargy the back part of the brain, whereas in this disease the front part, should be medicated. If it results from the deficiency and the destruction of its faculties, the front part of the head should be anointed with camomile, violets and roses boiled in water, with sandalwood and oil of roses and water of roses also. Before the patient a sweet sound should be made from [various] kinds of musical instruments, such as a bell, a fiddle and similar instruments. By these the soul is delighted and as a result of this delight the natural faculties are aroused.

1. he W. 2. lethargia, Isaac, letargia R *passim.* 3. WIsaac add: et. 4. RVWIsaac omit. 5. capitis V. 6. RIsaac omit. 7. violis et R. 8. camomilla in qua cocta sunt viola et rosa E, camomilla in aqua coctis viola et rosa W. 9. ungantur W. 10. prora capitis] RWEIsaac omit. 11. et aqua rosarum] RV omit. 12. sonus W. 13. R omits. 14. campanua V. 15. viola] rota RW, rota, viella V, rota, giga Isaac. 16. Isaac adds: omnibus. 17. condelectatur V. 18. exicatur R

The Arabic text mentions 'a rhythm (*īqaʿ*) such as the rhythm of the lute (ʿūd) and the *ṭunbūr* and those instruments of the kind that give pleasure'. The Greek text calls the instruments the *okta-khordē* and the *tambourion*. Constantine introduces this passage, along with several other chapters of the *Viaticum*, into his influential translation of al-Majūsī's *al-kitāb al-malakī* (= *Pantegni*), Practica, v.9,[5] but here the phrase mentioning the musical instruments reads: 'Ante infirmum dulcis sonitus fiat de musicorum generibus, sicut cum viella, lyra, simphonia, psalterio et huiusmodi.' (Before the patient a sweet sound should be made from [various] kinds of musical instruments, such as a fiddle, a lyre, a symphony, a psaltery and things of this kind.) The instruments appear to be a random collection, which Constantine or later scribes changed at will. The great variation in the list of the instruments from one manuscript of the *Viaticum* to another testifies to this fact.

II. A few chapters later on in the *Viaticum* there is a description of 'lovesickness' in which Ibn al-Jazzār quotes at length from a lost work of the Greek medical writer Rufus of Ephesus (fl. A.D. *c.* 100):[6]

---

[5] Ed. *Opera omnia Isaac* (Lyons, 1515), fol. 98ʳ.

[6] For this chapter see M. F. Wack, 'The *Liber de heros morbo* of Johannes Afflacius and its Implications for Medieval Love Conventions', *Speculum*, 62 (1987), pp. 324–44 and *idem, Lovesickness in the Middle Ages: the 'Viaticum' and its Commentaries* (Philadelphia, 1990), pp. 186–93. Both these works include editions of Constantine's translation, but use manuscripts different from those used here. The revised version of the chapter, which Wack attributes to Johannes Afflacius, adds nothing in respect to the musical references.

Viaticum, i.20: De amore qui dicitur hereos.[1]

... Quod[2] melius heriosos[3] adiuvat ne in cogitaciones profundentur nimias, vinum temperatum et odoriferum dandum est,[4] et audire[5] genera musicorum, colloqui dilectissimis[6] amicis, versus[7] recitatio, lucidos[8] videre hortos,[9] odoriferos et fructiferos,[10] currentem habentes aquam et claram,[11] spaciari seu deducere cum femina seu maribus pulcre persone ... Item[12] Rufus: non solummodo vinum[13] temperate bibitum[14] aufert tristiciam sed et[15] alia quidem[16] similia[17] sibi,[18] sicut balneum temperatum.[19] Unde fit ut cum quidam balneum ingrediantur, ad cantandum animantur.[20] Quidam ergo[21] philosophi dicunt sonitum esse quasi spiritum, vinum quasi corpus, quorum alterum ab altero adiuvatur. Dicunt alii quod Orpheus[22] dixit: imperatores[23] ad convivia me invitant[24] ut ex me se delectent,[25] sed[26] ego[27] condelector ex ipsis[28] cum quo[29] velim animos eorum flectere possim, sicut de ira ad mansuetudinem, de tristicia ad leticiam, de avaricia ad[30] largitatem, de timore ad[31] audaciam. Hec est ordinacio organorum[32] musicorum atque vini circa sanitatem anime.[33]

About the love which is called *hereos*.

... Because it helps lovesick men more effectively, so that they are not submerged in excessive brooding, tempered and fragrant wine should be offered, and hearing [various] kinds of music, speaking with dear friends, reciting poetry, visiting gardens which are bright, fragrant and fruitful, having clear running water [in them], and walking with or escorting a woman or men of fair character ... Likewise Rufus says: Sadness is taken away not only by wine drunk in moderation but also by other things like it, such as a temperate bath. Hence it is that when certain people enter a bath, they are roused into singing. Therefore certain philosophers say that the sound is like the spirit, the wine is like the body, of which the one is aided by the other. Others say that Orpheus said: 'Emperors invited me to feasts so that they might take their pleasure from me, but I am delighted by them, since I can turn their spirits in whatever direction I want to, for example from anger to gentleness, from sadness to happiness, from greed to generosity, from fear to boldness.' This is the application of musical instruments and wine in respect to the health of the soul.

1. erois W, ereos V. 2. Quid Isaac. 3. heryosos R, eriosos W, hereosos Isaac. 4. detur E, est ei dandum R, est dandum odoriferum V, W omits. 5. V adds: diversa. 6. dilectis RIsaac. 7. versuum WIsaac. 8. luciferos EVIsaac, iocundos R. 9. VW adds: et. 10. fructiferosos E, luciferos R, fructiferos et odoriferos W. 11. currentem habentes aquam et claram] currentem aquam et claram habere E, currentes aquam et claram videre R, currentem habentem aquam et claram V, currentes aquas habere et claram W. 12. Iterum E. 13. vino E. 14. ebibitum V. 15. WR omit. 16. quedam R. 17. consimilia W. 18. W omits. 19. temperatum] E omits. 20. ingreditur ... animatur W. 21. autem W, vero Isaac. 22. alii quod Orpheus] quidam Orpheum W. 23. W adds: sic. 24. invitaverant W. 25. delectant R, delectentur W. 26. E omits, et R. 27. W adds: quoque, Isaac adds: quidem. 28. eis W, R adds: et. 29. W adds: si. 30. in V. 31. in V. 32. organicorum Isaac. 33. circa sanitatem anime] R omits

So we see that singing in the bath has venerable antecedents! The

Arabic text (to the extent that it can be inferred from Dugat's translation) combines the first two remedies for lovesickness – '[the best remedy is] to drink while singing' – and omits the remedy of the stroll with a pleasant person. Where Constantine writes *dicunt alii*, Ibn al-Jazzār refers to the well-known 'Philosopher of the Arabs', Ya'qūb ibn Isḥāq al-Kindī, and Orpheus is described as 'the inventor of melodies (*alḥān*)'. Constantine included an abbreviated version of the *Viaticum* passage in *Pantegni*, Practica, v.21.

Another text referring to music therapy translated by Constantine of Africa is the *Maqāla fī 'l-mālīkhūliyā* (*De melancholia*), also written by a doctor who worked in Qairawān – Isḥāq ibn 'Imrān (d. before 907), who taught Ibn al-Jazzār's teacher.[7] Here we read: 'Alii amant equitare, diversa musicorum genera audire, loqui quoque cum sapientibus vel amabilibus.' (Others like to ride, to listen to various kinds of music; also to speak with intelligent men or with men of likable characters.) This is equivalent to an Arabic phrase which means: 'And they like riding and walking, gardens and listening to music (*al-samā'*), and the company of men.'[8] A little later in the work wine is added to the music therapy: 'Tollenda quae in anima sunt plantata cum diversa musica et vino odorifero, claro et subtilissimo.' (What has taken hold of the soul should be removed by different [kinds of] music and wine which is fragrant, clear and very fine.) In Arabic the prescription is simply 'the movement of music (*ḥarakat al-mūsīqī*) and the drinking of wine'.[9]

General references to musical instruments and their practice can be found in many of the astrological and magical works translated from Arabic into Latin in the twelfth and thirteenth centuries. Music and entertainment are ascribed to the planet Venus and the zodiac sign Virgo. In Adelard of Bath's translation of Abū Ma'shar's *Lesser Introduction to Astrology*, Virgo is described as controlling 'places of comedians and musicians' and Venus as providing 'ornaments and gold and silver and musical instruments and pleasures and delights'. In the *Greater Introduction* of the same Abū

---

[7] Sezgin, *Geschichte*, III, pp. 266–7; Ullmann, *Die Medizin*, pp. 125–6. The Arabic and Latin texts are placed side by side in Isḥāq ibn 'Imrān, *Maqālah fī l-mālīḫūliyā (Abhandlung über die Melancholie) und Constantini Africani Libri duo de Melancholia*, ed. and trans. K. Garbers (Hamburg, 1977).

[8] Ed. Garbers, pp. 124–5.

[9] Ed. Garbers, pp. 136–7.

Ma'shar, Virgo supervises places of women and entertainment and singers and pleasure gardens.[10] According to another astrologer, Sahl ibn Bishr, the 'voiced' signs of the zodiac agree with those who 'blow the flute (*nāy*) and strike the lute, and with singing'.[11]

More specific information concerning musical instruments is given in a bilingual table occurring in two manuscripts of the twelfth century, which gives predictions of activities depending on which sign of the zodiac a planet is in.[12]

(1) K72: *himag rebeb (samā' rabāb): audire liram*, 'to hear a rebec'.

(2) K93: *drab karamel (ḍarb 'karamel'*[13]*): tangere organum*, 'to play an organ'.

(3) K33: *drab arkela (ḍarb 'arkela'): sonitum tubarum*, 'the sound of trumpets'.[14]

---

[10] For these two references see C. Burnett, ed., *Adelard of Bath: an English Scientist and Arabist of the Early Twelfth Century*, Warburg Institute Surveys and Texts, 14 (London, 1987), p. 85 (reading *wa al-mutanazzahāt*).

[11] Sahl ibn Bishr, *kitāb al-ikhtiyārāt*, ch. 19a, edited and translated by C. M. Crofts, in '*Kitāb al-iḫtiyārāt 'alā l'buyūt at-iṯnai 'ašar* by Sahl ibn Bišr al-Isrā'īlī with its Latin translation *De electionibus*' (Ph.D. dissertation, University of Glasgow, 1985). The Latin translation runs: 'et signa quibus sunt voces conveniunt ei qui canit fistulam cum crudo et voci alhool et cantilenae'. This makes little sense: the *crudum* must be the Latin form of the Celtic instrument known as *cruit* (Irish) or *crwth* (Welsh); see C. Page, *Voices and Instruments of the Middle Ages* (London, 1987), p. 141. What the translator intended by *alhool* is unclear to me. For the division of the signs of the zodiac into 'voiced', 'semi-voiced', and 'mute', see W. Hübner, *Die Eigenschaften der Tierkreiszeichen in der Antike*, Sudhoffs Archiv, Beiheft 22 (Wiesbaden, 1982), pp. 165–9, and *idem*, *Varros instrumentum vocale in Kontexte der antiken Fachwissenschaften*, Akademie der Wissenschaften und der Literatur, Abhandlungen der Geistes- und Sozialwissenschaftlichen Klasse (Mainz, 1984).

[12] This was first noted by R. Lemay in 'A propos de l'origine arabe de l'art des troubadours', *Annales: Économies, Sociétés, Civilisations*, 21 (1966), pp. 990–1011. The table is edited by P. Kunitzsch, 'Eine bilingue arabisch-lateinische Lostafel', *Revue d'Histoire des Textes*, 6 (1976), pp. 267–304. See also the appendix to C. S. F. Burnett, 'A Note on Two Astrological Fortune-Telling Tables', *Revue d'Histoire des Textes*, 18 (1988), pp. 257–62. I give the Arabic and Latin phrases as they are found in the MSS, and suggest possible interpretations (note that the scribes often write *h* in place of *z*, which resembles *h* in their script). The numbers prefixed by K are those of Kunitzsch, and fuller interpretations of the phrases can be found in the aforementioned articles of Kunitzsch and Burnett. Two Latin phrases (and possibly three, see (5) below) have lost their Arabic equivalents: K58 *apprehendere musicam*, and K85 *componere metrum*.

[13] This presumably represents a Romance word deriving from vulgar Latin *calamellus* (= 'small reed'), the origin of the English word 'shawm'; see C. Sachs, *Real-Lexikon der Musikinstrumente* (Berlin, 1913), pp. 72 and 77.

[14] *'Arkal* is listed in the sense of '*duff* and *ṭabl*' by al-Ḥasan ibn Muḥammad al-Saghānī (d. 1252) in his *Al-takmila wa'l-dhail wa'l-ṣila li-kitāb Tāj al-lugha wa-ṣiḥāh al-'arabiyya*, v, ed. A. A. al-Ṭaḥāwī and I. al-Abyārī and revised by A. H. Ḥasan and M. Kh. Aḥmad (Cairo, 1977), p. 441, and in other Arabic lexica (I owe these references to Eckhard Neubauer).

(4) K45: *hiag tabor (samāʿ(?) ṭunbūr): sonitum cordarum*, 'the sound of string [instruments]'.

(5) K67: *drab keber (ḍarb kabar): monochordum mensurare*; the Arabic means 'the playing of a single-headed drum'; the Latin translation ('to measure the monochord') may have been misplaced.

(6) K27: *darbibok (ḍarb(i) būq): fistulare*; the Arabic refers to playing a horn whereas the Latin refers to playing a pipe.

(7) K8: *darbiduf (ḍarb(i) duff): tangere tympanum*, 'to play a drum'.

(8) K17: *gināantagib (ghinā' ṭayyib): cantilenas bonas*, 'good singing'.

In a text on the best time to undertake an activity – the *De electionibus horarum laudabilium* of ʿAlī ibn Aḥmad al-ʿImrānī (Haly) 'interpreted' by Abraham bar Ḥiyya in Barcelona in 1134[15] – after a chapter on choosing when to start teaching a child to write, and before a chapter on when to teach him to fish, there is a whole chapter on when to teach him to sing and play musical instruments:

Differentia 2 in eruditione cantilenarum et eorum que ad alacritatem pertinent.[1]
Aptanda est in hoc Venus et sit in aliqua suarum dignitatum, et similiter Mercurius sitque iunctus illi. Sit etiam[2] Luna in aliqua suarum dignitatum vel in Piscibus[3] separata /P p. 533/ a Mercurio et[4] iens ad coniunctionem Veneris, et sit[5] in aliqua dignitatum Veneris ascendens.[6] Si autem fuerit gradus ascendentis[7] dignitas Veneris et Mercurii, erit bonum. Luna vel Venus vel Mercurius non sint cadentes.[8] Si tamen fuerit Luna in nona,[9] que est domus sciencie, fortunata et fortis, erit bonum.[10] Significabit[11] enim perfectionem rei sicut[12] alii fortunati. Si vero fuerit dominus ascendentis in nono fortunatus et fortis, erit bonum. Dixit quidam necesse est in tactu[13] lyre ut sit Luna in Capricorno; in percussione autem atambur[14] et horum similium sit in fine Leonis; in tubis autem[15] sit in signis voce carentibus. Signa enim[16] voces habentia bona[17] sunt in cantibus et lectionibus[18] modulandis, et maxime Gemini et[19] Virgo. Et aptemus in hac re nonam et eius dominum. Et si fuerit intencio nostra[20] in hiis ad aliquid quod pertinet[21] ad opus[22] aptatio decimi erit bona. Quod etiam commendamus in omnis rei principio.

The second chapter: On teaching songs and those things which pertain to pleasure.
For this Venus should be taken, and she should be in one of her honour-

---

[15] The Arabic original of this text has not been found (see F. Sezgin, *Geschichte des arabischen Schrifttums*, VII (Leiden, 1979), p. 166). I quote the text after Paris, Bibliothèque Nationale, lat. 16204 (P), p. 532, *ibid.*, lat. 16208 (Pa), fol. 75ʳ, and Cambridge, Clare College 15 (C).

able positions, and the same with Mercury, and Mercury should be joined to Venus. And the Moon should be in one of her honourable positions or in Pisces, separated from Mercury and approaching conjunction with Venus, and the Ascendant should be in one of the honourable positions of Venus. And if the degree of the Ascendant is an honourable position of Venus and Mercury, it will be good. The Moon and Venus and Mercury should not be in a cadent house. However, if the Moon is in the ninth house – which is the house of learning – and if it is lucky and strong, it will be good. For it will signify the completion of the activity, just as other lucky [planets] do. But if the lord of the Ascendant is lucky and strong in the ninth [house], it will be good. Someone has said that it is necessary when playing the *lyra* that the Moon should be in Capricorn; but in striking the drum (*atambur*) and other [instruments] similar to this it should be in the last part of Leo; and in blowing trumpets it should be in signs lacking voice.[16] For the signs having voices are good for modulating songs and speeches, and this is especially true for Gemini and Virgo. And for this activity let us take the ninth [house] and its lord. And if our intention in these matters is [directed] towards something which pertains to action, the taking of the tenth [place] will be good. This is what we recommend also when beginning any activity.

1. in editione . . . pertinent] Aptatio ludi et instrumentorum eius C. 2. Sit etiam] Similiter P. 3. In Piscibus] Pisce Pa, ipsa C. 4. P omits. 5. C adds: ascendens. 6. C omits. 7. ascendens Pa. 8. Luna . . . cadentes] Nec sit Venus vel Mercurius aut Luna cadens PaC. 9. nono C. 10. erit bonum] erit laudandum Pa, non erit illaudandum C. 11. Significat P. 12. sicut] sint etiam Pa, sicut etiam C. 13. tastu P, retractu Pa. 14. athabur P, attaniluer Pa. 15. vero C. 16. autem C. 17. P omits. 18. el(ecti)onibus P. 19. P omits. 20. P omits. 21. pertineat Pa. 22. ad opus] P omits

This text was known to the translator, astrologer and magician of the early thirteenth century Michael Scot, the 'philosopher' of Frederick II in Sicily. In his encyclopedic introduction to astrology written for his royal patron, the *Liber introductorius*, Michael uses Haly's *De electionibus* as one of his sources, but he adds a detail which is not found in the manuscripts of that work known to me: the 'quidam' ('someone') is identified as the early Arabic astrologer ʿUmar ibn al-Farrukhān al-Ṭabarī.[17] The second part of the chapter runs:

[16] Presumably this is because it is possible to sing while playing the *lyra* or striking the drum, but not while playing the trumpet. Compare Marchetto da Padova, *Lucidarium*, ed. J. W. Herlinger (Chicago, 1985), ch. 13 (De sono qui non est vox): 'In [tuba et cimella] dicitur esse sonus qui non est vox.'

[17] ʿUmar was one of the astrologers who participated in making the horoscope for the founding of Baghdad in A.D. 762; see F. Sezgin, *Geschichte des arabischen Schrifttums*, VIII (Leiden, 1979), pp. 111–13. For the *Liber introductorius* I have consulted H. Meier's unpublished and incomplete typescript edition deposited in the Warburg Institute, and MSS Munich, Bayerische Staatsbibliothek, Clm 10268 (A.D. c. 1320), Oxford, Bodleian

Dixit enim philosophus qui Tabbari nominatur: Necessarium est in cantu lyre vel alterius instrumenti cordarum, si discipulus debeat bene addiscere et magister sit ei fidelis in docendo eamdem artem, ut Luna sit in Capricorno vel in Tauro prope cornua. In percussione bacilis vel tympani sit Luna in fine Leonis. In tubis Luna sit in signo carente voce. Carentia voce sunt mala in arte cantuum, habentia vero vocem bona sunt ad omnem cantum doctrinandum sicut in cantionibus et lectionibus ac modulationibus melodye, et maxime signum Geminorum et Lyre Celi.[18]

The philosopher who is called Tabbari has said: It is necessary when sounding the lyre or another string instrument, if the pupil has to learn it well and the (teacher is committed to teaching him the skill, that the Moon should be in Capricorn or in Taurus close to the horns. In beating a *bacile*[19] or tympanum let the Moon be in the last part of Leo. In blowing trumpets the Moon should be in a sign lacking voice. Signs lacking voice are bad in practising songs, but those having voice are good for teaching every song, just as [they are good] in chanting, public speaking and modulating a melody, and this is especially true for Gemini and the Lyre.[20]

The well-illustrated portion of the *Liber introductorius* devoted to the description of the heavenly constellations includes a group of stars which Michael calls *Figura sonantis canonem*, 'the figure of the Sounder of the *canon*'. This constellation does not appear in Michael's Latin sources and may be an invention of his.[21] The illustration in the Munich manuscript shows a seated figure holding a trapezoid *qānūn* or psaltery with three sound-holes, in a vertical position against the chest. The immediate source of the term *canon* used by Michael to describe this instrument is Arabic, and is next met with in a musical treatise written in the second half of the thirteenth century.[22] Like the modern Arabic *qānūn* the tuning

Library, Bodley 266 (15th century), St Petersburg, Public Library, lat. F.v.ix, no. 1 (A.D. c. 1275), London, British Library, Add. 41600 (15th century), and London, Wellcome Institute, 509 (c. 1510). The last three MSS contain only the portion of the *Liber introductorius* on the constellations, called *Liber de signis et imaginibus coeli*.

[18] Munich, Bayerische Staatsbibliothek, Clm 10268, fol. 135[va].

[19] In Medieval Latin *bacile* is a 'basin' or any basin-shaped receptacle. Hence it is an appropriate term to describe a drum of that shape.

[20] Lyra is not a sign of the zodiac but a constellation in the northern hemisphere. The Moon cannot therefore be said to be 'in' Lyra. It has probably replaced Virgo simply because it sounds good.

[21] See U. Bauer, *Der Liber Introductorius des Michael Scot in der Abschrift Clm 10268 der Bayerischen Staatsbibliothek München* (Munich, 1983), pp. 63–4.

[22] Aegidius Zamorensis, *Ars musica*, ch. 17, ed. M. Robert-Tissot (Rome, 1974), p. 103: 'canon et medius canon et guitarra et rabe fuerunt postremo inventa'. See also Page, *Voices and Instruments*, p. 123. Of course, the term is originally Greek. For its passage from Greek to Arabic, and back into Greek and the changes of its sense in the process, see R. Beaton,

pegs in the illustrations in the Munich, British Library and St Petersburg manuscripts are arranged in groups of three.[23] Michael describes the illustration and the position of the stars within the constellation, and then indicates the character of a person born under the constellation, as follows: 'Figura sonantis canonem habet stellas multas . . . Conceptus vel natus sub isto signo semper letam ducet vitam. Fiet ystrio cum pulsacione instrumentorum, et erit plus pauper quam dives, et tamen bene vestitus ibit.'[24] (The figure of the 'Sounder of the *canon*' has many stars . . . He who is conceived or born under this sign will always have a happy life. He will become an actor and a player of instruments, and he will be more poor than rich. Nevertheless he will be well dressed as he goes around.) The British Library and Wellcome manuscripts give a significantly different text: 'Figura sonantis canonem mulier est sedens in cathedra bene vestita et canonem sonans. Habet stellas multas . . . Natus sub hoc signo convenienter vivet in orbe. Efficietur pulsator instrumentorum. Et erit joculator et ei attribuentur multa bona sua bonitate. Et bene finiet vitam suam.'[25] (The figure of the 'Sounder of the *canon*' is a woman sitting on a chair, finely clad and playing a *canon*. It has many stars. . . He who is born under this sign will have a comfortable life in this world. He will become a player of instruments, and he will be a *jongleur*, and many good things will be given to him because of his good nature. And he will have a fine end to his life.)

For the most bizarre reference to musical instruments in an Arabic source translated into Latin we may turn to the handbook of magic known as *Picatrix*. This was translated in the court of Alfonso X of Castile in the late 1250s and includes the description of a wonderful instrument of the Indians called *alquelquella* (Arabic: *al-kankala*) which has one string [stretched] over one body, and from which you can produce any sound you desire.[26] Moreover, if

---

'Modes and Roads: Factors of Change and Continuity in Greek Musical Tradition', *Annual of the British School of Athens*, 75 (1980), pp. 1–11 (see p. 5).

[23]   In the Wellcome MS, fol 20^v, only a few oversized pegs are shown, but this time the strings are shown grouped in sets, two of five and one of four.

[24]   Munich MS, fol. 82vb, St Petersburg MS, fol. 11^r.

[25]   British Library MS, fol. 49^r, Wellcome MS, fol. 20^v.

[26]   *Picatrix*, II.v.2 (Arabic text, ed. H. Ritter, *Pseudo-Māğrīṭī, Das Ziel des Weisen* (Leipzig, 1933), p. 80; German trans., H. Ritter and M. Plessner, *'Picatrix': Das Ziel des Weisen von Pseudo-Māğrīṭī* (London, 1962), p. 84; Latin text, ed. D. Pingree, *Picatrix* (London, 1986), p. 46: 'Et similiter [Indi] habent instrumentum musice artis compositum, quod nominant

you wish to put to flight wolves or any other bad animals you may do this with a drum (*ṭabl*; *tamburum*) which has been specially made for the purpose, and you make it in this way: You take a sea-urchin (*duldul wa huwa al-qunfudh al-baḥrī*; *ericium marinum*) and, after killing it, take off the spines. Then you skin it and make from it a drum-skin – the kind that you would stretch over a silver-copper drum – and you should slay it at night.[27] And all bad beasts will flee at its sound, and all pests will die on hearing the instrument.[28]

II

The texts surveyed up to now refer to musical instruments and the practice of music. In the field of theoretical music very little was translated from Arabic into Latin. Perhaps this was because Europeans thought that everything had already been said by Boethius. In a work written or revised some time before the middle of the twelfth century by a 'magister A' and called *Liber ysagogarum ad totum quadrivium*, the author summarised the contents of the four subjects of the *quadrivium* – arithmetic, music, geometry, and astro-

---

alquelquella, et cordam armoniarum habens solam (v.l. monocordon), quo faciunt sonos et omnes eius subtilitates quemadmodum cupiunt et optant.' The *kankala* is described by Ibn Khurradādhbih in the following way: 'The Indians have the *kankala*. It has one string strung up over a gourd. [This instrument] holds [in India] the position of [our] lute and harp' (*apud* Maçoudi, *Les prairies d'or*, ed. and trans. C. Barbier de Maynard, VIII (Paris, 1874), p. 92). Other references to this instrument can be found in Abū'l-Farāj al-Iṣfahānī, *Kitāb al-Aghānī al-kabīr*, XVII, ed. ʿAlī Muḥammad al-Bajāwī (Cairo, 1972), p. 220; M. Ullmann, *Wörterbuch der klassischen arabischen Sprache*, I (Wiesbaden, 1970), p. 397; L. I. al-Faruqi, *An Annotated Glossary of Arabic Musical Terms* (Westport, CT, 1981), s.v. *kinkulah* (v.l. *gongolah, kirkalah, kankarah*), and Kunitzsch, 'Eine bilingue . . . Lostafel', p. 303 (*karkala, qarqal*).

27 The Latin text is slightly different from the Arabic, and may be translated: 'Then you will skin it and you should treat the skin as you would that of other animals. Then stretch the skin over the drum or bronze nackers (*nacara*), and put it aside ready for use. Then when you want to put such beasts to flight, beat the drum or nackers by night.'

28 *Picatrix*, IV.9.23, Arabic p. 413, German p. 420, Latin p. 227. I quote the Latin, which gives the fullest text: 'Ad fugandum lupos et omnia animalia mala. Hoc autem opus facias cum uno tamburo (v.ll. cambuco, tympano) ad hoc specialiter facto, cuius composicio talis est. Recipe [e]ricium marinum; ipsumque decollabis, et ex suis spinis spoliabis. Ipsum autem excoriabis, cuius corium aptetur et liniatur secundum confectiones aliorum coriorum. Postea accipe ipsum corium, quod optime extendas super tamburum (v.ll. tamburam, cambucum) vel nacaram eream; et usui reservabis. Cum vero predictas bestias fugare volueris, pulsabis dictum tamburum (v.l. cambucum) vel nacaram de nocte, quoniam omnes bestie male ad eius sonitum fugient et omnia reptilia predictum audiencia morientur.'

nomy.[29] In the case of arithmetic, the new Arabic numerals are introduced; for geometry, portions of a new translation of Euclid's *Elements* from the Arabic are included; and for astronomy, material derived from Hebrew and Arabic sources appears. For music, however, the author merely summarises a few chapters from Boethius' *De institutione musica*.[30]

Not only did the Latins not translate Arabic works dedicated to music, but also they left out portions of Arabic works which dealt with music. Thus, the section of Avicenna's *Shifā'* on music was never translated.[31] In the *Secreta secretorum* of Pseudo-Aristotle there is a chapter on spiritual medicine, which is a most interesting description of music therapy.[32] The *Secreta secretorum* was twice translated into Latin and was well known in the court of Frederick II, where an epitome of part of it was made by Theodore the court astrologer for his royal patron.[33] However, in both versions and the epitome the section on spiritual medicine was omitted.

One Latin translator, Hermann of Carinthia, had the arrogance to add musical examples from Boethius' *De institutione musica* to his translation of Abū Maʿshar's *Introductorium maius* ('Greater Introduction'). The Arabic of the text in question may be translated literally as:

And as for the philosophers, many of them have defined the half and the third as the greatest proportions (*ḥisābān*), and they have said that from these and the doubling of some of them, and from the relationship of one of them to the other according to the quantity of the half and the third, comes the relationship of the degrees of the circle which are the aspects.[34]

---

[29] This text has been edited by B. G. Dickey, in 'Adelard of Bath: an Examination Based on Heretofore Unexamined Manuscripts' (Ph.D. dissertation, University of Toronto, 1982), pp. 251–328; see Burnett, *Adelard of Bath*, pp. 38 and 173–4.

[30] Music and geometry together make up the fourth book of the work: 'Incipit quartus liber de musicis ac geometricis rationibus'. *De institutione musica*, ed. G. Friedlein (Leipzig, 1867), I.4, II.7–8 and II.12 are summarised.

[31] For the portions of Avicenna's *Shifā'* translated into Latin see M. T. d'Alverny, '*Avicenna Latinus I*', *Archives d'Histoire Doctrinale et Littéraire du Moyen Age*, 28 (1962), pp. 281–316. It may be significant that only the portions of the *Shifā'* which corresponded to, and therefore elucidated, works of Aristotle were translated into Latin. Since Aristotle did not write a book on music, scholars looking for a guide to Aristotelian philosophy would have had no interest in the section on music in the *Shifā'*.

[32] *Sirr al-asrār*, ed. A. R. Badawī, in *Al-Uṣūl al-yūnānīyah li'l-naẓarīyāt al-siyāsīyah fi'l-islām* (Cairo, 1954), pp. 115–16; English translation of the Arabic by A. S. Fulton in *Opera hactenus inedita Rogeri Baconi*, ed. R. Steele, v (Oxford, 1920), pp. 217–18.

[33] K. Sudhoff, 'Ein diätetischer Brief an Kaiser Friedrich II von seinem Hofphilosophen Magister Theodorus', *Archiv für Geschichte der Medizin*, 9 (1915), pp. 1–9.

[34] *Introductorium maius*, VI.3 (Arabic MSS Leiden 47, p. 193, and Carullah 1508, published by the Institut für Geschichte der arabisch-islamischen Wissenschaften, Facsimile C 21 (Frankfurt, 1985), pp. 335–6).

John of Seville, the first translator of the *Introductorium maius*, keeps close to the Arabic.[35] Hermann, however, substitutes *musici* for 'the philosophers' and translates as follows:[36] 'Musici vero dimidium et trientem maiores numeros appellant, eo quod duplam et sesquialteram proportionem reddant – moderatissimas dyapason et dyapente consonantias.' (But musicians call the half and the third the 'greater numbers' because they produce the proportions 2:1 and 3:2 – the most well-tempered consonances of the octave and the fifth.) Hermann's words take up the idea and some of the terms used by Boethius in *De institutione musica*, II.18: 'Igitur uni binarius comparatus proportionem duplicem facit et *reddit diapason consonantiam* eam quae est maxima et simplicitate notissima. Si vero unitati ternarius comparetur, diapason ac diapente concordiam personabit.' (Two measured against one makes the duple ratio and produces that consonance of the octave which is the most excellent, and, because of its simplicity, the most recognisable. If three is measured against one, it will give the consonance of the octave plus a fifth.)[37]

We see the same situation when we turn to the translators Adelard of Bath and Michael Scot. Adelard translated several mathematical texts from Arabic, and was himself a keen musician. He dedicated a treatise on the seven liberal arts – *De eodem et diverso* – to William, Bishop of Syracuse, in the early years of the twelfth century and devoted more attention to music than to any of the other arts. The theory of music in this work, however, derives almost entirely from Boethius' *De institutione musica* (with Martianus, Macrobius, and perhaps a commentary on Plato's *Timaeus*), whereas the anecdotes, fascinating as they are – of Adelard playing the *cithara* in front of the Queen of France, of the English catching fish by floating a bell on the surface of the water, and of taming a

---

[35] Cambridge, University Library, KK.i.1, fol. 37ᵛ, Paris, Bibliothèque Nationale, lat. 16204, p. 116, and Munich, Bayerische Staatsbibliothek, Clm 374, fol. 50ʳ: 'Quidam autem philosophi diviserunt medietatem et terciam – partes scilicet magnas – et dixerunt quia ex eis et ex duplicitate quarundam earum et ex affinitate unius earum in alteram et secundum quantitatem dimidii et tercii erit affinitas graduum circuli qui sunt aspectus.'

[36] I use the printed text, ed. Venice, 1506, fol. f1ʳ.

[37] *De institutione musica*, ed. Friedlein, p. 250; English translation adapted from that of C. M. Bower in Anicius Manlius Severinus Boethius, *Fundamentals of Music* (New Haven and London, 1989), p. 73. For further examples see Burnett, 'Hermann of Carinthia's Attitude towards his Arabic Sources, in Particular in Respect to Theories on the Human Soul', *L'homme et son univers au moyen âge*, ed. C. Wenin, Philosophes Médiévaux, 26 (Louvain-la-Neuve, 1986), pp. 306–22, see pp. 316–17.

wild hawk by playing a musical instrument – make no reference
to Sicily or the Arabs.[38]

Michael Scot expressed his interest in music by adding an
extensive chapter on 'the whole of the art of music' (*De notitia totius
artis musice*) to his *Liber introductorius*. Michael believed that music
was relevant to the astrologer in that instrumental music was ana-
logous to the music of the spheres. However, like Adelard, his
account of music is almost entirely based on Western sources – in
particular Boethius and Guido of Arezzo – and on his own observations of Italian musical practice.[39]

The three texts translated from Arabic into Latin dealing with
the theory of music which are regularly referred to in scholarship
are passages from (1) al-Fārābī's *Classification of the Sciences*,[40] (2)
the *De ortu scientiarum*, a work lost in Arabic, and attributed, probably falsely, to al-Fārābī in the one surviving Latin translation,[41]
and (3) the *Epistle on Logic* translated from the Arabic *Epistles of
the Brethren of Purity* (*Rasā'il Ikhwān al-ṣafāʾ*) under the title *Liber
introductorius in artem logicae demonstrationis collectus a Mahometh discipulo
aliquindi philosophi*.[42] These texts were concerned with the subdivisions of the science of music and its position in respect to other
academic disciplines. The passage from the *De ortu scientiarum*, in
addition, indicates the place of music in therapy.[43]

[38] See Burnett, 'Adelard, Music and the Quadrivium', *Adelard of Bath*, pp. 69–86.
[39] See F. A. Gallo, 'Astronomy and Music in the Middle Ages: the *Liber introductorius* by Michael Scot', *Musica Disciplina*, 27 (1973), pp. 5–9.
[40] The *Classification of the Sciences* was translated by Gerard of Cremona and revised by Dominicus Gundissalinus – both scholars working in Toledo in the second half of the twelfth century. The relevant passage has been edited and translated by D. M. Randel in 'Al-Fārābī and the Role of Arabic Music Theory in the Latin Middle Ages', *Journal of the American Musicological Society*, 29 (1976), pp. 173–88. Max Haas presents a revised Latin edition of the relevant passage and further comments in 'Studien zur mittelalter- lichen Musiklehre I', *Forum Musicologicum*, 3 (Basel, 1982), pp. 323–456, see pp. 420–3.
[41] Ed. C. Baeumker, *Alfarabi, Über den Ursprung der Wissenschaften (de ortu scientiarum)*, Bei- träge zur Geschichte der Philosophie des Mittelalters, 19 (Münster, 1918), p. 19.
[42] The relevant text is edited by H. G. Farmer, who cites the Arabic original and gives an English translation in *Al-Farabi's Arabic-Latin Writings on Music* (New York, 2/1960), pp. 63–4. Farmer pointed out that this passage was an abbreviation of a longer passage from the Ikhwān's *Epistle on Music*. The latter appears never to have been translated into Latin.
[43] *De ortu scientiarum*, ed. Baeumker, p. 19: 'Cuius [viz. music's] utilitas est ad temperandos mores animalium qui excedunt aequalitatem, et perficiendos decores eorum qui nondum sunt perfecti, et ad conservandum eos qui videntur aequales et nondum pervenerunt ad aliquod extremorum. Et est etiam utilis ad salutem corporis, eo quod quandoque corpus infirmatur languente anima et impeditur ipsa existente impedita; unde curatio corporis fit propter curationem animae et adaptationem suarum virium et temperationem suae

One theoretical text which, so far as I know, has not been discussed by musicologists is a short section from Avicenna's logic (part of the *Shifā*) incorporated into Gundissalinus' *De divisione philosophiae* as a chapter with the title *Summa Avicenne de conveniencia et differencia subiectorum*.[44] This chapter may be translated as follows:

1 The fourth [type of] division arises when the more special subject, rather than having the more general predicated of it, is accidental to a species of it, as in the case of musical tones (*nigham*) which, in relation to the subject of physics, belong (to the set of accidental features which happen) to some species of the subject of physics. **2** Yet musical tones are considered, in the science of music, under the aspect of something extraneous applied to them – something extraneous to them as well as to their genus [viz. sound in general], namely number. **3** Thus one looks for what pertains to musical tones inasmuch as that extraneous something applies to them, not for what pertains to them in their own right; for example, one looks in musical tones for consonance and dissonance. **4** In such a case [the special subject] must be placed, not under the science to whose subject it belongs, but under the science to which [the extraneous something] applied to it belongs; thus we place music under the science of arithmetic. **5** We said 'not in their own right' because to examine musical tones in their own right would be to examine accidental features of the more general subject [viz. physics] or accidental features of accidental features of some species of it (and this is part of physics, not the science under it). **6** The difference between this division and the previous one – i.e. the one exemplified by the moving spheres – is that such a science is not placed under the science examining the accidental feature applied to it, but under the science which examines the [subject] general to its own; for the science of moving spheres comes, not under physics, but under geometry. **7** By contrast, the latter [type of science] is placed under the science examining the accidental feature applied to it, in that music comes, not under physical science, but under arithmetic.[45]

substantiae ex sonis agentibus hoc et convenientibus ad hoc.' (The usefulness [of music] is in tempering the characters of animals when they go beyond equal temperament, and in perfecting the suitability of those which are not yet perfect, and in preserving those which are seen to be of equal temperament and have not yet diverged to either of the extremes. And it is also useful for the health of the body, since at times the body is unwell because the soul is sick, or [the soul] is hindered because of a [bodily] hindrance; hence the cure of the body comes about through the cure of the soul and the mending of its faculties and the tempering of its substance, as a result of sounds effecting this and appropriate to this.)

44 For the Arabic text see the edition of A. E. Affifi and I. B. Madkour in Ibn Sīnā, *al-Shifā*, *al-mantiq, V, al-burhān*, ii.7 (Cairo, 1956), pp. 164–5. For the Latin text see Gundissalinus, *De divisione philosophiae*, ed. L. Baur, Beiträge zur Geschichte der Philosophie des Mittelalters, 4.2 (Münster, 1903), p. 128. For an intelligent précis of this passage see H. Hugonnard-Roche, 'La classification des sciences de Gundissalinus', in J. Jolivet and R. Rashed, *Études sur Avicenne* (Paris, 1984), pp. 41–75 (see pp. 55–7).

45 I owe this translation to Dr Fritz Zimmermann.

Fritz Zimmermann explains the sense of this passage as follows.

I think what Avicenna is saying is that the celestial spheres being just a species of spheres, the subject of astronomy, which counts as a branch of geometry, is just a species of the subject matter of geometry. By contrast, music, which counts as a branch of arithmetic, is not about a species of numbers, but about an application of numerical ratios to [an accidental feature, viz. sound, of] the subject matter of physics. Hence relations between main subject and subordinate subject in the two cases are different.

Gundissalinus translates the passage in the following way:[46]

1 Quartus, cum de minus communi non predicatur communius, set ipsum *minus commune* est accidentale alicui rei specierum *communioris*, sicut neumata, que comparantur subiecto naturalis sciencie, quia sunt de universitate accidencium que accidunt alicui speciei subiectorum sciencie naturalis. **2** Cum hoc autem iam accipiuntur neumata in sciencia musice secundum quod adiungitur eis quiddam extraneum ab eis et ab eorum [Baur: earum] genere, quod est numerus. **3** Unde inquiruntur consequencia eorum secundum quod adiungitur eis illud extraneum; et hec sunt conveniencia et diversitas que queruntur in neumatibus. **4** Unde oportet ut ponatur *illa sciencia* non sub sciencia de cuius natura est subiectum eius, set sub sciencia eius quod adiungitur ei, sicut hoc quod nos ponimus musicam sub sciencia numeri. **5** Nec dicimus hoc 'quantum in se', quoniam consideracio neumatis quantum in se est consideracio accidencium subiecti sciencie communioris vel accidencium accidentibus suarum specierum; et hec est pars sciencie naturalis, non sciencia sub ea. **6** Differencia autem que est inter hanc partem et priorem – scilicet partem cuius exemplum posuimus speras mobiles – hec est: quod hec sciencia non est posita sub sciencia que considerat accidens quod sibi adiungitur, set sub sciencia que considerat id quod est commune in suo subiecto eo quod sciencia sperarum mobilium non est sub naturalibus, set sub geometria. **7** Hec autem est posita sub sciencia que considerat adiunctum sibi; musica vero non est sub naturali set sub numero.

As one can see, Gundissalinus' translation is very literal. However, he replaces Arabic pronouns or demonstratives with the nouns to which they refer in sentences **1** and **4**. He finds a Latin term for 'notes' which is close in sound to the Arabic term (*neumata* for *nigham*).[47] He translates the last phrase of sentence **1** as '*neumata*

---

46   I reproduce the text of Baur with one emendation. The words which Gundissalinus adds to clarify the Arabic text are in italics.

47   See E. A. Beichert, 'Neuma, philologisch-historischer Exkurs', appendix to *idem*, 'Die Wissenschaft der Musik bei al-Fārābī' (inaugural dissertation, University of Regensburg, 1931), pp. 47–52.

which are related to the subject of physics, because they belong to the set of accidental features which happen to one species of the subjects of physics'. In sentence **3** 'not for what pertains to them in their own right' is omitted, presumably because it was absent or accidentally overlooked in Gundissalinus' Arabic copy, for when Avicenna refers back to this phrase in sentence **5**, Gundissalinus also makes the same back-reference (*quantum in se*). Also in sentence **3** Gundissalinus shows his lack of respect for (or knowledge of) Latin musical terminology by translating the Arabic terms for 'consonance' (*ittifāq*) and 'dissonance' (*ikhtilāf*) as *conveniencia* and *diversitas*.[48] In sentence **4**, instead of 'to the subject of which it belongs' Gundissalinus writes 'of whose nature its subject is'. In sentence **5** both Avicenna and Gundissalinus give 'musical tone' in the singular (*naghma, neuma*) where one would more naturally expect a plural. In sentence **7** Gundissalinus omits 'accidental feature' and inappropriately introduces a contrast (*musica vero . . .*) in the last phrase.

This harvest of musical texts has been meagre, but not negligible. The works of Constantine the African were widely copied and helped to popularise music therapy.[49] There are scores of Latin texts on astrological interrogations and elections – whether direct translations from Arabic, or derivative from these translations – which remain to be investigated. Passages on musical instruments such as those from Sahl ibn Bishr and ʿAlī ibn Aḥmad al-ʿImrānī quoted in this article might be found in several of these texts. Finally, Dominicus Gundissalinus' text *De divisione philosophiae* became a regular companion to texts of the Latin Aristotle in the Middle Ages, and his account of the subalternation of the sciences, in which, as we have seen, the science of music provided an important example, must have prompted much discussion.

Warburg Institute, University of London

---

[48] For the use of *ittifāq* and *ikhtilāf* for 'consonance' and 'dissonance' see Ibn al-Akfānī (d. 1348), *Ad-durr an-naẓīm*, section 57 (ed. A. Shiloah, 'Deux textes arabes inédits sur la musique', *Yuval*, ed. I. Adler (Jerusalem, 1968), p. 236): 'music . . . is the science which teaches the conditions of notes (*nigham*) in their consonances (*ittifāqihā*) and dissonances (*ikhtilāfihā*)'. *Ittifāq* is given as the first translation of *concordia* in the twelfth-century 'Leiden Glossary'; *Glossarium latino-arabicum*, ed. C. F. Seybold (Berlin, 1900), s.v. 'concordia'.

[49] See Kümmel, *Musik und Medizin, passim*.

Early Music History (1993) Volume 12

OWEN REES

GUERRERO'S *L'HOMME ARMÉ* MASSES AND THEIR MODELS*

Of the three most important Spanish composers of the Renaissance – Morales, Guerrero and Victoria – it is undoubtedly Guerrero who has attracted the least musicological attention. The complete edition of his works begun in 1949 is still little more than half complete, and the only substantial published account of his life and output is over thirty years old.[1] As this article will show, at least one major work by Guerrero has managed hitherto to slip almost entirely through the musicological net, thanks to the general concentration on printed sources of his music at the expense of manuscripts.

The number of surviving masses by Guerrero is usually given as eighteen, these being the works that were published during his lifetime.[2] However, there have also been occasional references in the literature to a nineteenth mass, particularly intriguing since the mass concerned is reported to be a *Missa L'homme armé*.[3] The earliest of these references appeared as long ago as 1935 in J. B. Trend's article on Guerrero in the third edition of *Grove's Dictionary*,[4] where the list of manuscripts containing music by the com-

---

*Earlier versions of this article were delivered as papers at the University of Surrey in January 1992 and at the Twentieth Conference on Medieval and Renaissance Music, University of Newcastle upon Tyne, July 1992. I should like to thank a number of people whose help and advice assisted the research for this article: Iain Fenlon, David Fallows, Michael Noone, Bruno Turner and the Rvda Madre Guadalupe Marcos, archivist of the Monasterio de Sta. Ana in Avila.

[1] R. M. Stevenson, *Spanish Cathedral Music in the Golden Age* (Berkeley and Los Angeles, 1961), pp. 135–238.

[2] See, for example, R. M. Stevenson's article on the composer in *The New Grove Dictionary of Music and Musicians*, ed. S. Sadie, 20 vols. (London, 1980), VII, p. 788.

[3] The possible existence of such a work by Guerrero is mentioned nowhere, as far as I am aware, in published studies of the *L'homme armé* tradition.

[4] Ed. H. C. Colles, II, p. 477.

poser includes the following: 'Avila: R. Monasterio de Santa Ana; Mass, "L'homme arme" (4v.); Magnificat 1 toni (4v.); 3 motets (4v.); not found in any printed ed. (Tenor missing.)'. Fifteen years later, Robert Stevenson attempted to follow up this lead, but met with no success, reporting that 'the pertinent manuscript could not be found at Ávila'.[5] Unfortunately, as it turns out, Stevenson's statement (and his exclusion of the work from the *New Grove* article on Guerrero) was in some cases taken as the final word on the matter. As recently as 1982, José María Llorens Cisteró described the Avila source as lost in his introduction to the fourth volume of Guerrero's complete works.[6] However, it seems that Trend was not the only scholar to have seen this source: in 1968 Higini Anglès referred to Guerrero's mass and to the partbooks in which it was preserved.[7] The existence of the Avila source, and of the *Missa L'homme armé*, was finally confirmed in 1989, with the publication of a catalogue listing and describing the musical holdings of the Monasterio de Sta. Ana.[8]

If the mass preserved in Avila has languished in surprising

---

[5]   *Spanish Cathedral Music*, pp. 186–7.

[6]   *Francisco Guerrero: opera omnia*, IV, Monumentos de la Música Española 38 (Barcelona, 1982), p. 25.

[7]   *The New Oxford History of Music*, ed. G. Abraham, IV (London, 1968), p. 390, note 1. The fact that Anglès contradicts Trend in one important detail (stating that the missing book is the bass rather than the tenor) would seem to indicate that his information concerning the source was not merely derived from Trend's reference.

    The most detailed discussion of Guerrero's masses to date, Luis Merino's doctoral thesis, merely notes Anglès's reference to the *Missa L'homme armé*, without providing further information; see 'The Masses of Francisco Guerrero (1528–1599)' (Ph.D. dissertation, University of California at Los Angeles, 1972), p. 8, note 19.

[8]   Alfonso de Vicente Delgado, *La música en el Monasterio de Santa Ana de Avila (siglos XVI–XVIII): catálogo* (Madrid, 1989). The three partbooks (from an original set of four) containing the *Missa L'homme armé* attributed to Francisco Guerrero are described on pp. 52–6. The missing partbook is neither the tenor, as stated by Trend, nor the bass, as stated by Anglès. The remaining books bear the following (correct) part-names on their covers: 'tiple primero', 'tiple 3º' (i.e. 'tercero') and 'Baxo'. It thus emerges that the lost book was the 'tiple segundo' (a hypothesis confirmed by the existence of a different version of this *Missa L'homme armé*, described later in the present article). This vocal scoring suggests that the books may have been copied for a house of nuns, in all likelihood the monastery which still possesses the source. That this richly endowed monastery supported a polyphonic choir in the late sixteenth and early seventeenth centuries is demonstrated by a reference to 'una magnífica de canto de órgano' ('a Magnificat setting in polyphony') in the autobiographical writings of one of the nuns; see Olegario González Hernández (ed.), *Doña María Vela y Cueto: Autobiografía y Libro de las mercedes* (Barcelona, 1961), p. 237. From the fourteenth century onwards the monastery had also been provided with *capellanes* to assist in the singing of the services (*ibid.*, p. 47); it may be that the lowest part of the works in the source under discussion was taken by one of these *capellanes*.

obscurity, another – related – discovery has received still less attention. In 1982 there appeared a catalogue of the music manuscripts in the Biblioteca Pública Municipal in Oporto,[9] in which is described another source containing a *Missa L'homme armé* attributed to Guerrero (or, rather, to 'Guerreiro'[10]). The source in question, which bears the call-number MM 40, is a small choirbook compiled in Portugal, possibly at Braga Cathedral.[11]

Comparison of these two masses reveals that they are related, but that the relationship between them ranges from near-identity in some places to complete independence (apart, of course, from the common basis in the *L'homme armé* melody) in others. In general terms, the resemblance decreases during the course of the works. Thus, in the first Kyrie the variants are relatively few and superficial, while the settings of the Gloria correspond only intermittently, and those of the Credo merely for one brief phrase; the Sanctus and Agnus Dei sections are entirely different in the two masses. Where the pieces are related, the nature of the variants between them suggests that these variants are not the result of distortion during the process of transmission, but that we have here a case of revision by the composer.[12]

If this hypothesis is correct, which of these masses is the earlier work and which the revision? The answer is, as it happens, almost

---

[9]   L. Cabral, *Catálogo do fundo de manuscritos musicais*, Bibliotheca Portucalensis, 2nd series, 1, pp. 28–34.

[10] The Portuguese scribe consistently spells the name thus, and was certainly referring to Francisco Guerrero. Thus, the next work in the manuscript after the *Missa L'homme armé* – Guerrero's *Missa Dormiendo un giorno*, published in 1566 – is likewise attributed to 'Guerreiro'. Another Portuguese copyist, working at the Monastery of Santa Cruz in Coimbra, spelled the name 'gurreiro' (Coimbra, Biblioteca Geral da Universidade, MM 34, fol. 24ᵛ).

[11] It contains a large number of works by Manuel de Fonseca and Pedro de Gamboa, both of whom held the position of *mestre de capela* at the cathedral (the former in 1544 and the latter in 1587; see Robert Stevenson's introduction to *Antologia de polifonia portuguesa 1490–1680*, Portugaliae Musica 37 (Lisbon, 1982), pp. XXXIII and XXXVI).

      Although the editor of Guerrero's *opera omnia* had been informed in 1982 of the existence of the *Missa L'homme armé* in the Oporto manuscript, he was not then in a position to examine the work and, as noted above, believed the Avila source to be lost. See Llorens Cisteró, *Francisco Guerrero: opera omnia*, IV, pp. 24–5.

[12] It should be noted that the relationship between the two settings confirms beyond reasonable doubt that the attributions in the Oporto and Avila sources are correct, since these attributions (in sources which could not have been directly dependent upon one another, or even stemmatically close) can be seen as reinforcing one another. The recognition of the resemblances between the masses is particularly useful in another respect: where the settings are most similar one can use the Oporto mass as an aid to the restoration of the missing voice in the Avila mass.

startlingly obvious. The Oporto mass falls consistently far short of
the other in technical finesse; indeed, its occasional crudeness suggests that it cannot be a work of Guerrero's compositional matur-
ity, whereas the Avila mass is consistent with his mature style.
The possibility that the Oporto mass may be a 'student' piece
is considerably strengthened by the realisation that in writing it
Guerrero relied in a rather unusual fashion on another work: the
five-voice *Missa L'homme armé* by his teacher Morales. It should
be made clear that Guerrero's work is not a parody mass in the
conventional sense (as are no fewer than eleven of his other
masses) – that is, one which is filled with clear references to the
most prominent material of a short polyphonic original, and which
reworks that material in a fairly comprehensive way.[13] Instead,
Guerrero used the other mass as an occasional compositional prop,
raiding it for isolated motives which worked in imitation, good
countersubjects, cadence constructions, and ways to use the cantus
firmus as a structural device. Those passages which are closest to
the model provide a remarkably clear and detailed view of Guerrero's compositional habits and procedures, since in many such
cases it is possible to reconstruct the sequence of decisions made
by the composer. Moreover, the identification of Guerrero's model
and the study of how he used it provide a valuable opportunity to
observe a renaissance composer learning the elements of his craft
through emulation of an established master.[14]

[13] Luis Merino concluded from a comprehensive study of Guerrero's parody technique
that 'the parody Masses are characterized by a close proximity to the model. Like his
mentor Morales, Guerrero saturates his Masses with borrowed material, presenting it
in novel polyphonic combinations. Like Morales, he combines the motives from the
model' ('The Masses of Francisco Guerrero', p. vii). Robert Stevenson came to much
the same conclusions about Guerrero's parody technique (*Spanish Cathedral Music*, pp.
195–9).
   The Oporto mass is very atypical of parody masses in other respects: it is scored for
fewer voices than its model, and takes another mass as its model.
[14] In a study of a 'student' work and its model in Uppsala, Universitetsbiblioteket, Vokal-
musik i handskrift 76a, Howard Mayer Brown expressed the view that 'emulation –
using models to guide a student's initial efforts until he has mastered his craft – may
well have been as basic a principle of musical pedagogy in the sixteenth century as it
is now', and also made clear the distinction between such pedagogical imitation and
cases of 'one mature composer basing a new piece on an older piece by another mature
composer' ('Emulation, Competition, and Homage: Imitation and Theories of Imitation
in the Renaissance', *Journal of the American Musicological Society*, 35 (1982), pp. 8 and 10).
The significance of *imitatio* as an educational tool in the sixteenth century is discussed
by Michele Fromson in 'A Conjunction of Rhetoric and Music: Structural Modelling
in the Italian Counter-Reformation Motet', *Journal of the Royal Musical Association*, 117
(1992), pp. 209–46.

Before examining the relationship between Guerrero's mass and its model in greater detail, it is worth considering the circumstances in which the Oporto mass may have been written. Guerrero acknowledged Morales as his teacher in the following passage of the *Viage de Hierusalem* (the published account of his pilgrimage to the Holy Land in 1588–9):

Desde los primeros años de mi niñez me incliné al arte de la música, y en ella fuy enseñado de un hermano mío llamado Pedro Guerrero, muy docto maestro. Y tal priessa me dió con su doctrina y castigo, que con mi buena voluntad de aprender, y ser mi ingenio acomodado a la dicha arte, en pocos años tuvo de mí alguna satisfacción. Después por ausencia suya, desseando yo siempre mejorarme, me valí de la doctrina del grande y excelente Maestro Christoval de Morales, el qual me encaminó en la compostura de la música bastantemente, para poder pretender qualquier magisterio. Y assí a los diez y ocho años de mi edad fuy recebido por maestro de capilla de la Iglesia Catedral de Iaen.[15]

There has been some debate concerning exactly when Guerrero's studies with Morales took place: they could only have occurred either on the latter's visit to Spain (on leave from the papal choir) in 1540–1, or after his final return from Rome in the summer of 1545. (He obtained leave from the papal choir on 1 May.) Guerrero was just eleven or twelve years old on the first of these visits, while in the summer of 1545 he was seventeen. It is hence more likely that the advanced tuition mentioned by Guerrero was given at the later period, especially as the concluding two sentences of the passage just quoted imply that this tuition led more or less directly to Guerrero's first appointment at Jaen, an appointment which he secured in April 1546.[16]

[15] 'From the first years of my childhood I was inclined towards the art of music, and was instructed in that art by a brother of mine called Pedro Guerrero, a very learned master. And he imparted such skill to me through his teaching and correction that, given my willingness to learn and since my talents were well fitted to the said art, within a few years he drew from me rewarding results. Afterwards, owing to my brother's absence, and anxious always to improve myself, I availed myself of the teaching of that great and excellent master Cristóbal de Morales, who directed my progress in the composition of music to the level where I could aspire to any post of *maestro*. And so it was that at the age of eighteen I was appointed *maestro de capilla* at Jaen Cathedral.' This passage occurs on pp. 3ff in the 1596 Barcelona edition of the *Viage*, and is reproduced by Higini Anglès in *Cristóbal de Morales: opera omnia, I: Missarum liber primus (Roma, 1544)*, Monumentos de la Música Española 11 (Rome, 1952), p. 41.

[16] The possibility that Morales first became Guerrero's teacher on the visit of 1540–1 cannot, however, be ruled out, and Stevenson's attempt to do so (*Spanish Cathedral Music*, p. 138) lacks supporting evidence. Stevenson takes Guerrero's statement that he went to Morales for tuition only after the departure (to Italy) of his brother Pedro as an

We cannot prove that the Oporto mass was composed in 1545 or 1546 as a direct outcome of Guerrero's studies with Morales, but this does seem quite likely, particularly given the choice of polyphonic model for the work (as well as the way in which Guerrero made use of it). Morales returned to Spain in 1545 with two recently published books of his own masses (issued in Rome by Valerio and Luigi Dorico in 1544), the first (and only) such editions dedicated entirely to his works and published under his personal supervision.[17] Although these impressive folio-size volumes apparently failed to elicit any tangible reward from their respective dedicatees (Cosimo de' Medici and Pope Paul III), they seem to have proved useful to Morales when he arrived in his native country: there are indications that the Toledo Cathedral authorities were moved to grant Morales the post of *maestro* so speedily and without the usual competition largely because the Roman editions provided ample testament to the composer's skill.[18] Given, then,

indication that Morales could not have taught Guerrero until 1545; however, since we have no indication of the date at which Pedro left Seville, no such conclusion can be drawn.

The hypothesis that the tuition occurred between the summer of 1545 and April 1546 does pose one logistical problem: where did the lessons take place? By 31 August 1545 Morales had already secured the post of *maestro de capilla* at Toledo Cathedral, and one can presume that he spent some time in the city prior to this, even though the appointment apparently proceeded without the customary competition. This leaves very little time during which he could have taught Guerrero in Seville during the summer of that year. (As already noted, Morales obtained his leave from the papal chapel on 1 May.) In fact, an entry in the capitular acts of Toledo suggests that Morales did not visit his native city of Seville at all between his arrival in Spain and August 1546. (The relevant document is quoted by J. Moll in 'Cristóbal de Morales en España (Notas para su biografia)', *Anuário Musical*, 8 (1953), p. 19.) It is just conceivable that Guerrero went to Toledo in order to study with Morales; however, quite apart from the difficulty of obtaining leave from his post as a singer in Seville Cathedral, the journey of well over 200 miles between Seville and Toledo must have restricted the opportunities to make such visits. Previous writers on this subject are in disagreement: Stevenson (*Spanish Cathedral Music*, p. 138) believes that the tuition took place in Seville during 'the early summer of 1545', while Higini Anglès argues for Toledo as the likely site of the lessons ('Cristóbal de Morales y Francisco Guerrero', *Anuário Musical*, 9 (1954), pp. 62–3).

Interestingly, there are indications that Morales played a significant role in securing the Jaen post on behalf of his pupil, which sheds a new light on the conclusion of the passage from the *Viage de Hierusalem* quoted above; see Stevenson, *Spanish Cathedral Music*, p. 140.

[17] *Christophori Moralis Hyspalensis missarum liber primus* and *liber secundus*.

[18] The chapter act confirming Morales's appointment states that the decision was made 'atenta la abilidad y sufiçiençia del dicho Cristoval de Morales en la música, según consta por los libros de canto de órgano impresos en Roma' ('in view of the musical ability and competence of the said Cristóbal de Morales, as is made apparent by the books of polyphony printed in Rome'); see Moll, 'Cristóbal de Morales en España', p. 16. It seems quite likely, indeed, that Morales had made a gift of the two Dorico

that these two books were clearly Morales's compositional 'showcase' upon his return from Rome, it seems natural that he should have directed his pupil Guerrero to the volumes and suggested study of the works they contain. Of these works, the two *L'homme armé* masses (one in each book) provided perhaps the most useful basis of all for a compositional exercise (quite apart from the fact that an attempt to work with the *L'homme armé* melody would have been irresistible to a musician named 'Guerrero' – 'warrior'): firstly, the *L'homme armé* tune would have been well known to the young Guerrero (who, as demonstrated below, was certainly acquainted with Josquin's *Sexti toni* mass, and who could hardly have failed to be aware also of the *Missa L'homme armé* by his own most distinguished Sevillian predecessor besides Morales, Francisco de Peñalosa); secondly, the highly unusual exercise of basing a mass setting on both a monophonic and a polyphonic model (and hence the choice of a paraphrase and/or cantus firmus mass as polyphonic model) allowed Guerrero to practise techniques of handling and paraphrasing a cantus firmus while simultaneously using Morales's setting as a compositional support and a fund of contrapuntal and structural ideas.[19] At this early stage in his career, Guerrero apparently required more guidance in attempting so substantial a project than could be provided merely by the *L'homme armé* tune.

As mentioned above, the comparison between the Oporto mass and Morales's five-voice *Missa L'homme armé* proves most instructive where the resemblance between the two works is closest. Such passages occur at the openings of all three sections of the Kyrie, and in the Benedictus. Before proceeding, it will be useful to set out the version of the *L'homme armé* melody employed by Morales, and hence by Guerrero also (see Example 1, where the phrases of

volumes to the cathedral, judging by a further entry in the chapter acts dated 25 September 1545: 'Libros canto de órgano. Este dia, los dichos señores cometieron a los señores olvero y visitadores que vean lo que valen los libros de órgano que dió Morales, maes[t]ro de capilla, y se le pague de la obra lo que valeren' ('Books of polyphony. On this day, the said gentlemen commissioned Senhor Olvero and the Visitors to look into the value of the books of polyphony given by Morales, the *maestro de capilla*, and [agreed] that he be paid what the work is worth'); see Moll, 'Cristóbal de Morales en España', p. 18.

[19] There is, it should be pointed out, no certainty that Guerrero came to know Morales's mass through the Dorico print, since the work had previously appeared in two Venetian anthologies: *Quinque missae Moralis Hispani, ac Jacheti musici excellentissimi: liber primus, cum quinque vocibus* (Scotto, 1540) and *Quinque missarum harmonia diapente* (Scotto, 1543).

Example 1. The *L'homme armé* melody as found in Morales's five-voice mass and Guerrero's mass

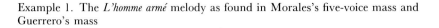

Example 2. Morales, *Missa L'homme armé*, opening of first Kyrie

the tune are labelled to assist the analysis which follows).[20] At the opening of his mass, Guerrero decided to reproduce exactly the opening phrase of Morales's topmost voice, a phrase which is freely based upon the beginning of *L'homme armé* (compare the superius in bars 1–4 of Example 2 with superius I in bars 3–7 of Example 3). The manner in which Guerrero developed this material, however, reveals clearly that his contrapuntal technique and imagination were still limited. Whereas Morales here employed imitative entries and countersubjects which are notably flexible in rhythm and distribution, Guerrero merely preceded the entry in the topmost voice with a pre-imitation at the unison in the second superius. This scheme, besides being rhythmically wooden and texturally

Example 3. Guerrero, *Missa L'homme armé* (Oporto version), opening of first Kyrie

[20] Morales's choice of tritus modality for his treatment of the *L'homme armé* melody was rather unusual within this mass tradition, although there was of course the precedent of Josquin's *Missa L'homme armé sexti toni*. The melody used by Morales and Guerrero departs from the more typical forms – including that found in the Josquin *sexti toni* mass – in omitting the fourth phrase which typically concludes the A section (and which in this mode would consist of the notes C–C–C–F).

bare, caused melodic problems for the second superius in bar 3 of Example 3: no doubt Guerrero would have liked to allow the second superius a smooth descent stepwise to f' after its suspension at the beginning of this bar (as later happens in the first superius), but he was prevented from so doing by the breve f' of the first superius entry. The second superius is thus stuck on a' until the end of the bar. Subsequently this voice lamely follows the first superius at the interval of a third, asserting no contrapuntal independence.

Turning now to the Christe, it is possible by comparing the respective openings of Morales's and Guerrero's versions to retrace the successive stages of Guerrero's adaptation in some detail. Morales built his Christe on a series of statements of phrase B1 and/or B2 of *L'homme armé* (as labelled in Example 1), these statements beginning alternately on f' and g' (see the alto parts in Example 4, where the first two statements are shown). As can be seen in Example 5, Guerrero copied the initial pair of structural entries, and retained the relationship between them (i.e. the second entry occurs in both masses at the point where the first entry reaches d'). He may originally have preserved the rhythms of these entries as they occur in Morales's passage. However, if this was indeed so Guerrero's next decision caused him to make rhythmic alterations. He must have realised that, given the long delay before the second imitative entry, he would have to provide – as had Morales – a countersubject to the first entry in order to lend some rhythmic life to the opening. In doing so, Guerrero evidently determined to copy the most striking technical feature of Morales's passage: as can be seen in Example 4, Morales had so devised things that the same countersubject is heard twice, first in the superius to accompany the f's of the structural entry's opening, and then beneath that entry in the tenor to accompany the e's.[21] Against all

[21] This countersubject is one of a number of motivic elements which appear also in Morales's *Missa Quaeramus cum pastoribus*, published in the same 1544 edition as the five-voice *Missa L'homme armé*. The idea of incorporating such cross-references was in all likelihood originally prompted by the close similarities between the opening material of Mouton's motet, of which the *Missa Quaeramus* is a parody, and phrases A2–3 of the *L'homme armé* melody. The countersubject under discussion appears towards the start of the first Agnus Dei in the *Missa Quaeramus*, accompanying a motive in the lowest voice almost identical with its equivalent in the Christe of the *Missa L'homme armé*, this motive being, of course, a reference to the opening of the *L'homme armé* tune. Other striking parallels between the two Mass settings include the bass subjects at the openings of the Credo settings, and the countersubjects at the very start of the Agnus Dei settings.

Example 4. Morales, *Missa L'homme armé*, opening of Christe

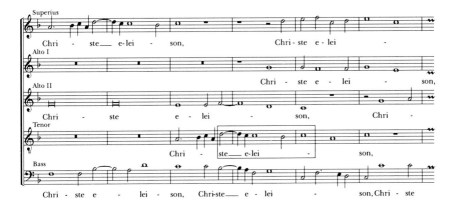

Example 5. Guerrero, *Missa L'homme armé* (Oporto version), opening of Christe

this Morales set another countersubject in the bass, the opening of which refers to the *L'homme armé* melody. Guerrero abandoned this bass countersubject, either because he wished to keep things simpler or because he had one voice fewer available than did Morales, and his lowest voice would be required to take on the role of Morales's tenor. However, he did preserve the plan of a countersubject heard first above and then below the cantus firmus entry. Guerrero's countersubject could not be the same as that of Morales, since the second breve of the latter's motive would no longer work without the bass countersubject to support it (see the superius and alto parts in the second bar of Example 4). Although Guerrero's solution in the superius (Example 5) appears to be wholly original at first glance, he probably arrived at the basic outline of his countersubject by adapting Morales's bass at bars 3–4 of Example 4; in other words, his first step after laying out the structural entries in the alto and second superius, and discovering that Morales's superius countersubject was no longer viable, was in all likelihood the addition of the lowest voice at bars 2–4 of Example 5. Next, he must have attempted to transfer this lower-voice countersubject to the first superius, against the opening of the structural entry in the alto. In order to make it fit, however, he was obliged to alter the rhythm of the alto (which he had copied from Morales) so that it reached *e'* earlier than in Morales's version. These opening four breves of the Christe were now complete except for the first superius in bars 3–4 of Example 5. Guerrero again adopted a simple and derivative solution, merely transposing Morales's tenor up an octave to provide his superius (as can be seen by comparing the boxed passages in Examples 4 and 5).

The openings of the final Kyrie settings reveal perhaps the closest correspondence of all between the two masses (Examples 6 and 7). Morales here returned to a simple cantus firmus layout, with the *L'homme armé* melody (section A') given to the second alto. The voice bearing the cantus firmus is the last to enter, and the other voices prepare for its arrival with pre-imitations based (with varying degrees of fidelity) on phrase A'1 of the melody. Guerrero followed his model in returning to cantus firmus treatment, and for his pre-imitation in the two outer voices he copied almost exactly Morales's tenor and superius entries. His only addition, the countersubject in the second superius, is itself derived from the opening of Morales's first Kyrie (see alto I in Example 2; it will be remembered that in composing his own first Kyrie Guerrero had omitted this countersubject). For the end of his countersubject (the suspended f' and its resolution) Guerrero turned from Morales's Kyrie I countersubject back to the tenor of Morales's final Kyrie (bar 3 of Example 6).

This heavy reliance on the model continues for several more breves; first, however, Guerrero dispensed with Morales's additional pair of pre-imitative entries (alto I and bass in bars 3–4 of Example 6), which he did not need since he had already brought in all three of his 'free' voices. Once the cantus firmus entry has begun, we can follow Guerrero's decisions closely. His second superius derived its rising phrase $f'-g'-a'$ from Morales's superius in bars 5–6 of Example 6; for the first superius Guerrero used the

Example 6. Morales, *Missa L'homme armé*, final Kyrie

Example 7. Guerrero, *Missa L'homme armé* (Oporto version), final Kyrie

suspension figure from alto I at the same point in his model, and then decided to retain Morales's striking superius phrase rising from *f'* to *d''* before settling to a cadence on *c''* (compare bars 7–9 of Example 6 with bars 5–7 of Example 7). Guerrero's upper voice may originally have retained Morales's rhythmic profile here, but if so it was later altered for reasons outlined below. Guerrero had now filled in two of his four voices at this point, since the alto bears the cantus firmus as in Morales's passage. Although we cannot be certain, it seems likely that his next step was the completion of the cadence at the end of bar 6 and the beginning of bar 7 in Example 7. It is often the case in the Oporto mass that – as happens here – Guerrero will suddenly preserve his model more or less intact at a cadence (presumably because one of his technical priorities was the acquisition of common cadential formulas). On this occasion Guerrero used Morales's alto I and tenor as his own superius II and tenor, as can be seen by comparing bars 8–9 of Example 6 with bars 6–7 of Example 7. This left him with only a small gap before the cadence in the second superius and a rather longer one (the second half of bar 4 and the whole of bar 5 in Example 7) in the lowest voice; it was probably this latter voice that he decided to tackle first, by inserting an imitative entry. However, if Guerrero had indeed at this stage retained Morales's rhythms for the rising phrase in the first superius, this tenor entry would not work, since the tenor reached *bb* while the superius was still on *a'*; also, the *g'* in the superius would have been excessively harsh as a minim passing note against the *f* in the lowest voice. It was for this reason, I believe, that Guerrero altered the rhythm of the superius, so that the offending *g'* on the second minim beat of bar 7 in Example 6 became just a crotchet (and hence inoffensive as a passing note; see bar 5 of Example 7), and the quavers at the end of the bar were replaced by crotchets, thus introducing the *bb'* earlier so that it coincided with the *bb* in the lowest voice. Only the second superius now remained incomplete, and Guerrero finished it simply with a rest and crotchet run.

In summary, we see that Guerrero practised contrapuntal skills through the manipulation of pre-existent materials, 'composing' substantial parts of his Kyrie setting by taking his model apart into single melodic or contrapuntal elements and adapting or reassembling these elements in different patterns. The evidence of the passages described above suggests that he rarely proceeded far with the working-out of a single voice (unless that voice was the basis of the structure, i.e. a phrase of the cantus firmus, or a particularly important imitative entry), but built up the texture in small stages, often leaving gaps in one or more voices to be filled later. His working method is seen at its most short-term and 'vertically' oriented – as one might expect – at cadences, where, as already noted, he will frequently retain or adapt the whole contrapuntal complex found in his model. Thus the very next cadence in Example 7, at bars 7–8, is also derived from the model (see bars 10–11 of Example 6), and another such case occurs in the Gloria, at 'bone voluntatis' (see Examples 8 and 9). Guerrero has here preserved Morales's statement of phrases A2–3 of the *L'homme armé* melody (including the rhythms), but has transferred it to the second superius. As the cadence approaches, the three 'free' voices (which had been independent of the model) quote Morales's version with some exactitude. However, while Morales's three free voices are the lowest three, Guerrero had a superius part available

Example 8. Morales, *Missa L'homme armé*, part of Gloria

Example 9. Guerrero, *Missa L'homme armé* (Oporto version), part of Gloria

as well as his two lower voices. He therefore transposed Morales's tenor up an octave to provide his superius.[22] (As in previous examples where Guerrero has indulged in such musical 'joinery', that joinery remains all too audible, producing in this case an oddly dislocated 'tail' to the first superius phrase (see the rest and leap in this part at bar 4 of Example 9, where the quotation of the tenor part begins); an almost identical dislocation occurs for similar reasons in the first superius at bars 2–3 of Example 5, where, it will be remembered, the same device – upward transposition of Morales's tenor at a cadence – had been employed.)

[22] Guerrero's tendency to quote from Morales's mass at cadences is seen again at the end of the first major section in the Gloria, at 'Jesu Christe', where he suddenly reproduces his model note for note (except that Guerrero's lowest voice is an octave higher).

The Oporto mass reveals its nature as an apprentice compositional exercise most clearly at those points where Guerrero attempted to surpass his model in artifice and symmetry. Such attempts usually brought with them contrapuntal problems which reveal that the young composer was not yet proficient at foreseeing all the consequences of a particular decision. A striking example occurs at the opening of the Benedictus (see Examples 10 and 11). As often, Guerrero adopted Morales's structural plan, assigning the B section of the *L'homme armé* melody to the middle of three voices, and preceding the first entry of this voice with a pre-imitation in the upper voice, accompanied by a countersubject in the lowest part. For the first two breves of this duet Guerrero followed Morales exactly; thereafter his countersubject is original. (Yet again, it will be noticed, Guerrero failed to conceal the join: he simply left a minim rest in the lowest voice.) At bar 5 of Example 11 in the upper voice Guerrero made his first attempt to improve on Morales's original, which here departs from the *L'homme armé* tune. However, while Guerrero does remain faithful to the tune, this has unfortunate results given his next revision of the model. As seen already in several other instances, he retained Morales's cadence at the end of the phrase (bar 6 of Examples 10 and 11), but on this occasion he swapped the two outer voices; as a consequence

Example 10. Morales, *Missa L'homme armé*, opening of Benedictus

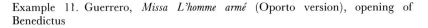

Example 11. Guerrero, *Missa L'homme armé* (Oporto version), opening of Benedictus

Guerrero's upper voice lamely repeats in bar 6 what it has just sung in bar 5.

Guerrero next introduced an element of neat symmetry missing in Morales's passage: he re-used as countersubject to the end of the inner-voice cantus firmus statement (bars 7–10 of Example 11) his newly composed countersubject first heard in the lowest voice at bars 3–6 (a device which, as noted above, he had copied from Morales at the opening of the Christe). It was presumably in accommodating this device that he altered the rhythm of Morales's cantus firmus statement, bringing forward by a semibreve the *d'* in bar 9 of Example 10 so that the rhythm corresponded to that of the earlier superius statement of this cantus firmus phrase. Once again, unfortunately, his good idea brought problems with it: this *d'*, unlike its equivalent at bar 5 of Example 11, cannot resolve down to *c'* twice, since that would distort the *L'homme armé* tune. (The equivalent superius melody at bars 5–6 is not, it should be remembered, a 'formal' statement of the tune, but merely a pre-imitation.) Since, however, Guerrero ended his countersubject as before with a suspension on *c''*, he this time landed on the *c''* as an unprepared dissonance, clashing with the obstinate *d'* of the cantus firmus statement.

Guerrero's skills in developing material taken from his polyphonic model and in constructing imitative counterpoint around cantus firmus statements had advanced noticeably by the time he came to set the Agnus Dei.[23] The opening of the first Agnus Dei reveals both of these skills. This passage is not related to Morales's Agnus Dei, but instead borrows a bass countersubject from the opening of Morales's Credo (see Examples 12 and 13). Guerrero had already made an attempt to work out his own version of this passage from his model, at the start of the Sanctus; there, he had relied heavily on Morales's version (Example 14), whereas in the

Example 12. Morales, *Missa L'homme armé*, opening of Credo

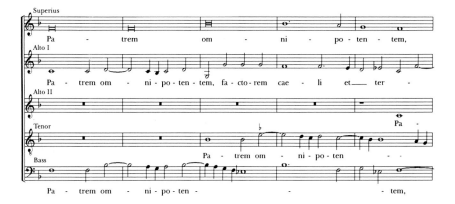

Example 13. Guerrero, *Missa L'homme armé* (Oporto version), opening of Agnus Dei

[23] One can, I think, be confident that the Agnus Dei was the last part of the Oporto mass to be written, given this increased technical competence.

Example 14. Guerrero, *Missa L'homme armé* (Oporto version), opening of Sanctus

Agnus Dei he is more adventurous, developing the opening three breves of Morales's lowest voice into a newly conceived imitative introduction and accompaniment to the cantus firmus statement in the bass.

The final Agnus Dei was, of course, traditionally a vehicle for some form of technical display (a lesson which Guerrero could have learned from the mass settings of his teacher). At this point in the Oporto mass Guerrero chose to employ a device – the presentation of the *L'homme armé* theme in retrograde in the lowest voice – which had the most eminent precedent, namely the extraordinary canonic Agnus Dei setting which concludes Josquin's *Missa L'homme armé sexti toni*.[24] As already noted, this mass is one of the few in the *L'homme armé* tradition to employ the tritus modality chosen by Morales and Guerrero, a factor which must have recommended it as a model. Furthermore, there are apparent references to the *Sexti toni* mass in Morales's five-voice *Missa L'homme armé*.[25] That Guerrero had Josquin's Agnus Dei in mind is suggested not only by his use of a retrograde cantus firmus statement in the lowest part but also by some motivic features of the upper voices. Two of the most prominent figures in the canonic upper voices of Josquin's setting are the rocking motive with which it opens (Example 15) and the falling scales which follow this motive and which are later developed independently (Example 16). Guerrero may have been thinking of the first of these figures when he devised the superius II countersubject at the opening of his Agnus

[24] Dufay's *Missa L'homme armé* likewise incorporates retrograde motion in its Agnus Dei.
[25] For example, at the opening of the Sanctus, where Morales added a new countersubject to Josquin's imitative entries.

Dei (Example 17), while a motive similar to the second figure occurs, as in Josquin's setting, in canonic stretto between the upper voices (Example 18).[26]

Example 15. Josquin, *Missa L'homme armé sexti toni*, Agnus Dei, opening motive of upper voices

Example 16. Josquin, *Missa L'homme armé sexti toni*, Agnus Dei, upper-voice motive

Example 17. Guerrero, *Missa L'homme armé* (Oporto version), opening of final Agnus Dei

[26] At the very end of the Oporto mass, Guerrero copied the device with which the lower two voices of Josquin's final Agnus Dei begin: against the retrograde statement in the lowest voice is fitted phrase B of the *L'homme armé* melody in the voice immediately above. Guerrero again took a leaf out of Josquin's book at the only point in the Oporto mass where canonic writing is attempted: in the Hosanna. The Spaniard here followed Josquin in constructing a canon between the two lower voices, based on the *L'homme armé* melody, while the upper voices engage in a looser canon.

Given these references, together with the heavy reliance on Morales's mass already described, it can be seen that the Oporto mass provides further evidence of the extensive practice of emulation existing within the tradition of *L'homme armé* masses. On this subject, see for example R. Taruskin, 'Antoine Busnoys and the *L'homme armé* Tradition', *Journal of the American Musicological Society*, 39 (1986), pp. 225–93.

As a measure of Guerrero's respect for Josquin, one might note that as late as 1586 he proposed to the Seville Cathedral Chapter that a book of Josquin's works be recopied; see R. M. Stevenson, *La música en la Catedral de Sevilla 1478–1606: documentos para su estudio* (Los Angeles, 1954), p. 52a.

Example 18. Guerrero, *Missa L'homme armé* (Oporto version), part of final Agnus Dei (upper voices)

At a later stage in his career Guerrero returned to his *Missa l'homme armé*, apparently with the intention merely of revising the work. Certainly (as already mentioned) he began in the Kyrie by making only the most superficial changes. However, it seems that as work progressed the numerous technical deficiencies of the original setting encouraged him towards increasingly drastic recomposition, and eventually to abandon the original almost entirely and compose afresh.

Guerrero's recomposition often resulted in a compression of the original, since one of his principal concerns was clearly to improve those points in the Oporto mass where the music lost momentum. (Thus the new Christe has been shortened by three semibreves and the final Kyrie by seven.)[27] A good example of the increased impetus achieved through such compression occurs in the opening Kyrie (Examples 19 and 20).[28] Two aspects of the original may

Example 19. Oporto mass, part of first Kyrie

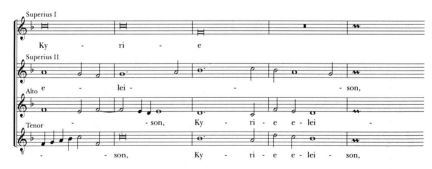

<hr />

[27] Those sections of the Avila mass which are partially or entirely new are also more concise than their equivalents in the Oporto mass, usually by as much as fifteen per cent. The one exception is the final Agnus Dei, which is longer in the Avila mass than in the earlier work; presumably Guerrero wished to provide a more fittingly expansive conclusion to his new setting.

[28] It will be noticed from these examples that the two superius parts have been reversed at this point in the Avila mass.

Example 20. Avila mass, part of first Kyrie

have prompted Guerrero to make alterations here: the sudden halt to rhythmic activity in bar 3 of Example 19 (this type of rhythmic hiatus being a common failing of the Oporto mass) and, in wider structural terms, the lack of any point of climax within the original Kyrie setting which would give it a purposeful shape. Guerrero's solution was to compress the second bar of Example 19 by removing the ornamental resolution of the suspension in the alto, and by making the consequent simpler resolution simultaneous with the rise from g' to a' in the superius. The quickening of harmonic rhythm which results creates the potential for climax, a potential fulfilled by the next alteration: the superius – unlike in the Oporto version – continues its scalic rise to reach d'', which is the peak-note of the superius parts in this mass. This melodic addition also serves to prevent the rhythmic stasis noted in bar 3 of Example 19; Guerrero is fastidious in filling such gaps in his new version of the mass.

By the time he reached the final Kyrie, Guerrero had begun to indulge in more substantial revisions of the Oporto mass, and as a result this section provides a fine example of his greater sensitivity to phrase-shape, climax, and pacing in the later work. It will be remembered that the opening of this Kyrie in the Oporto mass had been cobbled together from elements of Morales's first and final Kyrie settings. Although the musical joinery was accomplished with some ingenuity, the result is hardly organic (see Example 7 above): bar 4 repeats the harmonic gesture (including the suspension) of bar 3, and the superius-led climax which follows this is rather sudden and unprepared. Example 21 shows Guer-

Example 21. Avila mass, opening of final Kyrie

rero's revision of this passage. The opening pre-imitation has been drastically compressed, with a new countersubject (in superius I) adding to the rhythmic momentum, and the redundant extra cadence preceding the entrance of the cantus firmus has disappeared. Conversely, the succeeding climax is more sustained in the new version. Guerrero now uses the first superius a' in bar 3 of Example 21 as the natural springboard for the rise to the phrase's peak on d''. As a result, the first superius attains its climax earlier than before; however, the d'' has been lengthened from a crotchet to a dotted minim, making the whole gesture less perfunctory. The relationship between the outer parts has also benefited: the progression from F to B♭ in both of these voices in bar 5 of Example 7 had been too close to parallel octaves not to sound rather weak. The dissolution of this moment of climax has likewise been prolonged, and made melodically and harmonically more characterful. Guerrero achieved this by returning to Morales's mass at this point, reintroducing the bass figure with its leap of a fourth which he had removed in the Oporto mass (see bars 10–11 of Example 6, bars 7–8 of Example 7, and bars 6–7 of Example 21); this leap serves to accentuate the suspended dissonance with the superius.[29]

Although Guerrero had thus incorporated an additional reference to his original model in the new mass, this reference is of the most insignificant kind, and the overall effect of his recomposition of the climactic passage just discussed was the virtual destruction of a much more striking quotation from Morales's mass: as was shown above, the original climactic superius phrase here was derived directly from Morales. Many other revisions in the Avila mass produced the same result, so that – since in addition large portions of that mass were newly composed – the audible relationship between Guerrero's work and its original model could easily have disappeared almost entirely. However, Guerrero was clearly unwilling that this should be so, for he took steps which ensured that the new mass actually pays more overt homage to Morales than had the early version. Thus, for example, the Gloria now opens with an adaptation of the head-motive from the first three sections of Morales's work (compare Example 22 with Example 23). This reference to his teacher's mass is more immediately striking than any of those in the earlier setting, partly because of its position at the head of a complete section of the mass, partly because of the prominence of what it quotes (this head-motive being of greater significance than the opening of Morales's Benedictus which, as noted above, Guerrero had retained in the Oporto mass), and partly because the whole contrapuntal complex is retained more or less intact (unlike in the case of the relationship between the older Sanctus and Morales's Credo already mentioned: see Examples 12 and 14 above). We have here the type of open emulation – emulation which was designed to be noticed and thus to declare the new work's pedigree – which is an important feature of conventional parody technique, and which is, in the main, notably absent from the Oporto mass.

In general, the new Gloria reveals Guerrero's vastly improved skills in handling an extended musical structure. The aimless and monotonous impression created by the Gloria of the Oporto mass

[29] It should also be noted with regard to this passage that the end of the cantus firmus phrase in the alto, with its longer *d'*, now corresponds more closely to the rhythm of the *L'homme armé* melody than it had in the Oporto mass.

Example 22. Morales, *Missa L'homme armé*, opening of Gloria

Example 23. Guerrero, Avila mass, opening of Gloria

is due in large part to a lack of harmonic direction, of clear articulating cadences, and of textural variety. The contrast with the later work is often most impressive where this work re-uses material from the old, as for example at 'benedicimus te, adoramus te' (see Examples 24 and 25). Typically, there is no effective articulation between these two phrases of text in the Oporto mass: not only are the rising imitative motives too similar, but the non-motivic entries in the alto (bar 3) and superius I (bar 4) weaken the impact of the second text-phrase. When Guerrero wrote the equivalent passage in the later work, he exploited the cadential possibilities of bar 3 of Example 24 to create a point of articulation; while this potential cadence is avoided in Example 24 – the harmony remaining static from the end of bar 3 to the tactus beat at the beginning of bar 4 – in Example 25 the alto is altered to provide the cadence, an articulation emphasised by the silence of the outer voices and their subsequent entry in animated homorhythm.[30]

---

[30] It must of course be borne in mind that the second superius part is here editorial.

Example 24. Oporto mass, part of Gloria

Example 25. Avila mass, part of Gloria

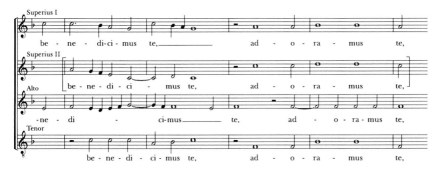

It will be remembered that Guerrero had begun the Avila mass by making only superficial changes to his earlier setting; thus the opening of the first Kyrie had, despite its melodic flaws and lack of rhythmic momentum, survived intact except for some minor alterations to improve the declamation. In the first Agnus Dei of the new mass, however, Guerrero took the opportunity to remodel this passage, and did so in a way which in terms of the coherence of the whole setting was a masterstroke. Although the Oporto mass had effectively made no use of a head-motive, Guerrero clearly realised, at this later stage in his career, the importance of such a device in linking the sections of a mass setting, and he had thus linked the Gloria and Credo of the Avila mass by basing their openings on the head-motive of Morales's mass. In so doing he paid homage to his master's piece in a manner conventional to parody technique, as already noted. His masterstroke in devising

45

the opening of the new Agnus Dei was to combine a reference to
Morales's head-motive (providing a link with his own Gloria and
Credo) with the reworking of his earlier Kyrie opening (thus also
linking the new Kyrie and Agnus Dei). The result can be seen in
Example 26. Comparison with Example 2 above shows that the
opening three breves are even closer to Morales's Kyrie than is the
start of Guerrero's new Gloria (Example 23). However, as the first
superius enters, his model becomes the Kyrie of his own early *Missa
L'homme armé* (see Example 3). Through his reference to Morales,
Guerrero removed the main fault of this original passage, namely
the bare sonorities and rhythmic inactivity caused by the layout
of the unison imitation between the superius parts. Although the
loss of the second superius makes it impossible to be certain, it
seems likely that the suppression in the new version of the second
note of the original first superius entry was designed to remedy
another less than felicitous aspect of the opening of the Oporto
mass: the inability of the second superius to descend by step after
its suspension figure in bar 3 (see p. 28 above). The alteration to
the first superius now made this smooth descent possible. Finally,
what had been the first imitative entry in the lowest voice was
brought forward by a semibreve in relation to the alto entry (bars
5–6 of Example 3 and of Example 26), removing the harmonic
repetitiveness of the original cadence at this point. After this Guerrero again abandoned his original version, and provided the Avila
mass with an impressively expansive conclusion in the form of a
canonic five-voice setting of the final Agnus Dei – a setting discussed further below.

Example 26. Avila mass, opening of Agnus Dei

As an epilogue to this study of Guerrero's *L'homme armé* masses, I would like to indulge in a brief speculation concerning probably the most famous incident with which Guerrero's name has been associated. This incident is described in Fray Prudencio de Sandoval's biography of the Emperor Charles V, and is assigned to the year 1556, when Charles was living in retirement at the Hieronymite monastery in Yuste. The passage concerned concludes an account of the emperor's love of music:

> Presentólo un maestro de capilla de Sevilla, que yo co[n]ocí, que se decía Guerrero, un libro de motetes que él había compuesto y de misas, y mandó que cantasen una misa por él, y acabada la misa envió a llamar al confesor y díjole:
> – Oh hi[jo]deputa, qué sotil ladrón es ese Guerrero, que tal pasó de fulano, y tal de fulano hurtó.[31]

One's faith in the accuracy of this account is increased by the fact that Sandoval knew Guerrero personally. (Sandoval was a sufficiently serious historian not to have invented such an acquaintance.) Clearly, if the account is accurate, the mass concerned was based upon more than one model. Of the eighteen masses published during Guerrero's lifetime, only one could conceivably fulfil this criterion – the *Missa Super flumina Babylonis* – and even in this case the evidence is very weak. The mass contains what may be thematic references to Gombert's motet of that title, but, as has been noted by Merino,[32] the relationship between mass and 'model' is far looser than is usual in Guerrero's parodies. It seems possible therefore that there was another, as yet undiscovered, model for the mass, a model which provided some of the recurring material that has no parallel in the Gombert motet. In the absence of further evidence, however, we shall have to look elsewhere in search of the mass performed at Yuste.

---

[31] 'A *maestro de capilla* from Seville called Guerrero, whom I knew, presented [to the emperor] a book of motets and masses which he had composed, and [the emperor] ordered them to sing one of the masses by him, and when the mass was finished he sent for his confessor and said, "What a son of a bitch, what a crafty thief is this Guerrero, for he stole this passage from so-and-so, and this passage from so-and-so." ' See D. C. Seco Serrano, ed., *Fray Prudencio de Sandoval: Historia de la vida y hechos del Emperador Carlos V*, Biblioteca de Autores Españoles 82 (Madrid, 1956), III, p. 498. Sandoval's biography was first published in Valladolid in 1604/1606; a second edition appeared at Pamplona in 1614.

[32] 'The Masses of Francisco Guerrero', p. 21.

There are reasons for believing that this mass may have been the *Missa L'homme armé*, in its later form. (Although the Oporto mass fits the criterion, since it refers to works by Josquin and Morales as well as to the *L'homme armé* melody itself, it seems most unlikely that Guerrero would have been satisfied to use this technically immature work as a showpiece for presentation to Charles.) It has already been pointed out that the new work includes prominent references to the five-voice setting by Morales, references which could hardly have been missed by anyone who knew this mass. In searching for a second model, there seemed to be an obvious place to start: it is striking that the new five-voice Agnus Dei with which the work ends is – surprisingly – entirely free of the *L'homme armé* melody, causing suspicions that it might be based on something else. A likely model does indeed exist in the form of a motet by Gombert, *Veni electa mea*. The opening of the motet and of Guerrero's Agnus Dei are given as Examples 27 and 28.[33] It will be seen that the initial motives in the upper voices are identical, and that the second imitative (or, in the case of Guerrero's piece, canonic) voice enters at the same point in both examples. A mass drawing on a motet by Gombert would in general terms have been an eminently suitable piece to perform before Charles, since Gombert had served the emperor as *maître des enfants* of the court chapel, and was effectively Charles's court composer for over a decade, writing works to commemorate several important events of the reign. As will be shown below, *Veni electa mea* may be just such an occasional motet – one that Charles would have been almost certain to recognise.

There is another, more significant, factor which would have made the *Missa L'homme armé* the perfect work to present to Charles, namely the cantus firmus itself. The theme of the armed man was a particularly appropriate one with which to flatter Charles, the great priorities of whose reign had been the crusades against the Turk and the protestant heretics, and who had been portrayed as a warrior king, leading his armies in person. The most famous encapsulation of this view in a work of art is the painting which

---

[33] The motet was first published in *Cantiones quinque vocum selectissimae* (Petrus Schöffer, Strasbourg, 1539). For a modern edition, see *Nicolai Gombert opera omnia*, VIII, ed. J. Schmidt-Görg, Corpus Mensurabilis Musicae 6 (Neuhausen-Stuttgart, 1970), pp. 137–43.

Example 27. Gombert, *Veni electa mea*, opening

Example 28. Guerrero, Avila mass, opening of final Agnus Dei

Charles commissioned from Titian to mark the defeat of the German Lutheran princes at the Battle of Mühleberg in 1547. The emperor is here shown in armour, spear in hand, and seated on his charger – the 'armed man'. Most tellingly for the present hypothesis, there exists one *Missa L'homme armé* which was certainly intended (at least in its published form) as a tribute to Charles the warrior emperor as represented by Titian. The work concerned is Morales's four-voice setting, published in Dorico's *Liber secundus* of 1544. As Stevenson has noted, 'the woodcut at the beginning of the four-voice *L'Homme armé* shows a crowned and bearded warrior, his eyes as well as his sword being uplifted. Atop his crown is a cross, and further above one reads the motto *plus ultra*'.[34] 'Plus

---

[34] *Spanish Cathedral Music*, p. 57.

ultra' was Charles's own motto, and a standard feature of the iconography surrounding him.[35]

There was almost certainly a further aspect to the identification of Charles as *L'homme armé*. Charles had adopted the heraldic device of which the motto 'Plus ultra' (originally the French 'Plus oultre') forms a part in 1516, specifically for the eighteenth chapter of the Order of the Golden Fleece held in Ste-Gudule in Brussels, this being the first chapter over which he presided as Master of the Order.[36] This new device showed the two columns of Hercules at the Straits of Gibraltar, which traditionally marked the limits of human exploration. The motto was therefore a declaration of Charles's power to surpass these limits in forging a greater Christian empire. Although the device was later seen as representing the conquest of the New World, at its inception it 'served primarily to express Charles's aims for the Order of the Golden Fleece',[37] which was dedicated to the fight against the Turk: 'as the prospective ruler of much of the Christian world, he could pledge more confidently than any previous Master to lead the knights of the Order against Islam and to cross the Straits of Gibraltar and to press on to the Holy Land'.[38] In all probability, then, it was as Master of the Order of the Golden Fleece that Charles was most directly associated with the figure of the 'armed man'. In recent years several writers have proposed a connection between the order – or, more specifically, its masters – and the tradition of *L'homme armé* masses;[39] it seems likely that at the very least Morales was aware of this connection when he oversaw the publication of his four-voice *Missa L'homme armé*.

Guerrero, in turn, must have recognised the significance of the visual 'dedication' made by his teacher in a book of masses which he is likely to have studied. Perhaps, then, it was this direct example that persuaded him (if Sandoval's story and the hypo-

---

[35] Gombert wrote a piece for two lutes under the title *Plus ultra*.
[36] See E. E. Rosenthal, 'The Invention of the Columnar Device of Emperor Charles V at the Court of Burgundy in Flanders in 1516', *Journal of the Warburg and Courtauld Institutes*, 36 (1973), pp. 201–3.
[37] Rosenthal, 'The Invention of the Columnar Device', p. 230.
[38] *Ibid.*
[39] See, for example, W. F. Prizer, 'Music and Ceremonial in the Low Countries: Philip the Fair and the Order of the Golden Fleece', *Early Music History*, 5 (1985), pp. 128–9; Taruskin, 'Antoine Busnoys', pp. 272–3; B. Haagh, letter in *Journal of the American Musicological Society*, 40 (1987), p. 143.

thesis just outlined are correct) to include his own *Missa L'homme armé* in the manuscript of masses and motets presented to Charles at Yuste.[40] Extending the hypothesis further, one wonders whether Guerrero's decision to recompose and improve his early *Missa L'homme armé* was prompted by the forthcoming visit to Yuste. If so, we could assign a date of *c.* 1556 to the Avila mass, which would thus postdate by a decade the Oporto mass.

At this point I would like to return to the reference in Guerrero's mass to Gombert's *Veni electa mea*. The motet's text is as follows: 'Veni electa mea, et ponam in te thronum meum, quia concupivit rex speciem tuam. Audi, filia, et vide, et inclina aurem tuam. Diffusa est gratia in labiis tuis: propterea benedixit te Deus in aeternum. Specie tua et pulchritudine tua intende, prospere, procede, et regna' ('Come my chosen one, and I shall place thee upon my throne, for the king has set his desire on thy beauty. Hear, O daughter, and see, and incline thine ear. Graciousness is poured out upon thy lips: therefore God has blessed thee for ever. Pay heed to thy fairness and thy beauty, prosper, go forth, and reign'). The bulk of this text comes from Psalm 44 (45 according to the English numbering),[41] which is a celebration of a royal wedding. The psalm falls into two sections. The first part is a song of praise for a young king, comely and eloquent, who is blessed by God; the king is victorious in battle, but his victories serve a righteous cause. In the second section the psalmist addresses the king's foreign bride, urging her to forget her father's house. After a description of her entry into the king's palace, the psalm ends with the prophecy that the union will be blessed with offspring, male heirs whom the king 'will appoint princes over all the earth'.[42] In March 1526 Charles travelled to Seville in order to marry Isabella of Portugal, daughter of King Manuel I. The motet text set by Gombert would certainly have been highly appropriate to the wedding festivities. However, the context from which the text was drawn – a context

[40] It should be pointed out that by 1556 Charles was no longer Master of the Order of the Golden Fleece, having passed the title to his son Philip.

[41] 'Audi filia ... tuam' is from verse 11 (according to the Vulgate versification) and 'Diffusa ... aeternum' from verse 3; 'Specie ... regna' is verse 5; in addition, 'Quia concupivit Rex speciem tuam' is similar to the first part of verse 12, 'et concupiscet rex decorem tuum'.

[42] For a commentary on this psalm as a 'royal wedding song', see for example A. Weiser, *The Psalms: a Commentary*, trans. H. Hartwell (London, 1962), pp. 362–4.

of which a contemporary audience would without doubt have been
aware – fits this occasion in a much more striking manner. As in
the psalm, the king marries a foreign bride, and their offspring will
rule over all the earth: as noted above, Charles's motto 'Plus ultra'
encapsulated the ceaseless expansion of his dominion in the New
World, Africa and the Near East, a theme represented on the seven
arches, each bearing a poetic gloss on 'Plus ultra', constructed to
line the route of the Emperor's and Isabella's entry into Seville for
their wedding.[43] Moreover the king described in the psalm is a
remarkably accurate portrait of Charles. The psalmist praises the
king as a great and victorious warrior, but – as already mentioned –
one who fights in a just cause. We have already seen that this was
exactly the manner in which Charles wished to be portrayed: the
'armed man' fighting, as Holy Roman Emperor and Master of the
Order of the Golden Fleece, in the most righteous of causes – to
defend catholic Europe from the infidel and from protestant heresy.
The previous year had witnessed the greatest military success of
Charles's reign up to this point, his defeat of the French at Pavia
and the capture of King Francis I. (It was on the very day of his
wedding in Seville that Charles granted Francis his freedom.) The
emperor as victorious christian warrior was the subject of the
second arch set up on Charles's route into Seville. This arch was
dominated by a statue of Charles in armour, sword in hand, with
the following Latin inscription beneath: 'Cessare fortitudine
potentissimae, postea quam ab inmenenti clade Rempublicam
Christianam liberavit, & Arabes, Armenos, Poenos, terrore late
concussit . . .'.[44]

The next part of the psalmist's eulogy of the king could likewise

---

[43] D. O. de Zúñiga reproduces detailed descriptions of these arches in *Annales eclesiasticos
y seculares de la muy noble y muy leal ciudad de Sevilla* (Madrid, 1677), pp. 483–8.

[44] 'To Caesar, most powerful in fortitude, since he has freed the Christian Republic from
imminent defeat, and has convulsed the Arabs, Armenians, and North Africans far and
wide with terror'. See Zúñiga, *Annales*, p. 484. This inscription suggests comparison
with the following passage in Psalm 44:

> Gird thy sword upon thy thigh, O most mighty!
> In thy splendour and glory.
> In thy glory ride forth triumphantly
> in the cause of truth and wronged right.
> May thy right hand teach thee dreadful deeds.
> Thine arrows are sharp; nations are subject to thee:
> the enemies of the king lose heart.

have been seen as particularly appropriate to Charles: 'Your throne is God's for ever and ever; the sceptre of your kingdom is a righteous sceptre: you love justice and hate wickedness. Therefore the Lord your God has anointed you with the oil of gladness above your fellows'. The office of Holy Roman Emperor was 'God's throne' in the sense of being divinely blessed, and was indeed set above other kingships.

In considering whether Gombert is likely to have composed *Veni electa mea* for the royal marriage in 1526, it is worth noting that the composer joined Charles's chapel in that very year,[45] and may therefore have participated in the wedding services. Further (as noted above), Gombert certainly provided works to mark other events in Charles's reign. It seems entirely likely that the piece was written for a royal wedding, and given all that has been said above about the correspondence between the themes of Psalm 44 and those of the 1526 wedding celebrations, the marriage of the emperor is surely the best candidate.

If this was so, Guerrero's reference to the motet comes to seem entirely felicitous: the motet, composed for the emperor's famous visit to Guerrero's native city,[46] carried associations (because of the main source of its text) with Charles the 'armed man'. Hence the incorporation of this quotation at the end of a *Missa L'homme armé*, far from representing an abandoning of the theme of the rest of the mass or an arbitrarily chosen reference to one of Charles's musicians, was wholly appropriate, and indeed served to make the entire mass a specific reference to Charles. Guerrero, in summary, could not have devised a better gift, a tribute from the Sevillian composer named 'warrior' to Charles the 'armed man'.

This view of Guerrero's purpose in quoting Gombert's motet makes it appear more likely that there is indeed some truth in Sandoval's story, and hence that the dating of the Avila mass to 1556 may be sound. If the dates proposed here for the composition of Guerrero's two *L'homme armé* masses prove dependable, they could act as invaluable yardsticks in plotting the early development of the composer's technique. However, even if the speculations upon which these datings are based were shown to be invalid, the

---

[45] See Stevenson, *Spanish Cathedral Music*, p. 24.

[46] Perhaps a copy of the piece, by means of which Guerrero might have come to know it, was preserved in Seville after the wedding.

bringing to light of the Oporto and Avila masses, and the recognition of the relationships between them and of the relationship with their principal model, should provide new impetus to the detailed study of Guerrero's style – in particular, his parody technique and the technical debt which his music owes to that of Morales. These discoveries also make, I believe, a valuable contribution to our understanding of musical pedagogy and compositional method in the middle of the sixteenth century.

University of Surrey

Early Music History (1993) Volume 12

KAY KAUFMAN SHELEMAY, PETER JEFFERY
AND INGRID MONSON

ORAL AND WRITTEN TRANSMISSION
IN ETHIOPIAN CHRISTIAN CHANT*

In memory of Howard Mayer Brown

Of all the musical traditions in the world among which fruitful comparisons with medieval European chant might be made, the chant tradition of the Ethiopian Orthodox Church promises to be especially informative. In Ethiopia one can actually witness many of the same processes of oral and written transmission as were or may have been active in medieval Europe. Music and literacy are taught in a single curriculum in ecclesiastical schools. Future

*This article is a revised and abridged synthesis of three separate papers presented at a session of the same title at the fifty-fourth Annual Meeting of the American Musicological Society at Baltimore, Maryland, in 1988. The material is drawn from a collaborative study carried out by the authors, for which Kay K. Shelemay served as project director, Peter Jeffery as project co-director and Ingrid Monson as research associate. The article has been edited by Kay K. Shelemay; sections written entirely by one member of the research team appear under his or her name, while the introductory and concluding remarks are drawn from all three articles. The authors acknowledge with gratitude a grant from the Research Division of the National Endowment for the Humanities, which supported their work, and the advice of Dr Getatchew Haile, who served as project consultant.

A note on transliteration of Gəʿəz terms: The transliteration system used here eliminates most diacritical markings in order to reduce confusion with notational signs. The seven Ethiopic (Gəʿəz) vowels (referred to as 'orders' when combined with one of the thirty-three basic symbols in the Gəʿəz syllabary) are represented as ε, u, i, a, e, ə and o. To avoid confusion in our transliteration of the written Gəʿəz sources, we have used ε (pronounced 'like the sound one makes while hesitating in speaking and which is represented in writing by "uh"'; W. Leslau, *Amharic Textbook* (Wiesbaden, 1967), p. 6) for all first-order vowels. The reader should be aware that ε is pronounced like that of the fourth-order (a) ('like the English exclamation "ah"'; Leslau, p. 6) on the laryngeal consonants (ʾ), (ʿ), (ḥ), (h'), (h). Additionally, the normally silent sixth-order vowel (pronounced 'like the "e" in "roses"'; Leslau, p. 7) is often pronounced in musical performance, and the consonants it accompanies often carry notational symbols as well. For this reason, we have included in our transliterations many syllables with sixth-order vowels that would not be articulated in normal speech. Popular spellings are used for modern place, tribal and personal names.

55

singers begin to acquire the repertory by memorising chants that serve both as models for whole melodies and as the sources of the melodic phrases linked to individual notational signs. At a later stage of training each one copies out a complete notated manuscript on parchment using medieval scribal techniques. But these manuscripts are used primarily for study purposes; during liturgical celebrations the chants are performed from memory without books, as seems originally to have been the case also with Gregorian and Byzantine chant.[1] Finally, singers learn to improvise sung liturgical poetry according to a structured system of rules. If one desired to imitate the example of Parry and Lord,[2] who investigated the modern South Slavic epic for possible clues to Homeric poetry, it would be difficult to find a modern culture more similar to the one that spawned Gregorian chant.

This article introduces the methods, materials and initial findings of a cross-disciplinary investigation of Ethiopian Christian chant. It was pointed out over twenty years ago that Ethiopian chant 'urgently needs investigating'.[3] Although scholars have long studied the history, literature and liturgy of the Ethiopian church,[4]

---

[1] As late as the fourteenth and fifteenth centuries in the West there were regulations obliging singers to perform without books (F. L. Harrison, *Music in Medieval Britain*, 4th edn (Buren, 1980), pp. 102–3). In the seventeenth century, Jacques Goar observed that 'while singing, the Greeks rarely look at, or even have, books written with musical notes' (E. Wellesz, *A History of Byzantine Music and Hymnography*, 2nd edn (Oxford, 1961, repr. 1971), pp. 4–5).

[2] A. Lord, *The Singer of Tales* (Cambridge, MA, 1960, repr. New York, 1965).

[3] F. L. Harrison, 'Music and Cult: the Functions of Music in Social and Religious Systems', *Perspectives in Musicology*, ed. B. S. Brook and others (New York, 1972), p. 315.

[4] The principal study of Ethiopian church history is Taddesse Tamrat, *Church and State in Ethiopia* (Oxford, 1972). For the considerable resources on Ethiopian literature, see E. Cerulli, *Storia della letteratura etiopica* (Milan, 1956); enlarged 3rd edn, *La letteratura etiopica* (Florence, 1968); Getatchew Haile, 'Religious Controversies and the Growth of Ethiopic Literature in the Fourteenth and Fifteenth Centuries', *Oriens Christianus*, 4th series, 65 (1981), pp. 102–36, and 'A New Look at Some Dates in Early Ethiopian History', *Le Muséon*, 95/3–4 (1982), pp. 311–22. Ethiopian Christian liturgy is discussed in E. Hammerschmidt, *Studies in the Ethiopic Anaphoras*, 2nd rev. edn (Stuttgart, 1987); B. Velat, *Soma Deggua, antiphonaire du carême, quatre premières semaines: texte éthiopien et variantes*, Patrologia Orientalis 32/1–2 (Paris, 1966); idem, *Études sur le Meʿerāf, commun de l'office divin éthiopien: introduction, traduction française, commentaire liturgique et musical*, Patrologia Orientalis 33 (Paris, 1966); idem, *Meʿerāf, commun de l'office divin éthiopien pour toute l'année: texte éthiopien avec variantes*, Patrologia Orientalis 34/1–2 (Paris, 1966); idem, *Soma Deggua, antiphonaire du carême, quatre premières semaines: introduction, traduction française, transcriptions musicales*, Patrologia Orientalis 32/3–4 (Turnhout, 1969); idem, 'Musique liturgique d'Éthiopie', *Encyclopédie des musiques sacrées*, ed. J. Porte, II (Paris, 1969), pp. 234–8. For a general history of the Ethiopian Church, see F. Heyer, *Die Kirche Äthiopiens* (Berlin, 1971).

which was founded in the mid fourth century, Ethiopian Christian liturgical music has received only intermittent scholarly attention from Ethiopianists.[5] The few investigations of Ethiopian sacred music (*zema*) in the musicological literature have combined data derived from Villoteau's landmark study with information from later secondary sources[6] and, occasionally, the writer's own observations.[7]

To be sure, the Gəʿəz language presented a substantial barrier to musicologists wishing to explore the surviving manuscripts. But beyond issues of linguistic competence and area expertise looms a larger epistemological issue. While musicological scholarship developed a sophisticated methodology for deciphering musical notation in manuscripts, it relegated to the area of 'performance practice' considerations of the relationship of notation to the unwritten or 'oral' features of this music. Ethnomusicologists, on the other hand, gained considerable experience in understanding orally transmitted musical traditions but rarely studied the systems of musical notation in which some of these traditions were encoded. This paradoxical situation has begun to change, as medievalists have become interested in the processes of oral transmission and its relationship to the development of Western musical notation.[8]

[5] A few Ethiopianists attempted to list the notational signs (*mǝlǝkkǝt*) they found within manuscripts, but did not investigate the melodies with which the signs were associated: H. Zotenberg, *Catalogues des MSS. éthiopiens de la Bibliothèque nationale* (Paris, 1877); A. Dillmann, 'Verzeichnis der abessinischen Handschriften', *Die Handschriftenverzeichnisse der Kgl. Bibliothek zu Berlin* (Berlin, 1878), III, pp. 31–2 and Tafel III; M. Cohen, 'Sur la notation musicale éthiopienne', *Studi orientalistici in onore di Giorgio Levi della Vida*, I (Rome, 1956), pp. 199ff; Tito Lepisa, 'The Three Modes and the Signs of the Songs in the Ethiopian Liturgy', *Proceedings of the Third International Conference of Ethiopian Studies*, II (Addis Ababa, 1970), pp. 162–87. An exception is M. Villoteau, 'De la musique (1) des Abyssins ou Éthiopiens', *Description de l'Égypte* (Paris, 1809), pp. 741–54, who both described the melodies of a small group of *mǝlǝkkǝt* performed by Ethiopian church musicians he interviewed in Egypt and transcribed several complete liturgical portions in Western notation. B. Velat (see note 4) published musical transcriptions of approximately half of the 500 melodies he recorded from informants during the preparation of his valuable studies of the Ethiopian liturgy (*Études sur le Meʿerāf*, and *Ṣoma Deggua*, 1969) but he did not correlate each melody with its respective notational sign.
[6] Notably F.-J. Fétis, *Histoire (générale) de la musique*, IV (Paris, 1874), pp. 101–16.
[7] E. Wellesz, 'Studien zur äthiopischen Kirchenmusik', *Oriens Christianus*, new series, 9 (1920), pp. 74ff; F. M. C. Mondon-Vidailhet, 'La musique éthiopienne', *Encyclopédie de la musique et dictionnaire du Conservatoire*, ed. A. Lavignac and L. de La Laurencie, I/5 (Paris, 1922), pp. 3179ff; M. Powne, *Ethiopian Music: an Introduction* (London, 1968); Ashenafi Kebede, 'La musique sacrée de l'Église Orthodoxe de l'Éthiopie', *Éthiopie: musique de l'Église Copte* (Berlin, 1969), pp. 3–14.
[8] L. Treitler, 'Homer and Gregory: the Transmission of Epic Poetry and Plainchant', *Musical Quarterly*, 60 (1974), pp. 333–72, and ' "Centonate" Chant: übles Flickwerk or E

Meanwhile, ethnomusicologists have shown increasing interest in non-Western notational systems.[9]

There is no doubt that this longstanding methodological impasse contributed to the scholarly neglect of Ethiopian Christian chant, since the only plausible method for studying this music and its notation is to approach them through the surviving oral tradition. Otherwise, the musical meaning of the notational signs and the relationships between them cannot be ascertained. The study of Ethiopian Christian chant and its notational system presented here has as a result drawn upon methods and sources of both ethno-musicology and musicology. The combination of ethnographic, palaeographic and documentary evidence provides a much fuller picture than that possible through only a single disciplinary matrix or set of sources.

Our findings suggest that the Ethiopian oral and written sources have interacted in a flexible yet surprisingly stable manner from at least the sixteenth century to the present. In the following pages we set forth what we have learned of this interaction and trace the new perspectives it provides both of the history and modern practice of this particular chant tradition and of the nature of musical transmission in its relationship to liturgical development, individual creativity and cultural change. In the context of the recent debate on issues of oral transmission, oral composition, memory and the history of notation in Gregorian chant,[10] the Ethiopian notational system also provides additional evidence that may be of broader interest to the scholarly community.

pluribus unus?', *Journal of the American Musicological Society* [hereafter *JAMS*], 28 (1975), pp. 1–23; H. Hucke, 'Toward a New Historical View of Gregorian Chant', *JAMS*, 33 (1980), pp. 437–67.

9   W. Malm, *Japanese Music and Musical Instruments* (Rutland, VT, and Tokyo, 1959); W. Kaufmann, *Tibetan Buddhist Chant* (Bloomington, IN, 1975); K. K. Shelemay, 'A New System of Musical Notation in Ethiopia', *Ethiopian Studies for Wolf Leslau*, ed. S. Segert and A. J. E. Bodrogligeti (Wiesbaden, 1983), pp. 571–82; T. Ellingson, 'Buddhist Musical Notations', *The Oral and the Literate in Music*, ed. Tokumaru Yosihiko and Yamaguti Osamu (Tokyo, 1986), pp. 302–41.

10   L. Treitler, 'The Early History of Music Writing in the West', *JAMS*, 35 (1982), pp. 237–79, and 'Reading and Singing: on the Genesis of Occidental Music-Writing', *Early Music History*, 4 (1984), pp. 135–208; D. Hughes, 'Evidence for the Traditional View of the Transmission of Gregorian Chant', *JAMS*, 40 (1987), pp. 377–404; K. Levy, 'Charlemagne's Archetype of Grergorian Chant', *JAMS*, 40 (1987), pp. 1–30, and 'On the Origin of Neumes', *Early Music History*, 7 (1987), pp. 59–90; A. E. Planchart, 'On the Nature of Transmission and Change in Trope Repertories', *JAMS*, 41 (1988), pp. 215–49; A. W. Robertson, '*Benedicamus Domino*: the Unwritten Tradition', *JAMS*, 41 (1988), pp. 1–62.

KAY KAUFMAN SHELEMAY

USING MODERN SOURCES TO ACHIEVE
HISTORICAL RECONSTRUCTION IN THE
STUDY OF ETHIOPIAN CHRISTIAN CHANT

Theory, modern sources and methodology. Most studies of oral transmission, in both music and literature,[11] have approached analysis through the examination of stereotyped musical or textual phrases, sometimes termed 'formulas', which are identified by the scholar through their repeated occurrence in surviving written sources. To the best of our knowledge, in prior studies the definition of these stereotyped phrases has been provided by the scholar studying a complete written 'text', whether of a Homeric epic or of a notated plainchant repertory.

In contrast, our analysis takes as its point of departure the smallest structural unit defined by the singer within the Ethiopian tradition we are studying. This unit is the *mələkkət* (sign) of the notational system. Each *mələkkət* consists of one or more members of the Ethiopic syllabary derived from the liturgical text of a well-known 'portion', or section of the chant book known as the *Dəggwa*, with which a particular melody is primarily associated; the *mələkkət* is placed immediately above words to which its associated melody should be sung. In the case of Ethiopian Christian chant, segmentation arrived at through these indigenous units also provides the critical link between oral and written aspects of the tradition: the *mələkkət* is at once an oral melody and a written sign.[12]

Our understanding of the Ethiopian musician's perception of the *mələkkət* was derived from oral and written materials I gathered during fieldwork in the Ethiopian capital, Addis Ababa, with *Ɛlɛqa* Berhanu Makonnen, the musician in charge of all church musical activity and the accreditation of its musicians. He is a leading

---

[11] In addition to Lord, *The Singer of Tales*, see also R. Finnegan, *Oral Poetry* (Cambridge, 1977), and *Literacy and Orality* (Oxford, 1988); W. Ong, *Orality and Literacy* (London, 1982); J. Goody, *The Interface Between the Written and the Oral* (Cambridge, 1977).

[12] Although text and melody are effectively fused, this relationship arises from association within the context of a liturgical portion. No prosodic rules govern text–melody relations, nor does a particular segment of text serve in any way of which we are aware to generate its associated melody.

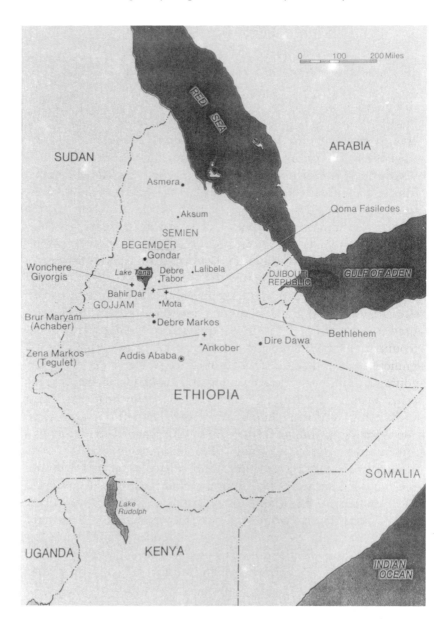

Figure 1   Map of Ethiopia

exponent of the vocal style predominating in the modern church, called the 'Bethlehem style' after the northern Ethiopian monastery with which it is associated, and his knowledge and performance practice exemplify both normative and virtuoso aspects of the Ethiopian chant tradition.[13]

In addition to systematically explaining aspects of Ethiopian Christian liturgical and musical practice, and performing chants drawn from all the major service books for all occasions in the annual liturgical cycle, Eleqa Berhanu gave me a complete list of the notational signs (*mələkkət*) that he had prepared for his classes at the Theological College in Addis Ababa and sang the melody associated with each sign. I tape-recorded all these sessions in full, which has facilitated the transcription, analysis and presentation of this material years after the primary research was completed.

Berhanu's list, of which I received a photocopy, was a mimeographed Amharic typescript on legal-size paper (8.5 × 14 in) incorporated within a longer document he had compiled entitled 'Sələqəddus Yared Tarik' (n.d.; 'Concerning the History of St Yared', hereafter SYT). The remainder of SYT contains an account of the life of St Yared (see below for discussion of his significance), explanation of the modal system, portion types and additional notational signs. Berhanu reports that he compiled SYT for his second-year Theological College students and that the list of notational signs was derived from a combination of his received knowledge of the notational system and from a review of the signs found in notated manuscripts in his possession.[14]

Compiled in writing as well as performed, this composite oral and written document revealed to us the materials of the Ethiopian

---

[13] Berhanu Makonnen is a third-generation *debtera* trained for thirty-one years in musical and liturgical studies, including twelve years at the Bethlehem monastery (see map, Figure 1). Following Ethiopian custom, we will often refer to him by his learned title, Eleqa, and his first name alone. To avoid bibliographic confusion, other Ethiopian scholars will be listed by their full names in first references.

[14] Interview, 2 June 1975, and correspondence with the author, 15 December 1988. Berhanu Makonnen's SYT, including the list of notational signs, appears to rely at least in part on the source or sources also used to prepare an obscure Theological College publication entitled *Yeqəddus Yared Tarikənna Yezemaw Mələkkətoch* (1959 E.C. [1967; hereafter *YYTYM*]). The complicated relationship between these two documents is discussed in detail in K. K. Shelemay and P. Jeffery, *Ethiopian Christian Liturgical Chant: an Anthology*, I (Madison, WI, forthcoming). Germane to the discussion here is the fact that both SYT and *YYTYM* appear to be only two of several attempts to list systematically the notational signs beginning in the 1960s, a development perhaps stimulated by pedagogical demands in the urban environment.

Christian musical and notational system. Furthermore, the structure of Berhanu's testimony set forth irrefutable evidence that a minimal structural unit, the *mǝlǝkkǝt*, existed in the mind of the Ethiopian musician, providing both a central hypothesis and the basis of a working methodology for our research. However, our dependence upon Berhanu's list of *mǝlǝkkǝt* raised other issues regarding the goals of this study and the management of the data that merit discussion.

The first issue is the nature of the relationship between an individual's knowledge of a tradition and the dimensions of the musical system at large. We have chosen to rely upon Ɛlɛqa Berhanu's view of the Ethiopian musical system as the anchor of our project because it is the only feasible way to sketch the boundaries of a tradition that necessarily vary from person to person. On a broader cultural level as well, Ethiopian concepts of the importance of the individual and the consistent emphasis on and respect for hierarchy supports such an approach.[15] This project therefore should be viewed on its most specific level as an effort to trace the major parameters of the normative Ethiopian Christian chant tradition in the late twentieth century, as understood and practised by one of its most accomplished musicians.

Aware of the limitations inherent in a study depending upon one main informant, I also recorded from Ɛlɛqa Berhanu and two other *dɛbtɛras* (church musicians) the same sample of fifty-seven *mǝlǝkkǝt* and selected liturgical portions from different service books. The other two musicians lived in the Ethiopian capital but were trained in schools of vocal style (Qoma and Achaber [probably Ach'abǝr]) associated with two different monasteries in north-western Ethiopia. This comparative material, discussed below by Ingrid Monson, confirms the existence of a shared core of notational and performance practice that transcends individual knowledge and schools of training, while graphically demonstrating the range of variation acceptable in performance of the Ethiopian chant tradition.

A second issue raised by the data from the oral tradition relates to the complexity of the Ethiopian Christian musical system. The 558 notational signs are divided into three categories of mode (*sǝlt*,

---

[15] D. Levine, *Wax and Gold* (Chicago, 1965), pp. 75, 274.

literally 'mode, manner, style'),[16] or, more generally, *zema*, 'chant, church song', with 287 signs in the *gǝʿǝz* mode (abbreviated G1–287), 142 signs in *ǝraray* (abbreviated A1–142), and 129 in *ʿǝzl* (abbreviated E1–129). The melodies associated with the signs are the building-blocks of the three modes and the smallest musical units discussed by Ethiopian Christian musicians. Thus issues of modality, which involve significant differences in pitch set, range, melodic contour, ornamentation and vocal style, become quite important in any discussion of the *mǝlǝkkǝt*. Conversely, this study of the *mǝlǝkkǝt* necessarily serves to illuminate and define the parameters of mode in this musical tradition.

The notation also provides insight into many aspects of musical and liturgical structure. In addition to the 558 *mǝlǝkkǝt*, there is a group of 114 signs called *bet* (literally, 'house', abbreviated B1–114), also derived from the syllabary. The *bet* appear in margins to indicate the 'family' of melody within a mode to which the particular chant melody belongs. There are also ten conventional signs, termed *yǝfidɛl qǝrs'*, that prescribe aspects of articulation, attack, decay, or placement of individual pitches or melodic patterns; they appear as interlinear signs interspersed between the *mǝlǝkkǝt* (see Table 1). Yet another notational component is references within the texts to the halleluya tables (*Ɛnqɛs'ɛ Halleta*) that indicate to which melody a halleluya should be sung; these melodies derive from the *bet* system. A final type of notational symbol is a number placed in the margin, called *mǝdgam*, which signals the singer to repeat that portion of text with instrumental accompaniment and dance.[17] To understand the *mǝlǝkkǝt*, therefore, is to confront the entire Ethiopian Christian musical system. Indeed, it can be argued that it is probably impossible to explicate fully Ethiopian Christian liturgical music without an understanding of the *mǝlǝkkǝt* and the other notational signs.

---

[16] Definitions are drawn from W. Leslau, *Concise Amharic Dictionary* (Wiesbaden, 1976), pp. 48, 179. Gǝʿǝz ceased to be a spoken language about the twelfth or thirteenth century; much of the terminology for Ethiopian music theory is therefore actually in Amharic, a related language that has become the official vernacular of modern Ethiopia.

[17] During the research sessions, all chants were sung without accompaniment as *qum zema* ('basic chant'). When performed in liturgical context during the offices that precede the Mass, certain chants are first sung unaccompanied and then repeated several times, accompanied in each subsequent rendition by the motion of the prayer staff (*mɛqwamiya*), the rhythms of the sistrum (*s'ɛnas'ǝl*) and drum (*kɛbɛro*), and liturgical dance (*ɛqqwaqwam*).

Table 1 *The ten conventional signs (yɛfidɛl qɘrs');*[a]
source: Berhanu Makonnen, 'Sɘlɛqɘddus Yared Tarik', p. 7

yɘzat	·	ch'ɘrɛt	)
dɛrɛt	⌣	hɘdɛt	⌣⁻
rɘkrɘk	⋰.	qɘnat	)
dɘfat	⌢	dɘrs (G261)	∩
qɘrt'	⊢	ɛnbɘr	⊏

[a] According to Berhanu Makonnen, *ch'ɘrɛt* and *qɘnat* share a sign. Velat does not list *qɘnat*, but provides the same sign for *ch'ɘrɛt* as does Berhanu (*Études sur le Me'erāf* (see note 4), p. 101). Lepisa presents *ch'ɘrɛt* as) and *qɘnat* as Ϛ (Lepisa, 'The Three Modes' (see note 5), p. 168). Although the cadential markers *dɘrs* and *ɛnbɘr* are classified as conventional signs, they are represented by characters from the syllabary; *dɘrs* is additionally included in the list of *mɘlɘkkɘt* as G261.

A third issue relates to the sheer amount of material provided by Berhanu Makonnen. Ɛlɛqa Berhanu sang all the notational symbols in his repertory, including the *bet* and *yɛfidɛl qɘrs'*, as well as over a thousand liturgical chants from the major service books. Because of the amount of material and the plethora of liturgical books and occasions involved, we decided to focus this initial inquiry primarily on the chants of the *Dɘggwa*, the most important collection as well as Berhanu Makonnen's primary area of specialisation.[18] The *Dɘggwa* is performed before the Mass on Sundays and holidays throughout the liturgical cycle. These chants form the non-monastic or 'Cathedral' Office, the most important occasion for music in the Ethiopian liturgy.

Our intent was to gain an overview of musical practice while learning in as much detail as possible what we could of the development of the notational system. Since a 'reading' of notation in manuscripts is clearly impossible without knowledge of the oral

[18] Although all *dɛbtɛra*s acquire general knowledge of the Gɘ'ɘz language, the basic service books and *zema*, it is traditional for a singer to specialise later in at least one area. Ɛlɛqa Berhanu, although primarily a master of *Dɘggwa* and a leader of the musicians (*marigeta*), received additional diplomas in liturgical dance and several other service books, and was further ordained as a priest.

tradition, we numbered all signs of the notational system from Berhanu's list and transcribed their melodies in a 'dictionary'. We then used this apparatus to analyse eighteen sample portions, balancing the choice to incorporate (1) a cross-section of liturgical occasions; (2) a representative sampling of portion types; (3) examples from the three modal categories; and (4) inclusion of portions with possible concordances in other Ethiopian and Eastern Christian traditions.[19]

Since this study employs an unorthodox methodology of working from the contemporary oral tradition backwards into manuscript sources, it seems appropriate to detail here our analytical procedures. Using the dictionary of signs constructed from Ɛlɛqa Berhanu's list, I identified the signs in the modern printed *Mɛs'h'afɛ Dəggwa*[20] from which Ɛlɛqa Berhanu sang. At the same time, I compared the dictionary entry for each sign with Ɛlɛqa Berhanu's realisation of the signs in performances of the complete portions, which I had also transcribed into Western musical notation. Meanwhile, Peter Jeffery used Berhanu Makonnen's list of signs to identify the *mələkkət* for each of the sample portions in a carefully selected group of manuscripts. After this first stage, we worked together to arrive at a final reading of the notation for each portion in all sources, checking Jeffery's reading of the notated manuscripts against my analysis of both the modern written sources and performance. We found that evidence from the dictionary of signs, the manuscripts, the modern notated books, musical transcriptions of complete portions, and Berhanu's explanations combined to provide an effective control on our readings of *mələkkət* from any single written source. Only occasionally were we unable to identify a sign after consulting our sources as well as the lists and transcriptions of signs prepared by others.[21]

Identification of the signs led in turn to consideration of a number of interpretative and historical issues. These can be illustrated briefly through discussion of one portion from our sample.

[19] The many issues raised by the process of transcribing both the Ethiopian *mələkkət* and the eighteen sample portions into Western staff notation are too complex for treatment here and are discussed at length in Shelemay and Jeffery, *Ethiopian Christian Liturgical Chant*.

[20] Addis Ababa (1950).

[21] Notably those of Lepisa ('The Three Modes') and Velat (*Études sur le Meʿerāf*, and *Ṣoma Deggua*, 1969).

Example 1. First portion for St John's day, 1 Mɛskɛrɛm (source: performed by Berhanu Makonnen, 2 June 1975)

Example 2. Bet 41 (source: performed by Berhanu Makonnen, 4 June 1975)

yət-fe-   ǩǩa-   h'ɔ   sɛ- ma- yə

Issues in analysis and interpretation. Here we shall examine the first portion of the *Dəggwa*, chanted on St John's day, the beginning of the liturgical year.[22] This chant is of particular analytical interest because Berhanu Makonnen, at my request, sang both the entire portion and then its constituent signs in order. Berhanu's 'analysis' of the signs in this portion helped us to answer some questions, and raised others in turn.

This portion, here termed portion 1, is preceded by a halleluya that corresponds to the first entry in the *Halleta* table under 'one halleluya'. There is also a *bet* indicated for this portion in the left-hand margin, *yə*, B41 (see also Example 2). Comparison of Examples 1 and 2 indicate that the melody of the halleluya, ornamented with vocal slides termed *rəkrək*, deviates considerably from the prescribed *bet*. This variation can probably be attributed to the tradition of elaborating chant incipits, especially one occurring at such an important point in the liturgy. This portion also contains separate notation at the end for a slightly varied repetition of the text, called a *məlt'an*, extending from the words *wəstɛ rə'əsɛ* to the end. The *məlt'an* notation here varies only on the words *tɛzkarəkɛ* and *ənǩa'ə*.

Although portion 1 contains a greater number of conventional signs (*yɛfidɛl qərs'*) than alphabetic signs (*mələkkət*), most of the melodic activity can be accounted for by the *mələkkət* alone. Comparison of notation for this portion in the manuscripts and modern printed sources demonstrates that the same sign may be represented by different characters from the same source text. That is, in one manuscript the sign may consist of the first two characters of its source text, while in another it will be represented by the final two characters, or some other combination. Such an example from our demonstration portion 1 can be seen in the notation of

---

[22]   See facsimile in Figure 2 and transcription in Western notation in Example 1. Peter Jeffery discusses the liturgical classification of this portion and its notational history below.

Kay Kaufman Shelemay, Peter Jeffery, Ingrid Monson

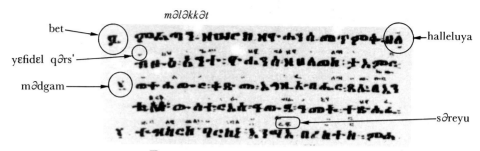

bet → yɛfidɛl qǝrs' → mǝdgam →

mǝlǝkkǝt

← halleluya

← sǝreyu

Figure 2 First portion for St John's day, 1 Mɛskɛrɛm (*Mɛs'h'afɛ Dǝggwa*, Addis Ababa, 1959 E.C.)

Translation: In one: Blessed are you, John, who had to know and walk before God. Pray for us. Your memorial has been inscribed on the beginning of the year's cycle. Bless me so that I may receive your blessing. *Mǝlt'an*: Your memorial has been inscribed on the beginning of the year's cycle. Bless me so that I may receive your blessing. (translation by Getatchew Haile)

G119 on the word *s'ɛlli*. G119 is derived from the source text *ɛwgǝr* (ኸወ ግር), and is most commonly represented by the sign *wɛ* (ወ) as seen here in Figure 2. Yet in two of the manuscripts (16D and 18D, see Jeffery below) in our sample, G119 is represented by the sign *gǝr* (ግር). In this case, it appears that the notational symbol itself changed over time, yet regional custom or individual idiosyncrasy may provide equally plausible explanations for such differences in other instances.

Some *mǝlǝkkǝt* may be confused in manuscripts as well as in performance simply because their source words are similar. See G269 (*gesɛt*, Example 3), the number which we have identified as

Example 3. *Mǝlǝkkǝt* G269 and G200 (source: performed by Berhanu Makonnen, 3 June 1975)

68

the sign actually performed in the rendition transcribed in Example 1 despite the appearance of G200 (*gesε*) in most of the manuscripts as well as the modern *Dəggwa* (20D, shown in Figure 2) from which Ɛlɛqa Berhanu sang. Although Ɛlɛqa Berhanu read notation for *məlǝkkǝt* G200, he actually sang G269. While in this case we can confirm the substitution because Berhanu sang both the portion and its constituent signs separately, we believe this is not an uncommon event.

In some cases Ɛlɛqa Berhanu's performance suggests that an older melodic tradition persists despite a change in the notation. This may be true of the first sign in the portion, G186 (*kah*), which remains constant throughout its notational history except for the inclusion of sign G88 (*z'u*) in our MS 16A. Comparison of dictionary entries (see Example 4) with the modern performance (Example 1) indicates that the melody of G88 may actually match the modern performance as closely as that of G186.

Finally, in a number of cases, we have found a close melodic relationship between the dictionary entries for different signs used on the same word in a portion. For example, G11 (*lεz*) is consistently used on the word *zεhεllεwεkkε* throughout our entire manuscript sample, while in one modern service book the melodically similar G60 (*qu*) is substituted (see Example 5). Additionally, the signs G86 (*bur*) and G17 (*lεgε*), appearing on the word *tεzkarǝkε*, have similar melodies (see Example 6). Their use may represent an intentional redundancy or slightly different options presented to the singer. Similar close relationships may have existed between signs in the past as well, and thus signs with similar melodies may have been freely substituted for each other.

Example 4. *Məlǝkkǝt* G186 and G88 (source: performed by Berhanu Makonnen, 3 June 1975)

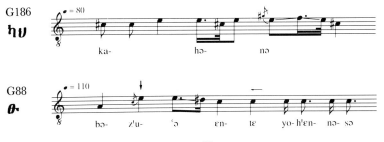

Example 5. *Məløkkət* G11 and G60 (source: performed by Berhanu Makonnen, 3 June 1975)

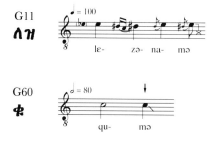

Example 6. *Məløkkət* G86 and G17 (source: performed by Berhanu Makonnen, 3 June 1975)

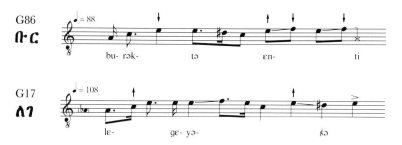

This brief analysis is intended to demonstrate that deciphering the *məløkkət* is an interpretative and not a mechanical act. Berhanu's list of *məløkkət*, and his performance of their melodies, provides a lens through which we can glimpse the inner workings of the Ethiopian Christian musical system. It allows us to describe the relationship between sign, source text and melody, and to reconstruct aspects of their interaction over time. Yet it must be emphasised that there is both intentional flexibility and unintentional confusion in use of the signs in manuscripts. Variation in performance practice by the singer introduces yet another level of differentiation that itself may eventually 'feed back' into the creation of a modified or new sign.

It is quite clear that the creativity of the individual musician is the critical link in the history of Ethiopian chant, with individuals like Berhanu Makonnen serving to consolidate, perform and transmit their knowledge of the musical system and its notation to the next generation. An individual *dɛbtɛra*, especially one whose own knowledge serves as a model for others, can indeed effect changes in chant performance and notation. A *dɛbtɛra* selects the precise *Dəggwa* portions to be performed on a given day from those of the required type and mode, and through this act may make decisions that ultimately promulgate specific texts and their associated melodies. As he copies his own *Dəggwa*, each man records his own understanding of the tradition in a source that may later influence others. Yet while the individual plays a potentially powerful role in transmitting and performing Ethiopian chant, and the system itself accommodates some flexibility, strong constraints have always encouraged and continue to guide the individual singer, who is taught to respect the models received from his own teacher, to obey the laws of the larger tradition of which he was a part and, ultimately, to revere the memory of St Yared.

Oral and written sources for the history of Ethiopian chant.
Nowhere does the Ethiopian Christian musical tradition acknowledge the role of the individual more than in its collective commemoration of St Yared, to whose inspiration is attributed the genesis of the Ethiopian chant tradition in the sixth century.[23] The Ethiopian Church celebrates a day each year in honour of St Yared, and colourful tales concerning his life and creative activity are recorded in the Ethiopian *Synaxarion*[24] and the *Gɛdlɛ Yared*[25].

Although oral traditions credit Yared with creating at least some of the *mələkkət*,[26] and a few written sources do mention music writing as one of his contributions,[27] we have found no *mələkkət* in any manuscript dating before the sixteenth century. Therefore, traditions concerning two sixteenth-century church musicians who are

[23] Getatchew Haile has recently questioned the traditional sixth-century chronology for Emperor Gɛbrɛ Mɛsqɛl, to whose reign Yared's musical activity is attributed, and has proposed instead a late ninth-century dating ('A New Look', pp. 318–19).

[24] E. A. W. Budge, *The Book of the Saints of the Ethiopian Church* (Cambridge, 1928).

[25] C. Conti Rossini, *Acta Yāred et Pantalewon: scriptores aethiopici*, IX–X, Corpus Scriptorum Christianorum Orientalium 26–7 (Louvain, 1955).

[26] Interview with Berhanu Makonnen (Addis Ababa, 1 September 1975).

[27] A. Dillmann, *Lexicon linguae aethiopicae* (1865, repr. Osnabrück, 1970), p. 1130; Ministry of Information, *Patterns of Progress: Music, Dance, Drama in Ethiopia* (Addis Ababa, 1968), p. 25.

said to have codified the notational system assume great significance.

An Ethiopian royal chronicle records that 'at the time of King Gɛladewos [1540–59] there appeared Azzaj Gera and Azzaj Ragu'el, priests trained in *zema*. And they began to make rules for the *məlɘkkɘt* of the *Dɘggwa* and taught the priests of Tɛdbabɛ Maryam, which this prince had built'.[28] A manuscript (EMML 2045) copied at the northern Ethiopian monastery of Hayq during the reign of Emperor Iyasu 1 (1682–1706) presents a somewhat different and lengthier description concerning Gera and Ragu'el's contribution, attributing it to a command of Emperor Sɛrs'ɛ Dɘngɘl (1563–97) and crediting the clerics with revising the *Dɘggwa* in the face of opposition within the church at that time.[29]

Documentary sources therefore strongly suggest that the clerics who lived and worked immediately following the Muslim invasion of Ethiopia (1529–41) were responsible at the very least for reconstruction and revision of the Ethiopian Christian notational system. This invasion, which led to the widespread destruction of churches and monasteries, and deprived Ethiopia of much of its literary heritage, must have severely disrupted liturgical performance and musical transmission.

In addition to the documentary sources, oral traditions also point to the mid sixteenth century as a period of revival in the church musical tradition. The pre-eminence of the musical style associated with the Bethlehem monastery is said to date from that period, precisely because it was the only place a notated *Dɘggwa* survived the Muslim invasion.[30] Both the documentary sources and

---

[28] R. Basset, 'Études sur l'histoire d'Éthiopie', *Journal Asiatique*, 7th series, 17 (1881), p. 336.

[29] EMML 2045 is described in G. Haile and W. Macomber, *A Catalogue of Ethiopian Manuscripts Microfilmed for the Ethiopian Manuscript Microfilm Library, Addis Ababa, and for the Hill Monastic Music Library (Collegeville)*, vi (Collegeville, MN, 1982), p. 42. Other manuscripts provide similarly conflicting information. A chronicle cited in Velat, *Ṣoma Deggua* (1966), p. 98, dates the two clerics to the reign of Gɛladewos (1540–59), while the rule of Sɛrs'ɛ Dɘngɘl is given in a St Petersburg MS described in C. Conti Rossini, 'Aethiopica (IIa Series)', *Rivista degli Studi Orientali*, 10 (1925), pp. 515–16, after B. Turaev, *Ethiopskiya rukopisi v S.-Peterburge* [Ethiopian Manuscripts in St Petersburg; in Russian], Zapiski Vostochnago Otdeleniya Imperatorskago Russkago Arkheologicheskago Obshchestva [Memoirs of the Oriental Section of the Imperial Russian Archaeological Society] 17 (1906), pp. 179–82.

[30] Berhanu Makonnen transmits a genealogy of Yared's successors and credits a *dɛbtɛra* named Lɘssane 'ɘphrat, a student dated by oral tradition to the eighth generation after Yared, with having notated a *Dɘggwa* during the reign of Emperor Zɛr'a Ya'ɘqob

surviving oral traditions therefore do at least raise the possibility that the sixteenth-century notational innovations may have drawn upon a pre-invasion model, perhaps one that arose a century earlier as part of an enormous surge of literary activity during the reign of Emperor Zɛr'a Ya'əqob (1434–68). However, we have not yet found any other firm evidence for this earlier dating.

We therefore suggest that many aspects of the modern notational system, as well as the hegemony of the Bethlehem musical style, date primarily from a period of renewal beginning after the Muslim invasion in the mid to late sixteenth century. Notation evidently emerged within a relatively short period after a major calamity, setting into motion a period of innovation that climaxed in the seventeenth century. Below, Peter Jeffery sets forth the manuscript evidence supporting this hypothesis.

Harvard University

PETER JEFFERY

THE MANUSCRIPT EVIDENCE (13TH–20TH CENTURIES)

Because the following discussion is the first attempt to trace the history of Ethiopian chant from written primary sources, it can do no more than locate tentatively some of the most prominent chronological landmarks in what has up to now been almost completely uncharted territory. In order to provide some objective basis for dating the various features of the chant and tracing their development, it was necessary first to assemble a corpus of datable chant manuscripts going back as far as possible. This was done by consulting published manuscript catalogues; the manuscripts chosen are listed in Table 2. While a few of the manuscripts listed

(1434–68). According to this tradition, only Ləssane Ǝphrat's notated *Dəggwa* survived the Islamic invasion in a place near the Bethlehem monastery. As a result, the emperor decreed that Bethlehem should be the place where *Dəggwa* training would be centred (interview, 3 September 1975, and SYT, p. 4). Others have gathered similar traditions, including one concerning a search for surviving liturgical books during the reign of Emperor Sɛrs'ɛ Dəngəl (1563–97) which discovered a *Dəggwa* and other service books at the Bethlehem monastery (B. Velat, 'Chantres, poètes, professeurs: les dabtara éthiopiens', *Cahiers Coptes*, no. 5 (Cairo, 1954), p. 27).

Table 2 *Ethiopian chant manuscripts arranged chronologically*

Siglum	Date (A.D.)	MS no.	Contents
13A[a]	XII–XIII[b]	EMML 7078	ɛrbaʼt arranged by melodic group
14A[a]	XIV	EMML 6944	Mz, liturgical order
15A[a]	XIV–XV	EMML 2095	ɛrbaʼt, liturgical order
15B[a]	XV	Paris, BN, eth. 92	several collections
15C[a]	XV	Vatican Aeth. 28	D, SD (incomplete)
16A	XV–early XVI	EMML 4667	D, SD
16B	XVI	EMML 1894	D, SD, Mr (Tɛgulɛt?)
16C[a]	XVI	EMML 2468, ff. 143–6	D fragments
16D	late XVI	EMML 2542	D, SD, Mr, Mw
17A	1653–4	EMML 3400	D
17B	1682–93	EMML 2077	Mr, Mw, Zm
17C	1695–6	EMML 2045	D, SD (revision dated 1563–97)
18A	1755–61	EMML 2474	SD, ab Mr for Lent
18B	1755–69	EMML 3440	D, Mr, Mw, Zm
18C	1760	EMML 512	D, SD, ɛryam list
18D	1787–8	EMML 759	D
18E	1779–1800	EMML 2519	SD, Mr for Lent
19A	1800	EMML 3160	D
19B	1820–1	EMML 2368	D, SD
19C	1884	EMML 35	D, SD
19D	XIX	EMML 2936	treatise on D, Bethlehem school
20A	1917, 1919–21	EMML 1262	D, Bethlehem school
20B	1936–41	EMML 733	D, SD, Bethlehem
20C	XX	EMML 1253	Mz, YT
20D	1947–50	*Mɛsʼhʼafɛ Dəggwa* (Addis Ababa, 1966–7)	
20E	XX	*Sʼomɛ Dəggwa* (Addis Ababa, 1968)	
20F	1957–8	*Yɛziq Mɛsʼhʼaf* (Addis Ababa, 1970)	
20G	XX	*Ɛmməstu Sʼɛwatəwɛ zemawoch* (Addis Ababa, 1968)	
20H	1975	MS by singer/informant of Achaber school	

Key to abbreviations: ab = Abbreviated   D = Dəggwa
EMML = Ethiopian Manuscript Microfilm Library, Collegeville, Minnesota
Mw = Mɛwasəʼt   Mz = Mɛzmur   Mr = Məʼraf
SD = Sʼomɛ Dəggwa   YT = Yɛ-qal Təmhərt   Zm = Zəmmare

[a] These sources have little or no musical notation.
[b] Roman numerals denote centuries.

are owned by European libraries, the majority are widely scattered in many locations throughout Ethiopia, some of them quite inaccessible rural monasteries. Fortunately these are available on microfilm through EMML, the Ethiopian Manuscript Microfilm Library in Addis Ababa and Collegeville, Minnesota.[31] From the seventeenth century to the present it was possible to select sources that can be dated to a very short span of years, because they contain prefaces or colophons that give specific dates or name the reigning kings and bishops. No such information is found in the extant manuscripts of the thirteenth to fifteenth centuries, which can only be dated more broadly by means of palaeographical evidence. However for this early period almost every known manuscript of the main chant collection (the *D∂ggwa*) has been included in the list.[32] Ethiopian manuscripts older than the fifteenth century are quite rare; most of the earlier sources that may once have existed seem to have been destroyed in the wars with Muslim and other invaders that took place at that time.

The formation of the Ethiopian chantbook (*D∂ggwa*). The Ethiopian repertory contains about two dozen categories of chants that Western scholars like to call 'antiphons', because they somewhat resemble the antiphons of Gregorian chant in length and textual content. The Ethiopian word for them (*εr'∂stε D∂ggwa*) means 'chapters' or 'portions', that is to say sections of the complete chant book, which is called the *D∂ggwa*, a name of uncertain etymology. It is impossible to say precisely how many categories[33] because

---

[31] For information on this very important microfilming project, see Haile and Macomber, *A Catalogue of Ethiopian Manuscripts* (Collegeville, MN, 1975–); also W. Macomber, 'The Present State of the Microfilm Collection of the Ethiopian Manuscript Microfilm Library', *Ethiopian Studies: Proceedings of the Sixth International Conference, Tel Aviv, 14–17 April 1980*, ed. G. Goldenberg (Rotterdam and Boston, 1986).

[32] One MS that was not included is a *D∂ggwa* of the sixteenth or seventeenth century, listed as MS 24 in J. Flemming, 'Die neue Sammlung abessinischer Handschriften auf der Königlichen Bibliothek zu Berlin', *Zentralblatt für Bibliothekswesen*, 23 (1906), p. 13. Another, Uppsala, Universitetsbiblioteket MS O Ethiop. 37 is a *S'omε D∂ggwa* copied some time between the mid sixteenth and the late seventeenth century. See O. Löfgren, *Katalog über die äthiopischen Handschriften in der Universitätsbibliothek Uppsala* (Stockholm, 1974), pp. 75–9; S. Uhlig, *Äthiopische Paläographie*, Äthiopistische Forschungen 22 (Stuttgart, 1988), pp. 445, 539–40.

[33] The number of genres is said to be 22 in the Amharic treatise in Vatican City, Biblioteca Apostolica Vaticana, Cod. Aeth. 244, fols. 9–12; see S. Grébaut and E. Tisserant, *Codices aethiopici vaticani et Borgiani, Barberinianus Orientalis 2, Rossianus 865*, 2 vols. (Vatican City, 1935–6), p. 754. Velat (*Soma Deggua*, 1969, pp. xv–xviii) also gives this number, but shows that some genres have more than one name, or fall into subgroups with different names.

Table 3 *The main types of portion or 'antiphon' in Ethiopian chant*

I. Used to begin an office hour or a structural unit within an office hour:
    A. Wazema ('Vespers'), sung at the beginning of Vespers
    B. Mεzmur ('Psalm'), sung at the beginning of Sunday Matins (Mεwεddǝs)
    C. Ɛbun ('Our Father'), sung at the beginning of Lauds and the Little Hours on weekdays
    D. 'ǝzl (named for its mode), sung at the beginning of Lauds (Sǝbh'εtε nεgħ)

II. Ecstatic chants which precede some of the above types on certain days:
    A. Ɛryam ('Highest Heaven') can precede mεzmur or abun
    B. Ɛngεrgari ('Frenzy?') or mǝlt'an ('litany') can precede mεzmur or 'ǝzl or even replace wazema
    C. Mǝsbak ('Proclamation') can precede wazema

III. Chants preceded by the refrain of Ps 135 [136]: 'Quoniam in aeternum misericordia eius [For his mercy endures forever]':
    A. Ǝsmε lε-'alεm ('Quoniam in aeternum'), sung at Lauds
    B. Qǝnnǝwat ('Nails' [of the Cross]'), sung at the Little Hours

IV. Chants named for the type of stanza used in the accompanying psalm:
    A. Bε-ħεmmǝstu ('in 5'), with stanzas of five lines
    B. Ɛrba't ('fourth'), with stanzas of four lines
    C. Ŝεlεst ('third'), with stanzas of three lines

V. Chants sung with specific psalms or canticles of the Ethiopian Psalter, from the incipits of which they take their names:
    A. Ǝgzi'εbh'er nεgŝε ('Dominus regnavit') with Ps 92 [93] at Vespers
    B. Yǝtbarεk ('Benedictus') with Daniel 3:52–6 at Vespers and Lauds
    C. Zε-εmlakiyε ('of Deus meus') sung with Ps 62 [63] at Matins and Ps 21 [22] at Lenten Sext
    D. Zε-yǝ'ǝze ('of Nunc [dimittis]') sung with Luke 2:29–32 at Lauds
    E. Mah'let ('Canticle') sung with Daniel 3:57–88 at Lauds
    F. Sǝbh'εtε nεgħ ('Glorification of the Morning') sung with Psalms 148–50 at Lauds

VI. 'Responsorial' chants (collected in a book called Mεwaŝǝ't)
    A. Mεwaŝǝ't ('Responses') sung before Gospel in morning office on important days and in services for the dead

VII. Chant sung at the end of each office
    A. Sεlam ('Peace')

VIII. Communion chants sung at Mass (collected in a book called Zǝmmare)
    A. Zǝmmare ('Psalmody'), hǝbǝst ('Bread') or sǝga ('Flesh')
    B. S'owa' ('Chalice') or dεm ('Blood')
    C. Mεnfεs ('Spirit')

Table 3 *continued*

VII. Chants used during Holy Week to replace improvised liturgical poetry
(qene), from the categories of which they take their names:
  A. Mibɛzẖu ('Quid multiplicati sunt'), sung with Ps 3 at Matins
  B. Mɛwɛddəs, named for Sunday Matins when it is sung
  C. Kwəlləkəmu, a short Mɛwɛddəs
  D. Kəbr yə'əti ('Gloria haec'), sung at Ps 149:9b
  E. 'ət'anɛ mogɛr ('toss of incense')

---

they are not mutually exclusive: some overlap with others, some
are subdivisions of larger and more varied categories, and some
are called by different names in different manuscripts or in different
liturgical circumstances. The liturgical characteristics of the various categories are not the subject of this paper; they are
summarised in Table 3 and will be discussed at length in a forthcoming book.[34] When only musical characteristics are considered,
however, many of the two dozen categories of portions can be
classified into one of two groups, which I have labelled 'Type I'
and 'Type II', as shown in Table 4. Those that belong to neither
type are grouped artificially under 'III'.

The earliest manuscripts in our list are devoted to collections of
individual categories of portions rather than to the complete
Dəggwa repertory. There were two possible ways of organising such
a collection: either by melodic group, somewhat as in a Western
tonary, or according to the days and times when the portions are
sung over the course of the liturgical year. Thus both 13A and 15A
are collections restricted to the *ɛrba't* category, but the former is
arranged by melodic group, while the latter is in liturgical order.
14A contains chants of several categories closely related to the
mɛzmur, arranged by liturgical year. 15B contains fragmentary collections of about ten different categories, brought together into a
single disordered volume. Some of its collections have the melodic
arrangement, others the liturgical one. Only with 15C do we have
for the first time a true *Dəggwa*, with all the chant texts of almost
all categories arranged according to the liturgical year, comparable
to the Western antiphoner or the Eastern tropologion. The *Dəggwa*
has remained the most important type of chant book down to the
present, though its contents naturally continued to develop and

---

[34] Shelemay and Jeffery, *Ethiopian Christian Liturgical Chant.*

Table 4   *Categories of Ethiopian chant portions, arranged by 'type'*

I. 'Type I' portions: utilising a system of 'melodic models'
  1. ɛrbaʿt
  2. ɛryam
  3. ṣɛlɛst

II. 'Type II' portions: with standardised melodic incipits organised into a system of *betoch* or 'houses'
  A. 'Type IIA' portions: usually preceded by one or more repetitions of the word 'halleluya' sung to standard melismas
    1. mɛzmur
    2. ɛbun
    3. məsbak
    4. wazema
    5. ɛngɛrgari or məltʾan
    6. əzl
    7. sɛlam
    8. mɛnfɛs

  B. 'Type IIB' portions: preceded by the refrain of Ps 135 [136], 'For his mercy endures forever', sung to standard melismas
    1. əsmɛ lɛ-ʿalɛm
    2. qənnəwat
    3. zəmmare

  C. 'Type IIC' portions: sung at communion at Mass, with the verse 'For nothing is impossible with God' (Luke 1:37)
    1. səwaʿ

III. 'Neither Type I nor Type II'
  A. Categories for which there are collections in 15B
    1. yətbarɛk
    2. zɛ-ɛmlakiyɛ
    3. səbhʾɛtɛ nɛgħ
    4. mɛwaṣəʿt
    5. əgziʾɛbhʾer nɛgṣɛ

  B. Categories for which there are no early collections independent of complete Dəggwa MSS
    1. zɛ-yəʾəze
    2. mahʾlet
    3. bɛ-ħemməstu
    4. mibɛzħu
    5. mɛwɛddəs
    6. kwəlləkəmu
    7. kəbr yəʾəti
    8. ʾətʾane mogɛr

change. In the eighteenth century it became normal to omit the chants for Lent from the complete *Dəggwa*, collecting them instead into a separate book, the *S'omɛ Dəggwa* or *Dəggwa* of the Fast.[35] But Lent was already omitted from some earlier sources, for instance our 17A. The tendency to put the Lenten material in a separate book may have been encouraged by the fact that another season, *ɛstɛmhəro* ('teaching'), expanded considerably during the seventeenth century, partly by reduplicating portions borrowed from Lent. Some categories of chant, notably the *mɛwaʃə't* (responses), *zəmmare* (psalmody) and certain categories of liturgical poetry, continued to be transmitted in collections that were independent of the *Dəggwa*.[36] The liturgical psalter (*Mə'raf*) is also a separate book; its original core, the psalms arranged and notated for chanting in the liturgy, has attracted some other material used for training the singers.[37] Although manuscripts of the *Dəggwa* and other collections continue to be copied on parchment even in the twentieth century, as an essential part of the training of Ethiopian singers,[38] printed chant books began to appear in the 1960s, most of them facsimiles of manuscripts copied in the 1940s and 1950s. The sources 20D, 20E, 20F and 20G in Table 2 fit into this category; both the date of printing and the date of the writing of the original manuscript (where known) are given in the Table.[39]

---

[35] First half edited in Velat, *Ṣoma Deggua* (1966), translated in idem, *Ṣoma Deggua* (1969).
[36] The earliest written *mɛwaʃə't* collections (14th–15th centuries) are in fact supplements to MSS of the Ethiopic Psalter, for instance: Paris, Bibliothèque Nationale, eth. 10; Vatican Aeth. 4; Vatican Aeth. 10; Vatican Aeth. 15. See Uhlig, 1988, pp. 241, 309.
[37] Complete text edited in Velat, *Me'erāf*, translated with extensive commentary in Velat, *Études sur le Me'erāf*.
[38] Sergew Hable Selassie, *Bookmaking in Ethiopia* (Leiden, 1981), p. 28. On p. 33 is an interesting list showing the amount of time taken to copy the various liturgical and chant books; a *Dəggwa* takes eighteen months. R. Curzon, who visited an Ethiopian monastery in Egypt in 1833, described traditional copying practices and published a sketch of the monastery library: *Visits to Monasteries in the Levant*, 5th edn (London, 1865), repr. with an introduction by J. J. Norwich, London, 1983), pp. 134–42. He reported, probably with some exaggeration, that 'One page is a good day's work' (p. 140). See also Velat, 'Chantres, poètes, professeurs'.
[39] Unless otherwise specified, dates in these articles are given according to the Gregorian calendar as used in North America and western Europe. The calendar followed in Ethiopia, which derives ultimately from the calendar of Pharaonic Egypt, is seven years behind the Gregorian from 11 September to 31 December, and eight years behind for the remainder of the year (E. Ullendorff, *The Ethiopians: an Introduction to Country and People*, 3rd edn (London, 1973), p. 177).

Table 5   *The history of Ethiopian chant: a chronological summary*

VIᵃ: Traditional date of the reign of Gɛbrɛ Mɛsqɛl (558–84), and of the life and work of St Yared

IX: Possible correct date of St Yared (G. Haile, 'A New Look' (see note 4), pp. 318–19)

XIII: Earliest extant written collections of Ethiopian chant texts, with each category collected independently (= 'Type I' Stage I; 'Type II' Stage I) – 13A, 14A, 15A, 15B

XV: One portion chosen as representative of each 'Type I' melodic group (= 'Type I' Stage II) – 15A, 15B

        Earliest extant Dəggwa, containing chants of almost all categories in liturgical order, all three 'modes' identified by name – 15C

XVI: Marginal signs for the 'houses' (i.e. the standard incipits of 'Type II' portions) begin to be written by the original scribe in Dəggwa MSS (= 'Type II' Stage II) – 16B

        Activity of Gera and Ragu'el, who invented or codified the məlǝkkǝt during the reign of Gɛladewos (1540–59) or Sɛrsɛ Dǝngǝl (1563–97)

XVII: Ɛstɛmhǝro section of the Dəggwa expanded, with many portions borrowed from the period of Lent (S'om) – 17A

        Written lists of the model melodies of 'Type I' portions compiled and incorporated into the Mǝ'raf (= 'Type I' Stage III) – 17B

        Written lists of halleluya formulas, linked to their respective houses and supplied with music notation, appear in Dəggwa MSS (= 'Type II' Stage III) – 17C

XVIII: Portions assigned to Lent now generally collected in a separate book (S'omɛ Dəggwa) – 18A, 18E

XIX: Late in the century, beginning of attempts to notate in greater detail by using more signs – 19C

XX: Printed editions of the Dəggwa and other chant books (actually facsimiles of recent MSS) published – 20D, 20E, 20F, 20G

        A list of the marginal signs representing the *betoch* published in 20D

ᵃRoman numerals denote centuries.

The 'Type I' portions. The Type I group includes three categories, the *ɛrbaʿt*, *ɛryam* and *ḱɛlɛst*. Each is distinct from the other
two in terms of textual form, melodic content and liturgical function. Yet all three have a similar history, which is included in the
chronology in Table 5. 13A is a collection of one of these three
categories, the *ɛrbaʿt*, representing what I call 'Stage I'. In 13A
we find the texts arranged according to their melodic groups, that
is to say they are grouped with other texts sung to similar melodies,
each group headed by the rubric *bɛzemahu* ('in its [own] melody'),
zɛhimɛ bɛzemahu ('this also in its [own] melody'), or *sǝrɛyu* (the
meaning of this term will be discussed below). Within each melodic
group the texts are arranged in the order of the liturgical year. 15B
includes, among other things, collections of texts belonging to all
three categories of Type I, arranged by melodic group as in 13A.
In Figure 3 we can see, after the third line of text, a line indicating
the beginning of a new melodic group. After that line is the rubric
'This also in its own melody', meaning that all the texts that follow
belong to the same melody, or rather melodic family. The individual portions of the group follow, arranged in the liturgical order
of their feasts, separated from each other by rubrics and by obeli
or 'daggers' in the margin. There has, however, been a new development, 'Stage II'. In each melodic group in 15B, one portion has
been singled out to serve as representative of the entire group; its
name is written in the top margin of the page the group begins on,
apparently in the hand of the original scribe. The incipit of the
group representative, which in Figure 3 is 'On this day', is followed
by the words 'in which one would say', meaning that the melody
of 'On this day' serves as the typical one for this entire group of
portions. Sometimes the first chant in the group (i.e. the one that
appears earliest in the liturgical year) was chosen arbitrarily to
represent the entire group. But in other cases, as in Figure 3, a
chant from elsewhere in the group was chosen, evidently because
it was somehow considered a more appropriate representative of
the group as a whole. These group representatives were dubbed
'melodic models' ('modèles mélodiques') by Velat.[40] We continue
to use this term until such time as a more profound understanding
of them may suggest a more appropriate one.

---

[40] *Études sur le Meʿerāf*, pp. 232ff.

81

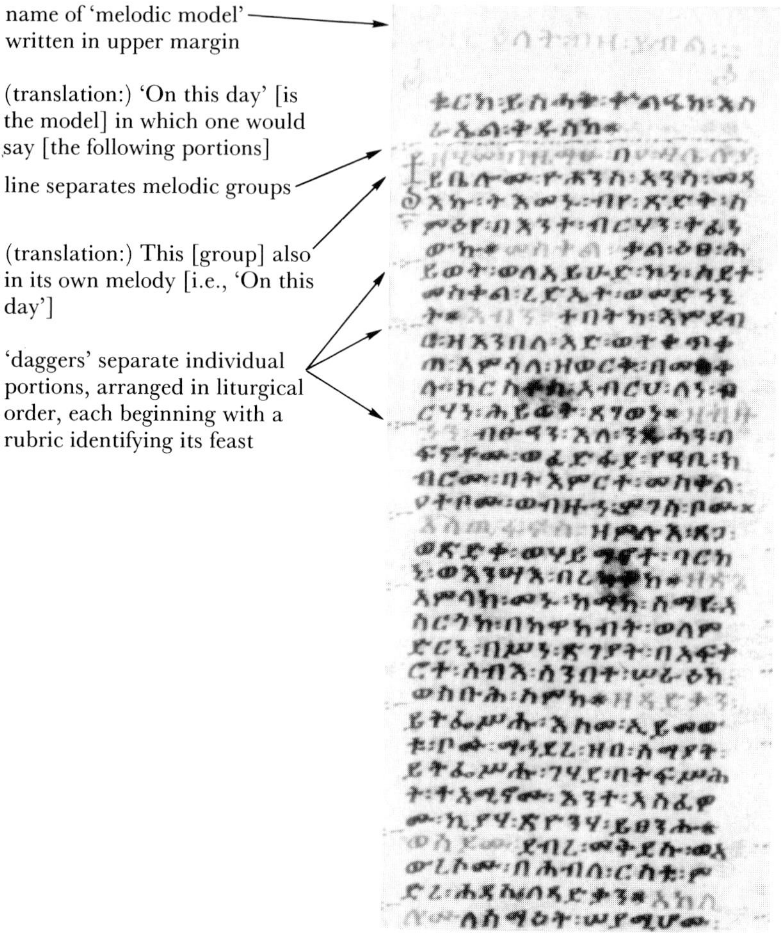

name of 'melodic model' —→
written in upper margin

(translation:) 'On this day' [is
the model] in which one would
say [the following portions]

line separates melodic groups

(translation:) This [group] also
in its own melody [i.e., 'On this
day']

'daggers' separate individual
portions, arranged in liturgical
order, each beginning with a
rubric identifying its feast

Figure 3   15B, fol. 10a, col. 2

Already in 15A, in which the ɛrbaꜤt portions are arranged
according to the liturgical year, each text is preceded by the text
incipit of its group representative or 'melodic model', written in
red. The page shown in Figure 4 contains chants for the feast of
the archangel Gabriel, each portion separated by a line. But each
is preceded by a rubric indicating its melodic group. The three
melodic groups shown here, 'On this day', 'John cried out' and
'At that time it was Sabbath' are each followed by the traditional
formula 'in which one would say'. The practice of giving the name

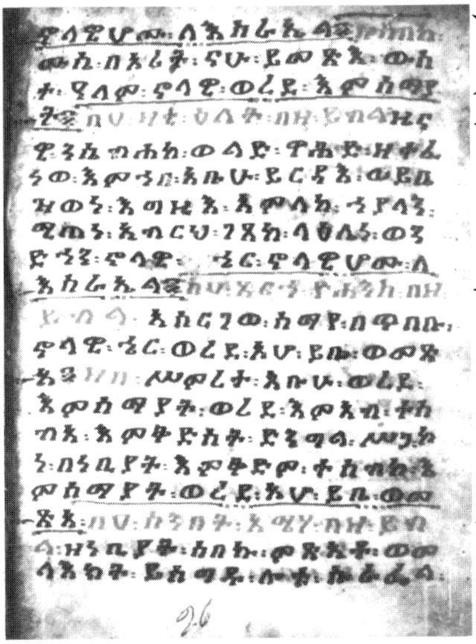

Oral and written transmission in Ethiopian Christian chant

lines separate individual portions

(translation:) 'On this day' [is the model] in which one would say [the following portion]

(translation:) 'John cried out' [is the model] in which one would say [the following portion]

(translation:) 'At that time it was Sabbath' [is the model] in which one would say [the following portion]

Figure 4   15A, fol. 26a, feast of the archangel Gabriel

of the melodic model in red before every text in the same group was continued in 15C, our earliest *Dǝggwa*, and in all other *Dǝggwa* manuscripts down to the present. It is interesting that the second model, 'John cried out', does not occur in more recent sources; its group has either disappeared or adopted a different portion for its model.

The practice of preceding a text with the name of a melody – a name derived from the incipit of a different text deemed the 'model' – will inevitably remind chant scholars of the Byzantine *heirmos* or the Syriac *resh qala*. As will be shown below, however, the relationship between an Ethiopian 'model' and its 'derivative' can be much looser, with much of the resemblance concentrated towards the beginning. The full range of possible relationships will not be known until there have been exhaustive studies comparing selected models with their complete 'family' of derivatives.

In 'Stage III' the texts of the melodic models themselves were being assembled into written lists. By the seventeenth century these lists were beginning to be written down and incorporated into an emerging type of liturgical book known as the *Mǝˁraf* ('sections' or 'stopping-places'), which primarily contains texts of the psalms pointed and notated for liturgical chanting. Our MS

17B appears to be one of the earliest examples.[41] The primarily oral character of these lists is still evident, however. Boys training to be ecclesiastical singers work at memorising both the texts and their melodies during the night when it is impossible to read. For this reason the lists, along with certain other material to be memorised, are called *Yɛ-qal Tǝmhǝrt* ('Oral Studies') or *Yǝ-mata Tǝmhǝrt* ('Night Studies').[42]

The 'Type II' portions. A much greater variety of categories makes up what I call Type II, listed in Table 4. It subdivides into further groups on the basis of a simple difference in performance practice. The categories of Type IIA, the first three of which are partly interchangeable, are usually preceded by the word 'halleluya', sung from one to ten times according to standard melodic formulas. The categories of Type IIB are preceded instead by one rendition of the refrain of Psalm 135, '*ǝsmɛ lɛ-ʿalɛm mǝh'rɛtu*' ('For his mercy endures forever'). Type IIC includes one of the three types of communion hymns. It is preceded by the Gospel verse 'For nothing is impossible with God' (Luke 1:37), apparently referring to the miraculous transsubstantiation of the eucharistic bread and wine.

The earliest collection of Type II portions, 14A, is arranged by liturgical year. It seems to show that the various subcategories of this type were perhaps not fully differentiated. On every feast there is a series of chant texts, including some that later manuscripts would assign to the *mɛzmur* or *ɛbun* categories, others that would later be assigned to the *ǝsmɛ lɛ-ʿalɛm* category, and sometimes a few that would later belong to other Type II categories. Rubrics indicating the category are rare in this manuscript, and there are no markings of any kind to separate the *mɛzmur* texts from the *ǝsmɛ lɛ-ʿalɛm* ones, which in any case are often intermingled. One can often recognise a *mɛzmur* or *ɛbun* text because it will be preceded by a numeral indicating the number of times the word 'halleluya'

[41] Berlin, Staatsbibliothek Preussischer Kulturbesitz, MS orient. oct. 1268 (= Hs. 40 in the catalogue of E. Hammerschmidt and V. Six, *Äthiopische Handschriften*, I: *Die Handschriften der Staatsbibliothek Preussischer Kulturbesitz*, Verzeichnis der orientalischen Handschriften in Deutschland, xx/4 (Wiesbaden, 1983)), is a MS dating 1563–97 that includes a *Mǝʿraf*, but Hammerschmidt and Six do not say whether the contents include the melodic models. On the palaeography see Uhlig, *Äthiopische Paläographie*, p. 462.

[42] These texts are edited without notation in Velat, *Meʿerāf*, pp. 34–68, and are translated and discussed in Velat, *Études sur le Meʿerāf*, pp. 218–66.

should be sung at the beginning, but this does not mean that any text lacking such a number must be an *ðsmɛ lɛ-ʿalɛm*. In a few places *wazema* and *ʿðzl* texts are clearly designated as such by a rubric (e.g. fol. 48a), but in other places they are not. The one type of category that seems to be consistently identified in the manuscript is the *qðnnðwat*, which always comes at the very end of the series of chants assigned to each feast. In later sources of the *Dðggwa*, on the other hand, the three series of *mɛzmur* or *ɛbun* texts, *ðsmɛ lɛ-ʿalɛm* texts and *qðnnðwat* texts will be fully segregated from each other, with each series clearly identified by a rubric at the beginning.

For two categories of Type IIA portions, *sɛlam* and *wazema*, substantial remnants of collections survive in 15B, both of which are organised by liturgical year. These, together with 14A, represent 'Stage I' in the history of Type II, corresponding to Stage I in the history of Type I. In 15C we find the texts of all the Type IIa and IIb portions already incorporated into the earliest *Dðggwa* manuscript. Since then they have remained among the normal contents of the *Dðggwa*, though separate collections of individual categories did not die out completely.[43]

At some unknown time, however, Type II chants also came to be understood as belonging to groupings known as *betoch* or 'houses'. Portions belong to the same house when they have the same melodic incipit; the house itself came to be named for the textual incipit of a representative chant from the group. 'Stage II' took place when these houses began to be designated by written signs, each appearing in the margin next to the first line of the portion to which it applied. The earliest appearance of such signs is in the *sɛlam* collection in 15B, in a hand different from that of the original scribe but nevertheless belonging to the fifteenth century. But, as can be seen in Figure 5, the written system had not yet been stand-

---

[43] See our sources 20C, which includes a collection of *mɛzmur*, and 20G, which includes collections of *mɛzmur* and *ðsmɛ lɛ-ʿalɛm*. The nineteenth-century source Paris, Bibliothèque Nationale, MS d'Abbadie 87 contains collections of: *mɛzmur* (fols. 1a–68b), *sɛlam* and *wazema* (69a–92b, though the rubric on 69a speaks of *sɛlam* and *mɛzmur*), *wazema* (92b–106b), *ʿðzl* (106b–120b), *zɛ-ɛmlakiyɛ* and *ɛrbaʿt* (120b–128b), *kɛlɛst* (128b–140a), *ɛryam* (140a–148b), *zðmmare* (149a–173b), *mðʿraf* (175a–195b) and *mɛwajðʿt* (195b–209a). This description is more accurate than the ones in C. Conti Rossini, 'Notice sur les manuscrits éthiopiens de la collection d'Abbadie', *Journal Asiatique* (Nov–Dec 1912), pp. 469–70, or M. Chaîne, *Bibliothèque nationale: catalogue des manuscrits éthiopiens de la collection Antoine d'Abbadie* (Paris, 1912).

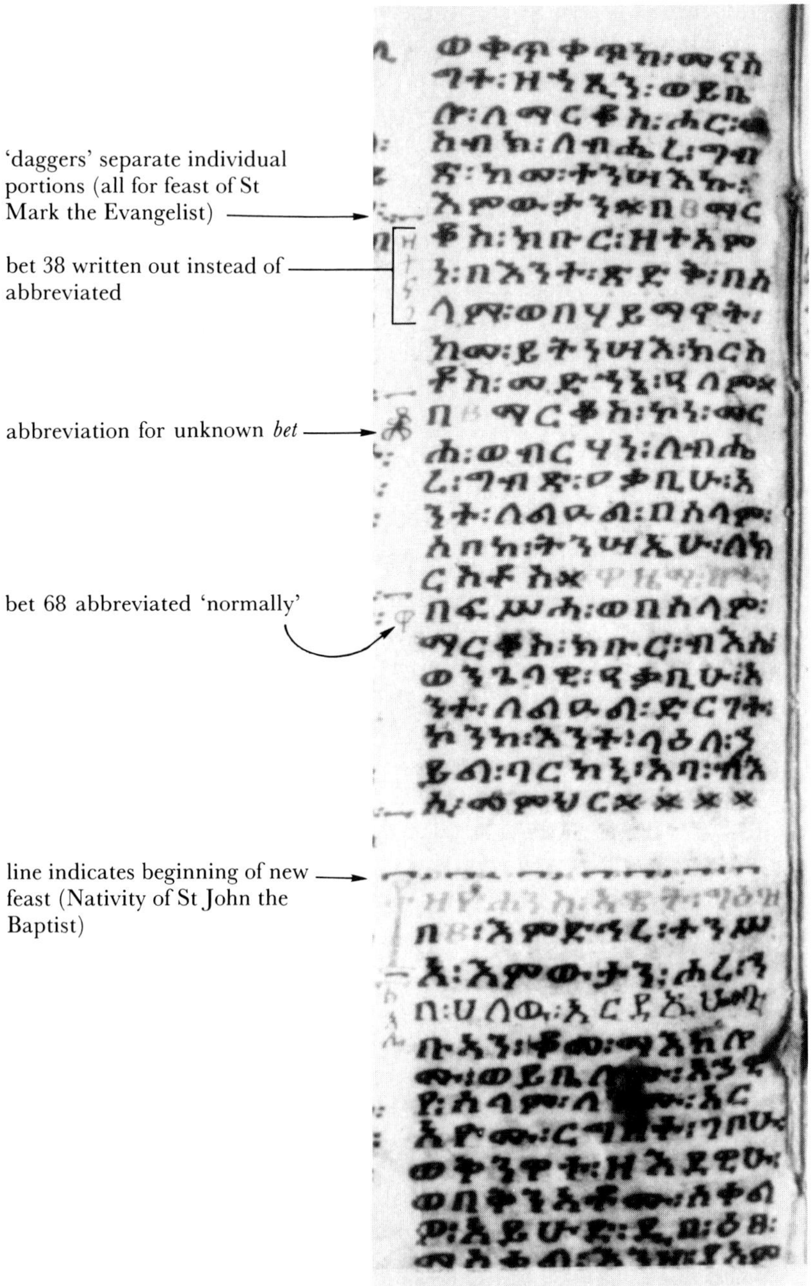

'daggers' separate individual portions (all for feast of St Mark the Evangelist)

bet 38 written out instead of abbreviated

abbreviation for unknown *bet*

bet 68 abbreviated 'normally'

line indicates beginning of new feast (Nativity of St John the Baptist)

Figure 5   15B, fol. 126b, col. 2

ardised. The first *bet* sign, B38 in our list, is completely written out except for its final letter – though it was this final letter that became the standard abbreviation in later sources. The second *bet* sign is an abbreviation of some sort (it consists of the letter *qo* written over the letter *mɛ*), but it cannot be identified with any *bet* known to us from twentieth-century sources of information.[44] On the other hand the third *bet* sign, B68 in our list, is already the one that became standard, the first letter of the complete word. The earliest source in which *bet* signs according to the standard system appear to have been written by the original scribe is 16B, but the majority of such signs even in this manuscript were clearly added by later hands.

The practice of classifying chants by melodic incipit is of course known also in medieval western Europe, where it competed with that of classifying melodies according to their final.[45] As Monson's discussion below indicates, the notion of 'final' is much less central in Ethiopian chant, though not completely absent. It is in any case quite useless for distinguishing the Ethiopian 'modes'. The *bet* system, on the other hand, is one of several indications that in Ethiopia it is the beginnings of melodies that are particularly important.

At some point the standard incipits of the *bet* system became linked to the standard melodic formulas with which the words 'halleluya' and 'For his mercy endures forever' were sung with each Type II portion. This was only natural, for in performance these prefatory formulas would have been followed immediately by the beginning of the portion itself. In Stage III, written lists of these 'halleluya' and 'For his mercy' formulas, supplied with musical notation, began to be drawn up, with each formula attached to its textual *bet* incipit, also with musical notation. Such a list is called *Enqɛs'ɛ Halleta* ('The gate of the halleluya material'), but because each halleluya or refrain melody is linked to a *bet* it also serves as a list of *bet* and a guide to the *bet* system as a whole. The earliest manuscript in our list of sources to include such a halleluya list is

[44] Bet 23 in our list, *ɛls'iqo*, is normally abbreviated *qo*, but there is no *mɛ* in this word. The Gǝʿǝz word *qomɛ* ('stop'), written exactly as shown in Figure 5, can be found in the margins of biblical manuscripts, where it signals the end of a pericope or liturgical reading (R. Zuurmond, *Research into the Text of the Synoptic Gospels in Geʿez*, II (Delft and Faringdon, Oxon., 1987), p. 48; Uhlig, *Äthiopische Paläographie*, pp. 91–2.
[45] M. Huglo, *Les tonaires: inventaire, analyse, comparaison* (Paris, 1971), pp. 72, 399–412.

Kay Kaufman Shelemay, Peter Jeffery, Ingrid Monson

17C, though a slightly earlier manuscript dates from A.D. 1667–8.[46] The list in 17C is already very similar to the *Ɛnqɛs'ɛ Halleta* lists normally found in *Dǝggwa* manuscripts from that time on. Not until printed books appear in the 1960s, however, do we find lists of the *bet* signs, giving all the marginal abbreviations according to 'mode' and identifying each with its fully spelled-out *bet*. This final development is 'Stage IV'. There are 123 *bet* signs in the list in 20D, but our chief informant evidently regarded some of them as duplications, for he sang only 114.

While we have not yet identified the sources of many of the *betoch*, it appears that they tend to be derived from portions of the *mɛzmur* category. Thus Bet 41, *yǝtfeṣsah' sɛmay*, to which the portion in our Figure 2 belongs, derives from the *mɛzmur* from the morning office (*Mɛwɛddǝs*) for Easter (Fasika).[47] There are however some exceptions. Bet 68, *wazema*, is used for many portions of the *wazema* category; its source may be the *wazema* of the feast of the Four Heavenly Creatures, 8 Ḥǝdar.[48] Bet 97.3, *ɛngɛrgari*, which appears to duplicate Bet 91, *qum ɛngɛrgari*, seems to be used for the *ɛngɛrgari* or *mǝlt'an* category in general and not to have a specific source in one particular portion. But there is at least one example of a *sɛlam* in this bet, sung at the end of the *wazema* (Vespers) office on Christmas (Lǝdɛt).[49] Bet 56, *qedami zema*, is derived from an *ɛryam* for Easter (Fasika),[50] even though the portions of the *ɛryam* category do not participate in the *bet* system.

The written history of the 'modes'. As explained above, all Ethiopian chants are assigned to one of three groupings that Westerners like to call 'modes', though in Ethiopic each grouping is called an 'order' (*sǝlt*) or 'chant' (*zema*).[51] Traditionally these three *zemat* are attributed to St Yared. But they may have emerged more recently, and there may once have been only two modal classifications. The

---

[46] Uppsala, Universitetsbiblioteket, MS O Ethiop. 36, described in Löfgren, *Katalog*, pp. 67–75. EMML 3890, which also contains an *Ɛnqɛs'ɛ Halleta*, is of about the same date as our 17C, 1693–1716.
[47] In our source 20D, it is located on p. 249, col. 1, line 16.
[48] 20D, p. 86, col. 1, line 23.
[49] 20D, p. 196, col. 1, line 25.
[50] 20D, p. 249, col. 1, line 1.
[51] The word *zema*, however, can also be used as the general term for the chant of the Ethiopian Orthodox Church. See K. K. Shelemay, *Music, Ritual, and Falasha History* (East Lansing, MI, 1986), pp. 99–101.

three modes *gəʿəz*, *ʿəzl* and *ɛraray* are all named in 15C. But earlier sources seem to know only *gəʿəz* and *ʿəzl*, as if there were a time when only these two modes were in use. These sources include 14A, the *sɛlam* collection in 15B and the early *Zəmmare* EMML 2091 of the fifteenth or sixteenth century. The *Mɛstɛgabʾə*, a selection of psalm verses memorised by boys in training as part of the Night Studies, also includes only *gəʿəz* and *ʿəzl* sections, though we do not know when this collection was assembled. The collections of Type I chants in 13A and 15B name none of the modes, but identify some melodic groups as being 'in the second zema' (*bɛ-kaləʾ zema*) as if there were then only two *zemat*.[52] The possibility that there may once have been only two modes suggests an explanation for the names *gəʿəz* and *ʿəzl*, which can be translated 'common' and 'apart' or 'special'.[53] The 'special' character of *ʿəzl* may be connected with the fact that it is associated with particular seasons of the year.[54] Perhaps, then, there were originally only two modes, one used generally, the other restricted to certain special occasions. The name *ɛraray*, thought to be an Amharic onomatopoeic term for crying in a high or loud voice,[55] may have arisen at a later time to designate the higher-range chants of the *ʿəzl* group. Support for this view may be found in Monson's observation, reported below, that there are only two 'background pitch sets', one for *gəʿəz*, the other for *ʿəzl* and *ɛraray*. This hypothesis needs to be confirmed by extensive investigation of the history of the modal designations and notations of portions now assigned to *ɛraray*. In any case, three modes with the modern names already existed at the time 15C was copied.[56]

[52] On the other hand, an alternative interpretation is suggested by the *sɛlam* and *wazema* collection in Paris MS d'Abbadie 87 (19th century). It is organised into *gəʿəz* (fol. 69a), *bɛkaləʾ zema* (77a), *ɛraray* (80a) and *ʿəzl* (89b), suggesting that the 'second *zema*' is here regarded as a subdivision within *gəʿəz*.

[53] Cf. Dillmann, *Lexicon linguae aethiopicae*, p. 1189. For more on the terminology, see Shelemay, *Music, Ritual, and Falasha History*, pp. 168–73.

[54] See the treatise in Vatican MS Aeth. 245, fol. 10a; the opening is translated into Latin in Grébaut and Tisserant, *Codices aethiopici*, p. 755. For some other theoretical literature on the modes see E. Cerulli, *I manoscritti etiopici della Chester Beatty Library in Dublino*, Atti della Accademia Nazionale dei Lincei, Classe di Scienze Morali, Storiche e Filologiche, 8th series, XI (1965), p. 300 (a MS of the seventeenth or eighteenth century), EMML 3434, fol. 114a (eighteenth century), our source 19D (EMML 2936).

[55] W. Leslau, *Comparative Dictionary of Gəʿəz (Classical Ethiopic)* (Wiesbaden, 1987), p. 39.

[56] Cerulli, *La letteratura etiopica*, p. 163, asserts that a late seventeenth-century revision of the *Dəggwa*, prepared by Qalɛ Ewadi at Debre Libanos, was especially concerned with the modes of the chant; but he cites no sources and we have no further information.

The development of the notation. Ethiopian traditions seem to say that the notation was invented by two priests, Gera and Ragu'el, who are said to have lived at some time during the sixteenth century.[57] The manuscript evidence is more or less consistent with this. Fifteenth-century manuscripts lack music notation altogether. The scribes who copied 16B and 16C evidently did not foresee the addition of notation, although it was added over some of their texts during the seventeenth century.[58] But in 16D and all subsequent manuscripts, the original scribe left space for the notation above each line of text, and this notation was actually entered during the copying of the text or shortly afterwards. The notation of 16A (late fifteenth or early sixteenth century) stands apart from that of all other known sources, however, and makes it an important manuscript for investigating the origins of the notation. Most of its *mələkkət* are not much later than the text itself, but they and especially the *yefidel qərs'* are notably more sparse than in other sources. The notator rarely bothered to indicate *ɛnbər* at the ends of portions, for instance, and he wrote other signs very sparingly compared with later manuscripts. Indeed, in not a few places additional signs have been put in by scribes of later periods. A number of features confirm the impression that 16A witnesses to an early stage when the notational system was not yet fully developed. The *yefidel qərs'* are especially sparse: *dəfat* occurs very rarely, while *dɛrɛt*, *rəkrək* and *hədɛt* seem not to have been used at all by the original notator. On the other hand, there are frequent vertical or slanted strokes both within and above the texts, which appear to have been deliberately intended to convey declamational information of some sort. Their frequency, combined with the limited use of the conventional signs, seem to indicate that this manuscript was notated at a time when the *mələkkət* system had already developed but the *yefidel qərs'* system was still being worked out.

The historical development of the *yefidel qərs'* and the *mələkkət* as written systems can be traced by following a single portion all the way through our series of dated manuscripts. Through such study one can learn much about the notational history of the chant.

---

[57] See discussion in note 29.

[58] Because most of the *mələkkət* are characters from the syllabary, they can be dated by the same palaeographical techniques used for dating Ethiopian texts; see Uhlig, *Äthiopische Paläographie*, pp. 539–40. However, the dating of scripts from before the seventeenth century is still difficult because dated landmarks are so rare.

Our Table 6 compares the notation of the first portion in the *Dǝggwa* (the one illustrated above by Shelemay) as it occurs in all the notated sources on our list in Table 2.[59] The text is given beneath the notation of 20D, because this is the source our informant used to perform the portion. We begin with the rubric indicating the category of the chant (*mǝlt'an* in most manuscripts, *wazema* or *mɛzmur* in some) and its assignment to the feast of St John the Baptist (1 Mɛskɛrɛm), the first day of the liturgical year. Then, most sources give the abbreviation for the *bet*, which is B41 in our list. After that, the indication 'in 1' means that the word 'halleluya' is sung once. Thereafter, the numbers preceded by a capital G represent *mǝlǝkkǝt* in the *gǝˤǝz* mode for which we have transcriptions. An asterisk after the number means that this particular place is the source (*sǝrɛyu*) of the melodic formula associated with this *mǝlǝkkǝt*. The underlined syllables are transliterations of *mǝlǝkkǝt* for which we have no musical transcriptions, because our informant did not include them in his list. All the other symbols – dots, brackets and the rest – are *yɛfidɛl qǝrs'*.

In the very earliest sources, the notation is sometimes inconsistent, as if a great variety of melodic traditions were in circulation. Our example is more consistent than most, perhaps because it is the first portion in the *Dǝggwa*. 16D contains an especially large number of variants throughout all the portions we checked, as if it represented a tradition quite different from the one that became more or less standard. The most noteworthy early variant is the very first *mǝlǝkkǝt* in 16B, which is the syllable *yu* for *sǝrɛyu*. A modern Ethiopian singer would presumably look to the text below and, seeing the words *bǝz'uˤǝ ɛntɛ yoh'ɛnnǝsǝ*, decide to sing the melodic formula he has memorised with these words. This would be formula G88 in our dictionary, but one that occurs at this place in no other source. Was it indeed what the scribe who notated 16B actually intended? The problem is complicated by the fact that *bǝz'uˤǝ ɛntɛ yoh'ɛnnǝsǝ*, 'Blessed are you John', is a textual formula, beginning a number of portions for this feast day and (with the name changed) many other feasts as well. But almost all of the portions for St John's day that begin with this incipit, in all sources including 16B, are notated with the same *mǝlǝkkǝt* as our portion

---

[59] The complete chart will be published in Shelemay and Jeffery, *Ethiopian Christian Liturgical Chant*. Here we reproduce the chart for only the first two phrases of portion 1.

Table 6 *The first portion in the Dəggwa*

15C									
	1a, 1, 13	məlt'an			in 1?	= = = = = = = = = = = = = =			
16A									
	1a	[first folio faded and illegible]							
16B									
	6a, 1, 29	məlt'an of John	*yo*		in 1	= = = = = = = = = = = = = =			
16D									
	5b, 1, 1	məlt'an of the evening	bet 41		in 1	= = = = = = = = = = = = = =			
17A									
	1a, 1, 16	məlt'an of the evening of St John	bet 41		in 1	= = = = = = = = = = = = = =			
17C									
	5a, 1, 21		bet 41		in 1	= = = = = = = = = = = = = =			
18B									
	5a, 1, 12				in 1	= = = = = = = = = = = = = =			
18C									
	5a, 1, 1	məlt'an of the evening	bet 41		in 1	= = = = = = = = = = = = = =			
18D									
	3a, 1, 13	wɛzema of John	bet 41		in 1	= = = = = = = = = = = = = =			
19A									
	4a, 1, 22	mɛzmur of the evening	bet 41		in 1	= = = = = = = = = = = = = =			
19B									
	3a, 1, 28	məlt'an of the evening on 1 Mɛskɛrɛm	bet 41		in 1	= = = = = = = = = = = = = =			
19C									
	4a, 1, 1	məlt'an of the evening			in 1	= = = = = = = = = = = = = =			
20A									
	7a, 1, 19	məlt'an of the evening on the feast of St John	bet 41		in 1	= = = = = = = = = = = = = =			
20B									
	6a, 1, 20	məlt'an of the evening of John	bet 41		in 1	= = = = = = = = = = = = = =			
20D									
	1, 1, 10	məlt'an of the evening of John the Baptist	bet 41		in 1	= = = = = = = = = = = = = =			
20F									
	7, 1, 4		bet 41		in 1	= = = = = = = = = = = = = =			
20D							:)	*gu'u:*		
						:	*gu'u:*	:	Ɛn
	392, 1, 28	[halleluya table]	bet 41*		in 1	ha-	lle	lu-	ya

Table 6   *continued*

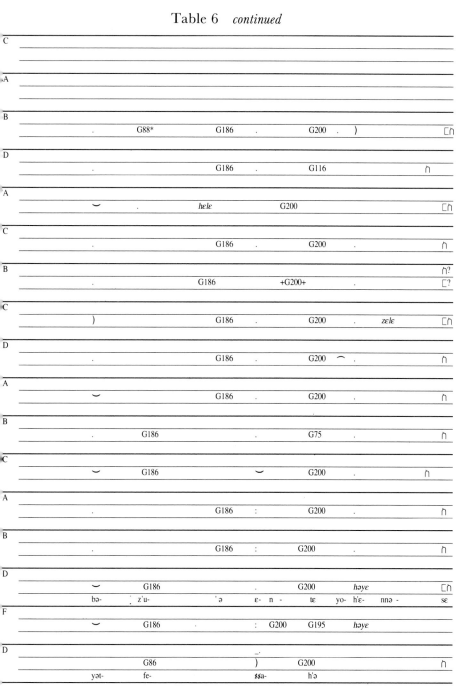

Table 6   *continued*

15C											
16A											
16B	.	.? .	G11	.	nɛd	⌐	.		⌐	)	.
16D	˙.	.	G11	.		⌐	.		na	)	.
17A	.	.	G11	.		⌐	.	. G61	G11		
17C	.		G11 .			⌐	.	G61		)	.
18B	.	.	+G11+	.		+⌐+		G61	+)+		.
									+rə+		
18C	.	.	G11	.		⌐	.	na		)	⌣
18D	.		G11		⌐			G61		)	
									= =		
19A		.	G11 .		⌒		.	G61		)	.
19B	.	.	G11	.		⌐	.	G61		)	.
19C	.	.	G11	.		⌐	⌣	.	G61)		⌣
20A	.		G11 .			⌐	.	)	G61		⌣
20B	.		G11	G60		⌐	)	G61	)		⌣
								2			
20D	həyɛ	.	G11	.		⌐	⌣	G61	)		⌣
	zɛ-	hɛ- llə-	wɛ-	kkɛ	ta'-	mə-	rə	2 wɛ- tɛ-	h'ɛ- wwə- rə	qɛdə-	mɛ
20F	G119 .		G11	G60		⌐	⌣	G61	)		⌣

1, namely G186 followed by G200. The source, or *sərɛyu*, of G88 is one of the *ɛrbaˤt* portions included in *Yɛ-qal Təmhərt*, assigned to the following Sunday.[60]

As the chart for portion 1 shows, much of the notation had stabilised by the seventeenth century, except at certain points that for some reason continued to vary over time. At one point in this portion, at the text *bɛˀənti'ɛnə wəstɛ rə'əsɛ* (not reproduced in Table 6), the manuscripts not only differ among themselves, but often contain *mələkkət* that are not to be found in our list. Once achieved, the overall notational stability lasted through the seventeenth and eighteenth centuries and into the nineteenth. In the late nineteenth and the twentieth centuries, many more signs came to be added to the notation, as if singers were beginning to lose their grip on the tradition, and compensated by attempting to notate as specifically as possible. Our example has experienced less of this than other portions, but on p. 2 it will be noted that the two most recent sources, 20D and 20F, contain *mələkkət* not found earlier: G195, the unlisted *mələkkət həya*, G119, G151. 20F also shares G60 with 20B.

Once the notation is understood it is possible to seek a better understanding of how the Type I and Type II groups actually function. Table 7 compares the notation of the first melodic model for the *ɛryam* category, portion 12 in our forthcoming anthology, with several other *ɛryam* texts that take the portion 12 melody for their model. Boxes outline places where the melodies agree with portion 12, and it will be readily observed that these are more common towards the beginning of each portion. The use of A1 for the final cadence is very common among portions in the *ɛraray* mode; its presence in four of our six examples should not be over-rated. However, only extensive study will determine how typical portion 12 is of the Ethiopian repertory as a whole.

Table 8 compares a Type IIa portion (our no. 1, the same one as illustrated in Table 6) with the portion that serves as the source of its *bet* (B15), where the notation represents no single source but is conflated from several twentieth-century manuscripts. The two

---

[60] For the text, see Velat, *Me'erāf*, p. 49 no. 15. For a translation see Velat, *Études sur le Me'erāf*, p. 246 no. 15. For its liturgical assignment (the Sunday after St John's day) see 20D 8, 2, 18. For the *mələkkət*, which have not been published, see EMML 1347, fol. 37b, col. 1, line 5.

Table 7 *Portion 12, a 'melodic model', compared with some derivative portions*

12	(	A39	:	A72	A19 A70	)	A69	A19	:	⌒
AA	˘	??	A115	A72	A19	.	A69	A19	:	A34*
BB	(	A19	A124	A72			A77		:	A122
CC	A19	A39	A19	A72			A116			A122
DD	.	A39	A115	A72			A116		:	⌒
EE	˘		??	A72					:	⌒

12	A32	A61	:			A1
AA	˘	A61	.	A19		A1
BB	A70	A124	A115			A120
CC	A83	A83	A15		:	A77
DD	A70	A54	A61	nəħə	:	A1
EE	A116	A19	A54			A1

Key: 12 – *ɛryam* for Easter, first in the series of 'melodic models' for the *ɛryam* category
AA – *ɛryam* for St John (first day of the year)
BB – *ɛryam* for Terce, first Monday in Lent
CC – *ɛryam* for Sext, first Monday in Lent
DD – *ɛryam* for None, first Monday in Lent
EE – *ɛryam* for the commemoration of Christmas one month later

Table 8 *Comparison of portion 1 with the source of its bet (= portion 15)*

1	bet	41	in 1	)	G186	.	G200	.	hƏya	⌐n		G151		G11	.	⌐		)		G61	)	)
15	bet	41*	in 1		G86	)	G200	.		⌐⌐	)	G182	)	G13	.		G88		.	G153	⌐	

1	.	G63	G11	. :	:	)	G119	G86	⌐n		...	ra	G160	)	G161	zƏye	G63	G86	G17
15	G195	G63	G11	.		)	G63	.	G274	G246	.	⌐⌐	G61	⌐		)			

1	G14 ⊢)	G84*	⌐		...	G165*	)	.	⌐ ⌐
15		G203*	)	G210	)	G108* ⊢)	G280	.	⌐ ⌐

have of course the same halleluya melisma, with the word 'halleluya' being sung only once. They agree in having G200 near the beginning, and G63 followed by G11 in the middle of the chant. Interestingly, they also agree in having the sources of two formulas (*sərɛyu*) close to the end (note the asterisks), though the two formulas are different in each case. Beyond that there is little similarity. Clearly the relationship between a Type II portion and the source of its *bet* is even looser than the relationship between a Type I portion and its melodic model. To the very limited degree that we can generalise from these two portions, it would seem that a *bet* is not a model at all, but governs only the halleluya and (loosely) the incipit. Indeed, comparison of Table 8 with Table 7 suggests that, in Ethiopian chant, similarities tend to cluster near the beginnings of the related portions. There is other evidence to support this impression. However, some of the other chants in our sample illustrate cases where portions sharing the same *bet* have a great deal more in common with each other than the two portions in Table 8.

Princeton University

INGRID MONSON

EVIDENCE FROM THE MODERN ORAL TRADITION

Ethiopian Christian chant is an example of a musical system whose notation was never intended to replace oral transmission. The alphabetic abbreviations known as *məlǝkkǝt* are used to index a corpus of conventionalised melodic phrases, which are themselves drawn from whole source chants. Unless the Ethiopian musician is performing the source portion itself, he must accommodate new text to the phrases while singing. Competence in Ethiopian chant performance, accordingly, is acquired by memorising a repertory of phrases, learning the alphabetical abbreviations for these melodies, and developing the ability to recall and sing these phrases on new texts with the aid of the *məlǝkkǝt* notation and a set of ten additional signs, *yɛfidɛl qǝrs'*, here termed 'conventional signs'.

Study of the notational system is carried out only after the Ethiopian church musician has learned many portions as whole chants. The notation, once learned, appears to facilitate the acquisition of additional repertory.

Transcriptions of eighteen liturgical portions, a pedagogical list of 558 *mǝlǝkkǝt* from the Bethlehem school (hereafter called the dictionary), and a comparative list of fifty-seven *mǝlǝkkǝt*, including performances by practitioners in the Qoma and Achaber schools, will be used here to illustrate various features of the musical system as perpetuated in the Ethiopian Christian oral tradition.

The first part of this discussion attempts to define 'mode' as it applies to Ethiopian chant. The second part discusses a single liturgical portion and its notation in detail. In the final section, a comparative sample is used to identify both the range of variation between renditions by one musician at different times, and between three different musicians performing the same material.

A definition of mode. The Amharic word *sǝlt*, which can be rendered as 'mode', applies to the indigenous classification of the *mǝlǝkkǝt* and portions into three musical categories. The word *zema*, which in its general sense means sacred chant, can also be used to mean mode. A metaphor associating the three modes with the Holy Trinity is operative in Ethiopian chant: the *gǝʿǝz* mode represents God the Father; *ʿǝzl* God the Son; and *ɛraray* the Holy Spirit.[61]

Musically, *gǝʿǝz* distinguishes itself from *ɛraray* and *ʿǝzl* by possessing a different background pitch set. *Ɛraray* and *ʿǝzl* are, in turn, differentiated from each other by liturgical function and register: they both use the same background pitch set, but *ʿǝzl* is employed primarily during Lent and Holy Week.

For the Ethiopian church musician the identity of the modes is expressed in the *mǝlǝkkǝt* melodies and the portions. There is no indigenous classification of the pitch material within these melodies, although a pitch set differentiation between *gǝʿǝz* and the other modes is tacitly and rigorously observed in practice. My description of pitch usage in the Ethiopian modes is therefore an

[61] Lepisa, 'The Three Modes', pp. 163–6.

analytical convenience and is not to be confused with indigenous notions of scale or melody type.

$G\partial^c\partial z$ is the most frequently occurring mode, accounting for approximately half (287) of the 558 signs in the dictionary. Example 7 sets out the pitch set used in $g\partial^c\partial z$. It consists of a series of thirds,[62] represented here as $a'-c''-e''$ (in semibreves) which serve as the most common points of resolution for $g\partial^c\partial z$ melodies ($g\sharp$ occasionally appears as a point of resolution as well). The chromatic auxiliary notes around the outer fifth ($g\sharp'$ and $b\flat'$ around a', and $d\sharp''$ and f'' around e'') embellish this mode, as can be seen in the example $m\partial l\partial kk\partial t$ shown in Example 7. There is often indifference over whether embellishment of the note is above or below the principal note, suggesting that for the Ethiopian musician variations of this type do not compromise the melodic identity of the sign (cf. example $m\partial l\partial kk\partial t$ G13, final three notes, and G25 on syllable $s\varepsilon$). The middle member of the series of thirds (c'') is not decorated by half-steps. This note is the returning tone, or final in the $g\partial^c\partial z$ mode.[63] In the notation, cadential patterns and the returning tone are indicated with $\varepsilon nb\partial r$, one of the ten conventional signs. The true distance of this pitch from the first in the series of thirds tends to be slightly larger than a minor third. On occasion it is as large as a major third.

---

[62] The expression 'series of thirds' is a modification of Curt Sachs's notion of 'chain of thirds' (Sachs, 'Primitive and Medieval Music: a Parallel', *JAMS*, 13 (1960), pp. 42–9; *The Wellsprings of Music*, ed. J. Kunst, repr. of 1962 edn (New York, 1977)). It is intended to describe the pitches which serve as points of melodic resolution in the $g\partial^c\partial z$ mode, in the absence of an indigenous term. Sachs defines 'chain' as follows: 'the melody has a formative kernel, usually a third or fourth; when the singer expands the range of his melody beyond this kernel, he often feels compelled to add a similar interval above or below, thus creating a double third or a double fourth and, onward, . . . [includes possibility of chain of 3–6 like intervals]' ('Primitive and Medieval Music', p. 45). Sachs's exposition requires revision for two reasons: (1) it does not include a notion of octave duplication (which occurs frequently in Ethiopian chant), and (2) it is used to articulate a theory for the historical development of melody cross-culturally on the speculative and evolutionary assumption that melodies expanded outward from small intervals and are filled in from larger ones (*The Wellsprings of Music*, pp. 143–58, 72, 51–2). H. van der Werf, *The Emergence of Gregorian Chant* (Rochester, NY, 1983), pp. 109–20, has apparently borrowed this term from Sachs along with aspects of Sachs's ideas concerning historical priority as applied to Gregorian chant. Sachs, however, includes the notion of points of melodic repose connected by 'passage' notes ('Primitive and Medieval Music', p. 45), which is useful in the Ethiopian case and is not included in the idea of 'octave species'. I thank Peter Jeffery for citations and for assistance in clarifying this point.

[63] In Ethiopian secular music, the term *melash* means 'returning tone' (A. Kebede, 'The Bowl-Lyre of Northeast Africa – Krar: the Devil's Instrument', *Ethnomusicology*, 21 (1977), pp. 389–91.

Example 7. 'Mode' in Ethiopian chant (source: dictionary of *mɑlɑkkɑt* performed by Berhanu Makonnen between June and October 1975)

101

Defining *εraray* and *ʿəzl* is more problematic, largely owing to difficulties in translating Ethiopian intonation into Western notation. *Εraray* and *ʿəzl* both use the same pitch set, *c′–d′–f′–g′–a′* or *c′–d′–e′–g′–a′*, as rendered in staff notation (see Example 7). Ambiguity in these modes, from the analyst's perspective, is the product of two factors. First, the actual intonation of the intervals *d′–f′* and *d′–e′* is often in between these two Western pitches, so much so that whether the Western ear should resolve the ambiguity towards the second or the minor third in the transcriptions has often been a point of disagreement in the research team. We had the interval measured on a Fairlight Voicetracker. It is indeed often exactly halfway between a major second and a minor third.[64] These two pitch sets, rendered in staff notation, are often observed as substitutes for one another. See, for example, Example 7, where the melody of sign A58 is shown in the dictionary using pitch set 1 and in one of the portions with pitch set 2. The signs proceed identically until the fifth pitch of the set is introduced. Secondly, the typical cadential gesture of a descent and return of a minor third can occur at two places within any given form of the pitch set: *c′* and *f′* within set 1, or *c′* and *g′* in pitch set 2, making it difficult to establish a returning tone for any *mələkkət* in isolation.[65] Selecting a comparative transposition level for the *mələkkət* was difficult, particularly in light of the fact that *εraray* is additionally said to be the mode with the highest register.[66] Only in the portions, which indicate returning tone with the symbol *εnbər*, has it been possible to observe the apparent predominance of pitch set 2 in characterising the mode. It may, in fact, be better to think of these modes as a pentatonic collection with a variable third degree.

The performance of a liturgical portion. To illustrate the many musical issues involved in performing Ethiopian chant, liturgical portion 7 from our sample will be examined in some detail. Portion 7 is an *εngεrgari* for Christmas in the *gəʿəz* mode. The word *εngεrgari* is evidently derived from an Amharic word which connotes agitation or excitement,[67] and is often used for chants that are linked to major feast days.

---

[64] We thank Dr Kathryn Vaughn, who carried out this work at the University of California, Los Angeles.

[65] This cadential gesture is observable at the end of each *mələkkət* in Example 7.

[66] Lepisa, 'The Three Modes', p. 166.

[67] Leslau, *Concise Amharic Dictionary*, p. 209.

Figure 6   Notation of portion 7, εngεrgari for Christmas (Yεziq Mεs'h'af, Addis Ababa, 1962 E.C.)

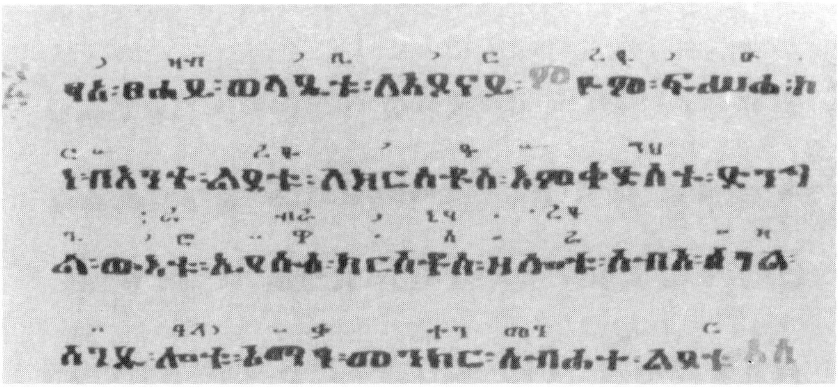

Translation: There is joy today because of the birth of Christ from the Holy Virgin. He is Jesus the Christ before whom the Magi prostrated themselves. Truly the glory of his birth is wonderful. (translation by Getatchew Haile)

An internal textual-musical repeat called a m∂lt'an is a formal feature that portion 7 shares with many others in our sample. The musical repeat is usually notated in one of two ways – either with a double line of notation over the part of the text to be repeated, or by placing the abbreviation for m∂lt'an (m∂l) at the end of the portion. When the latter convention is used, the second part is written out again. In our example, Ɛlɛqa Berhanu sang from a source called Yεziq Mεs'h'af, a collection of important parts of the D∂ggwa for holidays.[68] This particular source has an incomplete double line of notation beginning at the m∂lt'an; consequently, Ɛlɛqa Berhanu did not sing the repeat. The m∂lt'an, however, is notated in all but five of the manuscripts examined by Peter Jeffery. The notation that Ɛlɛqa Berhanu sang from is shown in Figure 6. Throughout the portions analysed for this project, the music for the m∂lt'an repeat is generally very similar to the first presentation, despite some notational contrast.

Portion 7 is one of the shorter chants in our sample, partly because Berhanu Makonnen chose not to sing the repeat. The top line of each system of Example 8 presents a transcription of Ɛlɛqa Berhanu's singing of portion 7. The bottom lines show the diction-

---

[68]   Addis Ababa, 1962 E.C., 20F in our MS sample.

Example 8. Portion 7, *ɛngɛrgari* for Christmas (source: performed by Berhanu Makonnen, 23 September 1975)

ary entry for each *mǝlǝkkǝt*. The *mǝlt'an* would begin on system 3 (marked with an M). In each section, portion and *mǝlt'an*, the *mǝlǝkkǝt* move to gradually lower points of resolution. In the first section of the portion the *mǝlǝkkǝt* come to rest first on c'' (as notated here), then $g\sharp'$, and finally on e' just before the *mǝlt'an*. At this point Berhanu returns to the opening e'', emphasising the high register until coming to rest on c'' (beginning of third system). From this moment onwards, Berhanu sings a gradually lower set of melodic resolutions that are more extended than those of section 1. The melisma on *lo* of *zelottu* (beginning of system 4) comes to rest on a'; the melisma on *tu* of *lottu* (beginning of system 5) comes to a halt on e'. The last phrase continues the descent to come to rest on c', the lowest note of the portion. This sequence of progressively lower melodic resolutions with lengthier melismas in the second half of portions or subsections of portions is a common feature of *gǝ'ǝz* mode portions, and appears to be a conventionalised practice.

Portion 7 exhibits a very high degree of correspondence between the dictionary *mǝlǝkkǝt* and the signs as performed in the portion. Allowing for octave displacement, eight signs match the dictionary entries with great exactness. These signs are marked with an asterisk on the dictionary lines of Example 8. Three signs are examples of *sǝrɛyu*, a designation indicating that this occurrence is the source text of the sign. These *mǝlǝkkǝt* are marked with an 'x' in Example 8.

In system 2 and the beginning of system 3, it will be noted that signs G279, G182 and G13 apply to the same musical phrase. The dictionary entries for these *mǝlǝkkǝt* are all very similar. Since G13 is the only sign that begins on the same pitch as the portion melody, it appears that Ɛlɛqa Berhanu has chosen to sing G13 and to bypass G279 and G182. Likewise, in system 3, G249 and G261 resemble each other very closely. Berhanu has apparently chosen G261, although in this case the signs are nearly identical. Such situations, including examples where the skipped *mǝlǝkkǝt* does not resemble the chosen sign, are quite common throughout the eighteen portions in our sample. A knowledge of which *mǝlǝkkǝt* are substitutable or equivalent to one another appears to be essential to the performance practice of Ethiopian chant.

In performance, one also finds contraction and expansion of the melodies associated with the signs. The portion melody for G66 (system 3) makes use of only the first word of the dictionary entry for the sign (cf. *wə'ətu* in the portion with *bɛdɛro* in the *mələkkət*). In contrast, the portion melody for G230 (see system 4, *zɛlottu*) represents an expansion of the dictionary version of the *mələkkət*. Finally, G122 (system 5, beginning) corresponds to the last part of the dictionary entry only: the melisma on the last syllable of the sign.

The sign in the margin of the notation (*ri*) is a *bet* or 'house' sign. It indicates a melodic incipit, which in this case exactly matches the *mələkkət* G259.[69] In portions with halleluyas, the *bet* indicates the melody to which a halleluya is sung. In some portions in our sample these incipits recur at phrase beginnings, even if the beginnings of the *mələkkət* are somewhat modified in the process. In this way the *bet* seem to provide a source of melodic continuity and may aid the singer in synthesising the portion.

For most signs, the *mələkkət* melody is applied to a different text and consequently the singer must adjust the text of the portion to the melody of the sign. The textual placement in the sign seems to guide that of the portion, but often discrepancies exist between the length of the portion text and that of the sign. Syllabic quantification does not appear to play a critical role in such accommodation. The conventional signs of *yɛfidɛl qərs'*, however, appear to play an important role in textual placement.

Example 9 presents examples of five of the ten conventional signs drawn from the portion sample. The musical contexts in which these signs appear in the portions have helped us to draw some tentative conclusions about their functions. I will start with the most consistent sign, *ch'ərɛt* (see Example 9a). In every case, *ch'ərɛt* indicates the syllable on which a melisma begins. *Hədɛt* (Example 9b) apparently indicates that many syllables must be quickly sung in the *mələkkət* melody. *Yəzat* (Example 9c) is somewhat puzzling. It occurs frequently in the portion sample, yet not in a uniform musical context. Berhanu's definitions – 'you must stop' or 'you must hold your voice on one letter'[70] – suggest that

---

[69]   This *bet* corresponds to one that Berhanu Makonnen did not sing (B97.3, *ri*), possibly because he regarded it as duplicating B91 (*quri*) to which the portion's opening melody corresponds exactly.

[70]   K. K. Shelemay, unpublished fieldnotes and recordings: interviews with Berhanu Makonnen, 2 June–10 October 1975 (Addis Ababa), 7 June 1979 and n.d., p. 7.

Example 9. The conventional signs (*yɛfidɛl qɔrs'*) (source: portions 7, 17 and 6 as performed by Berhanu Makonnen, 3 September, 27 June and 12 July 1975)

(a) *ch'ɔrɛt*)

G259   )   G195   )   yu G279   )   G66
yo- mə fə-   ʦʦə- h'ɛ   tu lɛ krəs-   to- sə   wə- 'ə-   tu

)   [G261   A19)   [G261   A19   )
lɛ-ma-rə-   ya-mə   əg-zi- 'ɛ lɛ-sen-   bɛ- tə z'o-rɛ- tto   bɛ

E5   )   E51   )   [   )
-fɛ-   qqəd- z'ɛ   h'a-yɛ   wɛ-bər-   ha-nə   yət-fɛ-qqɛd   əm-wɛy- nə

(b) *hɔdɛt* ∿

ur̄   G76   ur̄   G182   G13
be'ən-tɛ lə-de- tu   əm- qə-ddəs-tə dən-gə   lə

ur̄   [ur̄
yɛh'ɛ-wwə-ru ɛh'-za- bə   ʦər- gu- tə

(c) *yɔzat* .

.   G261   ..   G249   .   G230   ..   G122   )
krəs-   to- sə   i- yyɛ- su- sə   zɛ- lo-   sɛ- gɛ-   du- lo-   ttu

108

(c) *continued*

men-kə-rə   gər-ma   lə- ʿu-lə s'ɛ-llɛ-la-   wɛ-ʾɛ- bu-ha lɛ-   wə'ə-- tu-ni   qɛ- de- sa

A47   A41a   A41a

ɛ-   ma-nə   bɛ- ʿɛ- ma

A105a

(d) *dərs*

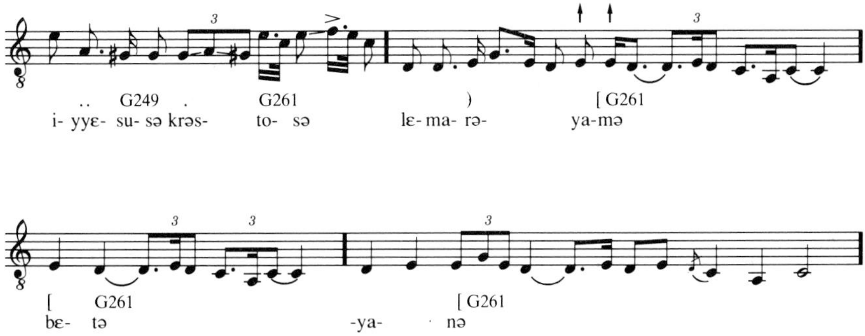

i- yyɛ- su- sə krəs-   to- sə   lɛ-ma- rə-   ya-mə

G249   G261   G261

bɛ-   tə   -ya-   nə

G261   G261

(e) *ɛnbər*

ko-   nɛ   lə- dɛ- tu   -lə s'ɛ-llɛ-la

llə-lə-   wwa wɛ- wɛ-   r-ha   zi ʾɛ-   ha

Note: these examples are drawn from portions in each mode; portion 7 is in gəʿəz, portion 17 in ɛraray and portion 6 in ʿəzl. Hədɛt was not available in all three portions.

it may indicate a stressed or prolonged syllable, although in many portions this is not very audible. Two conventional signs, *dərs* and *ɛnbər*, have specific melodies associated with them (Example 9d and e). These signs, which indicate that a melodic cadence should be sung, have versions appropriate to each mode: one version serves for *ɛraray* and *ʿəzl*; another serves for *gəʿəz*. *Dərs* actually has an equivalent in the *mələkkət*: G261; several other *mələkkət* appear to have functions that relate to the conventional signs as well. This suggests that there has been a tendency for the *mələkkət* to incorporate some of the musical features originally indicated by conventional signs.

The most important observations emerging from this discussion are (1) that the Ethiopian musician makes many of his own decisions in the course of realising the *mələkkət*, (2) that the conventional signs are most important in textual placement and indication of important melodic cadences, (3) that musical structure follows textual structure very closely and (4) that the *bet* may play an important role in the musical continuity of portions which use them.

A comparative sample. Fifty-seven *mələkkət* sung by representatives of the three extant regional styles – Bethlehem, Qoma and Achaber – provide comparative data for this study. The Bethlehem singer, Berhanu Makonnen, is the same musician who sang the dictionary. Comparing Ɛlɛqa Berhanu's renditions of the signs on two occasions several months apart allows us to see what type of variation occurs in his singing of the signs themselves. Of twenty-nine *mələkkət* in the *gəʿəz* mode, for which we have comparative information, only two exhibit variations that threaten the identity of the sign. Two are more extended in one rendition than the other. Example 10a displays two *mələkkət* sung by Berhanu Makonnen three months apart. G198 shows variation that affects the identity of the melody, while G219 is an example of melodic extension in one version. Allowing for equivalences in mode, general rhythmic character and octave displacement, the remaining *mələkkət* are nearly identical. In the *ɛraray* and *ʿəzl mələkkət* in the sample, extension of the sign is the only significant type of variation. Ɛlɛqa Berhanu is remarkably consistent in his rendition of the signs.

The melodies of the *mələkkət* as compared among the three

Example 10. Comparative renditions of *mǝlǝkkǝt*

(a) Different renditions of two *mǝlǝkkǝt* (source: performed by Berhanu Makonnen, 2–7 June and 8 September 1975)

(b) Comparative renditions of four *mǝlǝkkǝt* in Bethlehem (B), Qoma (Q) and Achaber (A) styles (source: performed by Berhanu Makonnen, Berhanu Abiye and Tekle Mesheshe, 8 September 1975)

111

Example 10 *continued*

(c) Different renditions of two *mələkkət* by Berhanu Makonnen and Velat's informant (sources: performed by Berhanu Makonnen, 2–7 June 1975; transcribed in Velat, *Études sur le Meʿerāf*, p. 629; note: the two items from Velat have been transposed for purposes of comparison)

112

regional styles – Bethlehem, Qoma and Achaber – exhibit greater variety, as might be expected. Example 10b shows four *məlǝkkǝt* from the comparative sample. The Qoma and Achaber styles tend to be more melismatic and extended than the predominant Bethlehem style, confirming singers' testimony that these two minority styles are 'longer' than Bethlehem. There is both sufficient general and specific correspondence between the signs, however, to suggest that the three schools are closely related (cf. G170 and G248; A97 and A140). While both oral tradition and documentary sources suggest that Bethlehem is the oldest style, it is important to note that similarities are probably the product of both common ancestry and contact in the modern performance tradition. It is not uncommon for church musicians from different regional styles to sing in the same church in the Ethiopian capital.[71]

There is one more comparative sample that should be mentioned. In 1951, Bernard Velat recorded an accomplished Bethlehem *dɛbtɛra* singing more than 500 of the *məlǝkkǝt*. He published transcriptions of about half of them.[72] I have compared many of these transcriptions with my own and have found a great deal of consistency in the *məlǝkkǝt*. Example 10c includes two *məlǝkkǝt* as rendered by Berhanu Makonnen and Velat's informant. While there is more variation than between Berhanu's two samples, given three months apart, the melodies are readily recognisable within the parameters previously mentioned. These transcriptions, made twenty-five years before our *məlǝkkǝt* were recorded, suggest that the Ethiopian notational system succeeds in transmitting a relatively stable musical corpus. The *məlǝkkǝt* seem to confine melodic variation to relatively small units.

University of Chicago

CONCLUSIONS

These observations, and indeed our entire project, have only scraped the surface of Ethiopic chant, which is in almost every way a subject as vast as Gregorian chant. We felt like archaeologists

[71] Shelemay, unpublished fieldnotes and recordings: interviews with Berhanu Makonnen, Berhan Abiye and Tekle Mesheshe, 8 September 1975 (Addis Ababa).
[72] Velat, *Études sur le Mĕʿerāf*, and Ṣoma Deggua (1969).

digging test pits in order to plan an excavation; the excavation itself has barely even begun.

Concerning the nature of Ethiopian chant as a musical and notational system, it appears that it intends to transmit a relatively fixed corpus of chants with identifiable and reproducible melodic content. We have seen that the melodies of the *mələkkət* seem to be quite stable within and between schools. The variations observed do not compromise the audible identity of the melody in most cases, and as such illustrate a distinction developed by Bruno Nettl and discussed by Harold Powers, between 'performing a version' of something and 'improvising upon something'.[73] Both are species of improvisation, in the sense that new melodic material may be constructed, but the intention of the former is to realise something relatively fixed and stable, while the latter actively values new invention. If, in order to describe degrees of improvisation, a continuum from nearly fixed to nearly random is posited, Ethiopian chant would occupy a position not far from the fixed end of the spectrum.

It may be asked to what extent the Ethiopian musician carries the musical tradition in his memory as whole chants, or to what extent he re-synthesises portions with the aid of the *mələkkət* notation each time he performs. Whether the macro- or micro-context is viewed as the one that generates musical performance, the musical content of this tradition is carried completely in the memory of the singer, since the text-based character of the *mələkkət* notation provides no visual indication of the contour of the melody.

If the *mələkkət* are seen as the building-blocks from which the singer creates a chant, there is ample evidence of oral compositional decisions. The Ethiopian musician must know which *mələkkət* resemble one another, which *mələkkət* are redundant, when to sing only the beginning or end of a sign, how to interpret the conventional signs, when and how to make use of the *bet*, how to place the text, and when melismatic extensions are appropriate – all of this in addition to knowing and being able to recall the 500-plus *mələkkət* themselves.

If the macro-context is viewed as potentially more important, it might be argued that the Ethiopian musician does not synthesise

---

[73]   H. Powers, 'Language Models and Musical Analysis', *Ethnomusicology*, 24 (1980), pp. 42–6.

a portion anew each time he sings, any more than a pianist is 'reading' a piece he or she has played innumerable times. The pedagogical tradition of the repertory also suggests this viewpoint: children learning the tradition begin by acquiring portions as a whole. Only after there has been some mastery at that level does the student begin a study of the notation. Apprehension of the notation, in turn, facilitates the learning of additional repertory.

If transmission in whole chants appears to be the most important process, however, the analyst must explain the persistence of the *məlakkət* system of notation over several centuries. Surely, a system that is not useful would not survive. It therefore seems only reasonable to suggest that the macro- and micro-musical memories of this tradition effectively reinforce one another; this, in fact, may be the central utility of the Ethiopian notational system. The Ethiopian church musician learns repertory in an order which integrates memories of whole chants with memories of chants in fragments – from two directions, as it were. If global memory fails, the *məlakkət* notation can serve as a means by which the musician re-synthesises vaguely remembered chants, and if local memory fails, recollection of the broader outline of the chant may help reconstruct the detail. There is probably much individual variation in which type of memory prevails.

The many contributions by individual musicians to the perpetuation and performance of the Ethiopian chant tradition took place within a broader historical framework. In the earliest recorded stage ('Stage I'), the different categories of portions were assembled into separate collections that could be organised either by melodic group or by liturgical year. The oldest such collection is from about the thirteenth century, and we do not know how much farther back such collections may once have existed, either orally or in writing.

By the fifteenth century, a representative portion had been identified for each melodic group ('Stage II'), becoming either a 'melodic model' in the case of Type I chants or the source of a *bet* or 'house' in the case of Type II. However, the 'models' system of Type I had achieved its standard form by the fifteenth century, whereas the house system of Type II – at least the written signs for it – did not stabilise until the sixteenth century. The first liturgical chant book incorporating all the categories is from the fifteenth century.

The notation was apparently developed in the sixteenth century, and has been an integral part of chant manuscripts ever since. It was also in the seventeenth century that written lists of the melodic models and the houses began to be made ('Stage III') providing overall structures for both systems. Thus the Ethiopian chant repertory had achieved its classic written form by the seventeenth century, which is called the 'Gondar period' by Ethiopian historians after the name of the new Ethiopian capital established at Gondar by the Emperor Fasilidas in 1635.

There is no doubt that the Ethiopian chant tradition and changes in its transmission process have been directly shaped by events in Ethiopian cultural history. The emergence of notation in the sixteenth century, although perhaps anticipated by earlier developments, appears to represent a direct attempt to sustain the musical tradition in the tragic aftermath of the Muslim invasion.

Available documentary sources suggest that the first seventy-five years of the Gondar period, culminating in the reign of Emperor Iyasu I, saw the construction of churches and castles as Gondar both influenced and absorbed an array of regional styles.[74] Royal support and demand for artistic and liturgical artefacts encouraged musicians to produce more notated manuscripts just as it encouraged the development of distinctive Gondarene styles of painting and iconography.[75] The technological innovation represented by the *mǝlǝkkǝt* and their proliferation during the Gondar period can be seen as part of a broader cultural trend towards literacy, but one that at the same time continued to encode meaning simultaneously in oral transmission. Likewise, the increasing numbers of manuscripts containing musical notation dating from the eighteenth and nineteenth centuries are only part of the residue of a broader transition from oral transmission to increased use of writing.[76]

---

[74] Merid Wolde Aregay, 'Southern Ethiopia and the Christian Kingdom 1508–1708, with Special Reference to the Galla Migrations and their Consequences' (Ph.D. dissertation, University of London, 1971), pp. 534–6, 542–8.

[75] J. Leroy, *Ethiopian Painting* (London, 1967), pp. 28–30.

[76] A recent analysis of the Amdǝmta Commentary corpus, a body of vernacular commentaries on Gǝʿǝz biblical and patristic texts, suggest that these commentaries were initially orally transmitted but reached their definitive written form during the Gondar era. R. Cowley, *The Traditional Interpretation of the Apocalypse of St. John in the Ethiopian Church* (Cambridge, 1983), pp. 23, 31.

Despite the decline of the Gondar monarchs' power in the late eighteenth century, their city continued to be a cultural centre and a site for musical innovation. But with the shift of the Ethiopian capital to Addis Ababa in 1887, the impact of governmental policies of centralisation[77] also encouraged increasing consolidation of the chant tradition.

In the late twentieth century, few *dɛbtɛra*s perpetuate regional chant traditions as the Bethlehem style increasingly predominates. There is little doubt that the twentieth-century transmission of the chant tradition in Addis Ababa has served both to standardise and to normalise surviving oral tradition, while encouraging increasing notational detail. The 1974 revolution and the end of the monarchy that patronised the church introduced a dramatic new socio-economic situation that has already altered transmission of the church musical system.[78]

Ethiopian chant is an example of a musical system whose notation was never intended to replace oral transmission. The *məlǝkkǝt* can be viewed as a conventionalised melodic repertory that assists and succeeds in the goal of transmitting a relatively fixed and stable liturgical corpus. The development of this notational system occurred in a specifically Ethiopian context and reflects particularly Ethiopian values concerning orality, flexibility and authority. The value of Ethiopian chant to comparative studies may lie in the portrait it provides of a highly constrained, notated, literate, yet orally transmitted repertory.

[77] Levine, *Wax and Gold*, pp. 46–7.
[78] For a detailed discussion of the Ethiopian revolution, including its impact upon the church, see J. Harbeson, *The Ethiopian Transformation: the Quest for the Post-Imperial State* (Boulder, CO, and London, 1988).

Early Music History (1993) Volume 12

ANDREW WATHEY

THE MOTETS OF PHILIPPE DE VITRY AND THE FOURTEENTH-CENTURY RENAISSANCE*

Towards the end of August 1350, Petrarch wrote from his home at Padua to Philippe de Vitry, chastising his friend for a letter that he had sent to their mutual patron, Cardinal Guy de Boulogne, papal legate in Italy. Vitry's mind has slowed since their first acquaintance, writes Petrarch, so that he now considers even a glorious absence from France undesirable. The man who, when asked where he was from, answered that he was a citizen of the world, now thinks any departure from France an exile. The dust of France lies too heavily on his shoes; the Petit-Pont in Paris, 'its arch not quite in the shape of a tortoise shell', is too appealing to him, and the murmur of the Seine delights his ear too much.[1] Worked into this elegant rebuke, however, there is also high praise

*This article originated as a paper read in different versions at the Annual Meeting of the American Musicological Society, Chicago, 8 November 1991, and the XVth Congress of the International Musicological Society, Madrid, 4 April 1992. For their help and encouragement at various stages of this project, I am grateful to David d'Avray, Margaret Bent, Bonnie Blackburn, Charlotte Brown, Leofranc Holford-Strevens, David Howlett, John Nádas and Nigel Palmer. The following abbreviations are used in the article:

A-Wn   Vienna, Österreichische Nationalbibliothek
AH   *Analecta hymnica*
D-B   Berlin, Staatsbibliothek Preussischer Kulturbesitz
D-W   Wolfenbüttel, Herzog August Bibliothek
F-Pn   Paris, Bibliothèque Nationale
IMU   *Italia medioevale e umanistica*

[1] *Epistole familiari*, ix.13. See V. Rossi, ed., *Francesco Petrarca: Le familiari*, 4 vols. (Florence, 1933–42), ii, pp. 246–56; also A. S. Bernardo, trans., *Letters on Familiar Matters, IX–XVI* (Baltimore and London, 1982), pp. 35–44. For Petrarch's other letter to Vitry (*Epistole familiari*, xi.14), sent from Avignon on 23 October 1351, see Rossi, ii, pp. 354–5. See in general on these letters E. H. Wilkins, *Studies in the Life and Works of Petrarch* (Cambridge, MA, 1955), pp. 66, 82, 90, 113, 171; E. H. Wilkins, *Petrarch's Correspondence*, Medioevo e Umanesimo 3 (Padua, 1960), pp. 5, 64, 67.

for Vitry's poetic activities. More than once Petrarch mentions his literary work, commending to him the cardinal, who has provided a 'testing ground for his talent and material for his pen', and alluding indirectly to texts that he has sent him. Most striking, Petrarch hails Vitry as the only true poet among the French ('Tu, poeta nunc unicus Gallicarum . . .'). It is true that not all of the traditions of the *Epistole familiari*, in which this and another letter to Vitry were later incorporated, include this passage.[2] Nonetheless, it was taken seriously both by contemporaries and by the humanist scholars of the later fourteenth century. In a commentary on Petrarch's *Bucolicum carmen* completed in 1394, Francesco Piendibeni da Montepulciano, chancellor of Perugia, makes clear not only that Vitry's reputation had survived into the first generation of Petrarch scholarship, but also that it was rapidly established in the exegesis of the poet's works. Identifying Vitry with the 'Gallus' of the Fourth Eclogue – 'Gallus hic fuit Phylippus de Victriaco, clarissimus musicus et philosophus et Petrarce summe notus' – Piendibeni comments that 'Gallus erat unus famulus francigena musicus qui Petrarcham infestabat assidue ut poesym et rhetoricam edoceret'.[3] These remarks are important in themselves, but

---

[2] The considerably shorter text of this letter in the later γ tradition substitutes 'Tu domino nostro compatris . . .' for this passage; for this version, see Rossi, *Le familiari*, II, pp. 267–75. The α version is not limited to Paris, Bibliothèque Nationale, MS lat. 8568, as Schrade claims ('Philippe de Vitry: Some New Discoveries', *Musical Quarterly*, 45 (1956), pp. 330–54, on p. 331 n. 3).

[3] 'This Gallus was Philippe de Vitry, most famous musician and philosopher, and well known to Petrarch', and 'Gallus was a servant, born in France, a musician who pestered Petrarch to teach him poesy and rhetoric'. Rome, Biblioteca Apostolica Vaticana, MS Pal. lat. 1729, fol. 7^r; printed in A. Avena, *Il Bucolicum e i suoi commenti inediti* (Padua, 1906), p. 264, and most recently discussed in N. Mann, 'In margine alla quarta egloga: piccoli problemi di esegesi petrarchesca', *Studi Petrarcheschi*, new series, 4 (1987), pp. 17–32, esp. pp. 26–7. See Mann, pp. 22–4, 26, for the commentary on this passage in the *Epitomata* attributed to Donato degli Albanzani ('Gallus fuit quidam proprio nomine dictus Philippus in musica summus artifex, a Gallia Gallus in hoc loco cognominatus'), and for that of the anonymous *Intentiones* ('Per Gallum intelliget quendam francigenam in scientia musica valde doctum'). For the anonymous commentary on this passage in Florence, Biblioteca Laurenziana, MS Plut. 52, 33 ('fuit quidam gallicus nomine filippus vitrinj [sic], musicus eximius et vir licteratus et ditissimus et amicus vatis ipsius franciscj petracce'), see Avena, p. 201. See also N. Mann, 'The Making of Petrarch's "Bucolicum carmen": a Contribution to the History of the Text', *IMU*, 20 (1977), pp. 127–84. For Piendibeni, a clerk in the chancery at Perugia until 1392, papal secretary from 1396, and Bishop of Arezzo 1414–33, see C. M. Monti, 'Una raccolta di "exempla epistolarum" I: lettere e carmi di Francesco da Fiano', *IMU*, 27 (1984), pp. 121–60, on pp. 138–40; also G. Billanovich, 'Giovanni del Virgilio, Petro da Moglio, Francesco da Fiano', *IMU*, 6 (1963), pp. 203–34, on pp. 212–15, 219, 225; R. G. de Witt, *Hercules at the Crossroads: the Life, Works and Thought of Coluccio Salutati*, Duke Monographs in Medieval and Renais-

they gain added weight set against Piendibeni's position in early Petrarchan scholarship. A regular correspondent of Salutati, and a pupil of Pietro da Moglio, who was himself a pupil of Petrarch, Piendibeni enjoyed privileged access to the traditions and truths surrounding the poet's works. He was also well placed to foster their dissemination.

Philippe de Vitry's friendship with Petrarch, and the question of its creative legacy, first received serious attention from Pierre de Nolhac in the early years of this century;[4] it was also taken up at length by Alfred Coville, in his 1933 biographical study of Vitry, which set the literary activities of the two men firmly in the context of service to the Avignon popes, and, in particular, within the cultural circle surrounding the court of Clement VI (1342–52).[5] Since then, however, this subject has been largely ignored. Schrade was content to leave the issue virtually untouched, and more recent musicological work has tended to perpetuate this omission, preferring to regard Vitry the musician and Vitry the writer as separate beings. In literary studies the subject of Vitry's poetic output has been taken up mainly by a revisionist historiography inclined to minimise his role in the world of letters.[6] Only very recently has

sance Studies 6 (Durham, NC, 1983), pp. 15, 284–5, 396. On the fourth eclogue, see T. G. Bergin, trans., *Petrarch's Bucolicum carmen* (New Haven and London, 1974), pp. 223–5.

[4] *Pétrarque et l'humanisme*, 2nd edn, 2 vols., Bibliothèque Littéraire de la Renaissance 1 (Paris, 1907), i, p. 66; ii, pp. 285, 310.

[5] 'Philippe de Vitri: notes biographiques', *Romania*, 59 (1933), pp. 520–47, on pp. 526, 531–3, 543.

[6] See for example Schrade, 'Philippe de Vitry', pp. 330–54; L. Finscher, 'Die "Entstehung des Komponisten" zum Problem Komponisten-Individualität und Individualstil in der Musik des 14. Jahrhunderts', *International Review of the Aesthetics and Sociology of Music*, 6 (1975), pp. 29–45, on pp. 32–3. See also S. Fuller, 'A Phantom Treatise of the Fourteenth Century: the Ars nova', *Journal of Musicology*, 4 (1985–6), pp. 23–50, on p. 47. F. J. Jones, 'Petrarch, Philippe de Vitry, and a Possible Identification of the Mother of Petrarch's Children', *Italianistica*, 18 (1989), pp. 81–107, deals with the relations between Petrarch and Vitry less credibly. For literary views see among others E. H. R. Tatham, *Francesco Petrarcha: his Life and Correspondence*, 2 vols. (London, 1926), ii, p. 43, n. 2; C. de Boer, ed., *'Ovide Moralisé': poème du commencement du quatorzième siècle*, 5 vols., Verhandelingen der Koninklijke Akademie van Wetenschappen te Amsterdam 15, 20, 30, 37, 43 (Amsterdam, 1918–38), i, pp. 9–11; F. Simone, *Il rinascimento francese: studi e richerche*, Biblioteca di Studi Francesi (Turin, 1961), pp. 55, 242; E. Pognon, 'Philippe de Vitri', *Dictionnaire des lettres françaises*, ed. G. Grente, 7 vols. (Paris, 1951–72), i, pp. 585–6; G. Ouy, 'In Search of the Earliest Traces of French Humanism: the Evidence From Codicology', *The Library Chronicle: University of Pennsylvania*, 43 (1978), pp. 3–38, on p. 5. But see also C. Samaran, 'Pierre Bersuire', *Histoire littéraire de la France*, 39 (1962), pp. 259–450, on pp. 289–90, 292; D. Cecchetti, *Il primo umanesimo francese*, Collana di Critica Linguistica e Poetica 5 (Turin, 1987), pp. 20, 29.

Vitry the poet come under renewed scrutiny, in work by Margaret Bent and David Howlett, whose analyses of the words and music of the motets open new perspectives on Vitry's scholarship and intellectual life, and on the creative processes behind his oeuvre. These analyses, demonstrating a high degree of adherence between the motets' musical and poetic structures, moreover encourage the important conclusion that the music and the words that it sets were the work of a single hand.

What has not apparently been noticed, however, is that the texts of Vitry's motets were circulated, independent of their music, within a literary tradition that was primarily Petrarchan in content and origin. Taken up with vigour by German scholars in the fifteenth century, Vitry's texts entered the bloodstream of the humanist tradition at an early date, almost certainly within his own lifetime. The literary copying of his Latin poetry therefore stands in some measure as the legacy of his relationship with Petrarch. Less directly, it may also provide evidence of the wider cultural milieu surrounding their friendship, and of Vitry's relations with the early humanist movement as a whole. The relatively random survivals of the motet poems in literary copies – fourteen sources containing seventeen texts – are not of course the whole of this story.[7] They do however constitute a substantial portion of the total reception of Vitry's oeuvre, and provide a number of revisions to the Vitry canon, supplying evidence for attribution, and for versions of the motets now lost. The literary copies of Vitry's motet texts present patterns of distribution markedly different from those of the musical sources, and thus also revise current notions of what that canon later became. Finally, the uses made of these texts in literary transmission hint with more accuracy than do the musical sources alone at the functions of their polyphonic settings and at the range

---

[7] See Table 1. The majority of these texts and sources are listed in H. Walther, *Initia carminum ac versuum medii aevi posterioris latinorum: Alphabetisches Verzeichnis der Versanfänge mittellateinischer Dichtungen*, 2nd edn, Carmina Medii Aevi Posterioris Latina 1 (Göttingen, 1969), and in the supplements by J. Stohlmann in *Mittellateinisches Jahrbuch*, 7 (1971), pp. 293–314; 8 (1972), pp. 288–304; 9 (1973), pp. 320–44; 12 (1977), pp. 297–315; 15 (1980), pp. 259–86; 16 (1981), pp. 409–41. Of these sources, only Darmstadt, Hessische Landes- und Hochschulbibliothek, MS 521, and *F-Pn* MS lat. 3343, were known to Schrade ('Philippe de Vitry', p. 353; see also E. Pognon, 'Ballades mythologiques de Jean de le Mote, Philippe de Vitri, Jean Campion', *Humanisme et Renaissance*, 5 (1938), pp. 385–417, and *Bibliothèque nationale: catalogue général des manuscrits latins V (nos. 3278 à 3535)* (Paris, 1966), pp. 236–48).

Table 1 *Literary sources for Vitry's motet poetry*

Schrade[a]	Voice	Text	Walther, *Initia*	Edited[b]	Literary sources
V3	I	Tribum que	19428		*D-LÜs* 152 (lost), fol. 263^v
V4	I	Firmissime	—	*AH*, xxxiv, p. 45	*D-DS* 521, fol. 228
V8	II	Hugo, Hugo	8524	Bertalot, pp. 158–9	*D-Ju* Buder 4° 105, fol. 221
V9	I	Colla iugo	3019	Bertalot, p. 158; Wattenbach, 'Geistliche Scherze', col. 326; Huemer, 'Iter', pp. 79–80	*D-B* lat. 2°. 49, fol. 88^v *D-Ju* Buder 4° 105, fol. 221 *A-KR* 149, fol. 285^v *A-Wn* 3244, fol. 169^v
	II	Bona condit	2214	Wattenbach, col. 326	*D-B* lat. 2° 49, fol. 88^v *A-Wn* 3244, fol. 169^v
	CT	Egregius labor	5291	Wattenbach, col. 326; Walther, *Sprichwörter*, no. 7013; Heinemann, ii, p.16	*D-B* lat. 2° 49, fol. 88^v *D-TRs* 804, fol. 49 *A-Wn* 3219, fol. 118^v *A-Wn* 3244, fol. 90 *A-Wn* 3244, fol. 169^v *D-W* Helmst. 525, fol. 69 *D-W* Helmst. 608, fol. 156^v *Signum quindecim horribilis* . . . (Cologne, after 1500), sig. B[4]^r
	T	Libera me		Wattenbach, col. 326	*A-Wn* 3244, fol. 169^v *D-B* lat. 2° 49, fol. 88^v
V11	I	Impudenter	8816	*AH*, xxxii, pp. 112–13; Huemer, 'Lateinische Rhythmen', p. 291	*A-Wn* 883, fol. 77
	II	Virtutibus	20611	*AH*, xxxii, p. 232	*D-LÜs* 152 (lost), fol. 260^v *A-Wn* 883, fol. 77
V12	I	Petre clemens	14027	Denis, i/3, cols. 2769–72	*F-Pn* lat. 3343, fol. 50 *A-Wn* 4195, fol. 157
	II	Lugentium	10464	Denis, i/3, cols. 2769–72	*A-Wn* 4195, fol. 157
	T	Non est inventus		Denis, i/3, cols. 2772	*A-Wn* 4195, fol. 157
[V15]	I	Phi millies	—	Pognon, pp. 50–2; Schrade, *Commentary*, pp. 119–21	*F-Pn* lat. 3343, fol. 71^v
	II	O creator	—	*ibid.*	*F-Pn* lat. 3343, fols. 71^v–72
	CT	Quam sufflabit	—	*ibid.*	*F-Pn* lat. 3343, fol. 72
	T	Iacet granum	—	*ibid.*	*F-Pn* lat. 3343, fol. 72
IV8 =[V13]	I	Quid scire	15892	De Poorter, *Catalogue*, p. 297	*B-BRs* 258, fol. 1 Matthias Flacius, *Carmina vetusta* (Wittenberg, G. Rhau, 1548) Matthias Flacius, *Pia quaedam* (Magdeburg, Michael Lotter, 1552) Matthias Flacius, *Varia doctorum* (Basel, J. Oporinus, 1557).
IV15	I	Flos ortus	6705	*AH*, xlii, p. 248	*D-DS* 521, fol. 235^{r-v}
	II	Celsa cedrus	2699	*AH*, xlii, p. 247	*D-DS* 521, fol. 235^v

[a] Numbers prefaced 'V' are those of the internal sequence of Vitry's presumed works in L. Schrade, ed., *The Roman de Fauvel: The Works of Philippe de Vitry: French Cycles of the Ordinarium Missae*, Polyphonic Music of the Fourteenth Century 1 (Monaco, 1956), and its separate commentary volume; numbers prefaced 'IV' follow the order of works in Ivrea.

[b] For full references, see Appendix.

of contexts available for their use. In what follows, I wish to comment on aspects of the literary tradition in the Latin texts of Vitry's motets, and, although conclusions here must remain tentative, to draw out of the survivals at present available a loose structure for their integration within Vitry reception as a whole. I wish then to examine the consequences of this tradition, direct and indirect, for the musical settings of the motet texts, and for the fourteenth-century motet repertory more generally.

The surviving literary copies of Vitry's motet texts afford glimpses of two facets of their reception in humanist circles, in all probability isolated fragments of a wider and more continuous tradition. A copy of the texts of *Petre clemens / Lugentium siccentur*, the sole representative of a very early phase of copying, survives in a collection of sermons written in Avignon in the late 1340s, where Vitry and Petrarch had both been present in 1342 and 1344. (It was from this volume, now *A-Wn* MS 4195, that the motet texts were printed in 1795 by Michael Denis in his catalogue of the manuscripts in the Vienna library, in versions considerably more accurate than those of Ivrea used for Polyphonic Music of the Fourteenth Century.)[8] The second is represented by a group of humanist anthologies, the work of German scholars active in Italy, and disseminating at home what they had gathered in the Schools further south.[9] Alongside the motet texts, these later books contain dictaminal treatises, copies, excerpts and digests of classical works, letters and other short pieces of Latin verse and prose; through their compilers, they are closely linked with the fledgling humanist traditions at the German universities, particularly those at Erfurt

---

[8] *Codices manuscripti theologici bibliothecae palatinae vindobonensis latini aliarumque occidentis linguarum*, 2 vols. in 6 (Vienna, 1793–1802), i/3, cols. 2769–72; see also Appendix, no. 12.

[9] For books of this type see generally P. Wilpert, 'Die Entstehung einer Miscellanhandschrift des 15. Jahrhunderts', *Mittellateinisches Jahrbuch*, 1 (1964), pp. 34–47; A. Sottili, 'I codici del Petrarca nella Germania occidentale: I', *IMU*, 10 (1967), pp. 411–91, on pp. 415–17; A. Sottili, 'Wege des Humanismus: lateinischer Petrarchismus und deutsche Studentenschaften italienischer Renaissance-Universitäten', *From Wolfram and Petrarch to Goethe and Grass: Studies in Literature in Honour of Leonard Forster*, ed. D. H. Green, L. P. Johnson and D. Wuttke, Saecula Spiritalia 5 (Baden-Baden, 1982), pp. 125–49. The contents of anthologies of this type remain imperfectly surveyed; several, however, receive detailed descriptions in V. Rose, *Verzeichniss der lateinischen Handschriften der Königlichen Bibliothek zu Berlin*, 3 vols. in 5 (Berlin, 1893–1919). For brief identifying descriptions see also Sottili, 'I codici ... I[–X]', *IMU*, 10 (1967), pp. 411–91; 11 (1968), pp. 345–448; 12 (1969), pp. 335–476; 13 (1970), pp. 281–467; 14 (1971), pp. 313–402; 15 (1972), pp. 361–423; 18 (1975), pp. 1–72; 19 (1976), pp. 429–92; 20 (1977), pp. 413–94.

and Heidelberg. The earliest, lost in 1945, appears to have been copied in Erfurt by Simon Baechtz between 1449 and 1456 and formed part of his bequest to the town of Lübeck in 1464.[10] The latest date from the 1480s and 90s, although a subgroup containing a text transmitted elsewhere as part of *Colla iugo / Bona condit* includes books copied in the early sixteenth century.[11] Among these anthologies is the principal source, copied in the 1460s and in part possibly autograph, for the letters of Peter Luder, a former pupil of Guarino in Ferrara, later a student in Padua, and grammar master at Heidelberg, Erfurt and Basel, who was himself instrumental in securing the acceptance of the *Studia humanitatis* in the German universities.[12] A second book written in Heidelberg in the mid 1480s, now in Berlin, MS lat. 2° 49, including works by Samuel Karoch of Lichtenberg, and one now in Kremsmünster may be closely related to this volume.[13] Finally, and most revealing of the source of this later tradition, the manuscript now Jena, Universitätsbibliothek, MS Buder 4° 105, was copied in the late 1450s while its owner, Lorenz Schaller, was a student in Pavia.[14] In the contents

---

[10] Lübeck, Stadtbibliothek, MS 152; see Appendix, no. 6. This anthology was, however, used for Walther, *Initia*, and for L. Bertalot, *Initia humanistica latina: Initienverzeichnis lateinischer Prosa und Poesie aus der Zeit des 14. bis 16. Jahrhunderts* (Tübingen, 1985–); see also P. O. Kristeller, *Iter italicum* (London and Leiden, 1965–), III, pp. 598–601. For Baechtz see E. Kleineidam, *Universitas studii Erffordensis: Überblick über die Geschichte der Universität Erfurt im Mittelalter, 1392–1521*, 2 vols., Erfurter theologische Studien 14, 22 (Leipzig, 1964–9), I, pp. 246, 319; F. Wiegand, 'Arnoldus Sommernat de Bremis, Symon Baechtz de Homborch, und Joannes Osthusen de Erffordia: drei Erfurter Universitätsjuristen des 15. Jahrhunderts als Ratssyndiker von Lübeck', *Beiträge zur Geschichte der Universität Erfurt (1392–1816)*, 7 (1960), pp. 45–59.

[11] See Table 1, and below, pp. 142–4.

[12] *A-Wn* MS 3244; Appendix, no. 11. For Luder, see W. Wattenbach, 'Peter Luder: der erste humanistische Lehrer in Heidelberg', *Zeitschrift für die Geschichte des Oberrheins*, 22 (1869), pp. 33–127; F. Baron, 'Peter Luder', *Die deutsche Literatur des Mittelalters: Verfasserlexikon*, ed. K. Ruh *et al.* (Berlin and New York, 1978–), V, cols. 954–9. Parts of the book may have been copied by Matthias von Kemnat, one of Luder's close associates in Heidelberg (F. E. Baron, 'The Beginnings of German Humanism: the Life and Work of the Wandering Humanist Peter Luder' (Ph.D. dissertation, University of California at Berkeley, 1967), pp. 84–6; K. Hartfelder, 'Matthias von Kemnat', *Forschungen zur deutschen Geschichte*, 22 (1882), pp. 331–49).

[13] *D-B* MS lat. 2° 49 (Appendix, no. 2); Kremsmünster, Stiftsbibliothek, MS 149 (Appendix, no. 5).

[14] For this book see L. Bertalot, *Humanistisches Studienheft eines Nürnberger Scholaren aus Pavia (1460)* (Berlin, 1910), reprinted in *Studien zum italienischen und deutschen Humanismus*, 2 vols., ed. P. O. Kristeller, Storia e Letteratura: Raccolta di Studi e Testi 129 (Rome, 1975), I, pp. 83–161; Kristeller, *Iter italicum*, III, p. 411; Appendix, no. 4. For Schaller see also Sottili, 'L'Università di Pavia nella politica culturale sforzesca', *Gli Sforza a Milano e in Lombardia e i loro rapporti con gli stati italiani ed europei (1450–1535): Convegno internazionale, Milano, 18–21 Maggio 1981* (Milan, 1982), pp. 522–3, 540.

of this book and in two other anthologies a clear strand associated with Milan/Pavia emerges. Together with letters of local concern by Petrarch, Bruni, Lorenzo Valla, Vergerius, Guarino and others, Schaller copied a substantial collection of Milanese state correspondence. Other material linked with Milan, principally letters and addresses to the Sforza dukes, appears in the Luder miscellany, and much of this is duplicated in a third source of Vitry's motet poetry, *A-Wn* MS 3219. To these humanist anthologies can be added two fifteenth-century collections of private religious poetry and hymns, each of which incorporates one of Vitry's motet texts, apparently included (as were some of Petrarch's verses in similar collections) for their devotional content.[15]

The origins of the literary tradition in Vitry's motet poetry are unclear, but two important structural points emerge nonetheless. The first is the initial dependence of this tradition on copies including music, demonstrated most clearly by the inclusion of voice labels in the earliest of the text-only sources, and in three others from the fifteenth century.[16] Whether a separate manuscript of Vitry's motet poetry, now lost, stands at the head of the literary tradition, or whether at this early stage poems were circulated individually, remains unclear. Either way, however, it seems evident that the copying of texts as literary objects, but with clearly designated musical identities, succeeded rather than preceded the motets' composition (although texts were probably written out in verse as part of the compositional process). It is also probable that the fifteenth-century copies were made from text-only sources of the motet poetry, rather than from music manuscripts. The blind copying of voice-labels as part of the poetic text (and their absence in musical sources) encourages this view. So does the textual integrity of the copies in the later literary sources: while sources of the motets with music often transmit bizarrely corrupt versions of the poetic texts, the literary copies, from the pens of literati who understood what they were writing, present versions that are mainly

---

[15]   Darmstadt, MS 521; *A-Wn* MS 883 (Appendix, nos 3, 9).

[16]   In *A-Wn* MS 4195 the texts 'Petre clemens', 'Lugentium siccentur' and 'Non est inventus similis illi' are labelled 'Triplum', 'Motetus' and 'Tenor' respectively. In both *D-B* MS lat. 2° 49 and *A-Wn* MS 3244 the text 'Egregius labor' is labelled 'Contra' (see also below, pp. 143–4). In *F-Pn* MS lat. 3343, the texts 'O deus creator', 'Jacet granum', 'Quam sufflabit' and 'Phi millies', are labelled 'Motetus', 'Tenor', 'Contratenor' and 'Triplum'.

cleaner and more homogeneous in their readings. For these to derive contemporaneously from copies with music, sources with better texts than those of many now surviving would have had to be available. Moreover, the texts of single voices were circulated separately (never labelled), and were paired with single-voice texts from other motets; while this pattern possibly discloses earlier links between motets, it too argues for the independence of the later tradition from copies including music.

Second is the isolation of the literary tradition in Vitry's motet poetry. A substantial number of the texts set in the thirteenth-century motet and conductus repertories were circulated in sources without music. Several were also printed between 1548 and 1558 by Flacius, the sixteenth-century owner of W_1 and W_2, in poetic collections for a Lutheran readership, where the texts' criticisms of the Roman church found an easy resonance.[17] By contrast, however, the texts of motets from the early fourteenth century have almost no independent literary circulation – with the sole exception of the texts of motets that have since come to be associated with Vitry's name. This pattern persists well into the following century, and is broken only when newly composed liturgical poetry begins to appear in polyphonic settings. (A small number of motet texts set by Dufay nonetheless appear in anthologies of devotional poetry within larger miscellanies.[18]) Vitry's texts survive singly or in pairs;

[17]   First appearing in *Carmina vetusta ante trecentos annos scripta, quae deplorant inscitiam Evangelij, et taxant abusus ceremoniarum, ac quae ostendunt doctrinam, huius temporis non esse novam* . . . (Wittenberg, G. Rhau, 1548) and, in revised and expanded versions, in *Pia quaedam vetustissimaque poemata partim antichristum, eiusque spirituales filiolos in sectantia* . . . (Magdeburg, Michael Lotter, 1552) and *Varia doctorum piorumque virorum de corrupto ecclesiae statu, poemata, ante nostram aetatem conscripta* . . . (Basel, J. Oporinus, 1557), pp. 29–89 (of which an annotated copy, with emendations to *Quid scire*, is London, British Library, [pr. bk.] 238. m. 29). See further on these books W. Preger, *Matthias Flacius Illyricus und seine Zeit*, 2 vols. (Erlangen, 1859–62), II, pp. 239ff, and M. Mirković, *Matija Vlačić Ilirik*, Djela Jugoslavenske Akademije Znanosti i Umjetnosti 50 (Zagreb, 1960), pp. 341–2; see also pp. 58–73, 336ff. For Flacius' ownership of W_1 and W_2 (*D-W* MSS Helmst. 628 and 1099) see G. Reaney, *Manuscripts of Polyphonic Music, 11th – Early 14th Century*, Répertoire International des Sources Musicales, B/IV/1 (Munich and Duisburg, 1966), pp. 97–8, 171.

[18]   The majority of sources without music for the texts of Dufay's motets are liturgical or devotional collections. Other manuscripts containing these texts include: Erfurt, Wissenschaftliche Bibliothek, MS Amplon. 12° 4; Oxford, Bodleian Library, MS Laud. misc. 542; Pavia, Biblioteca Universitaria, MSS 351 and 355. For lists, see the critical commentaries in G. de Van, ed., *Gugliemi Dufay: opera omnia 1–2: Motetti qui et cantiones vocantur*, 2 vols., Corpus Mensurabilis Musicae 1 (Rome, 1947–8), omitted from the Besseler revision (Rome, 1966).

Andrew Wathey

the poems set in thirteenth-century motet and conductus repertories are generally transmitted in larger groups, or in collections devoted exclusively to this material. Even so, the two traditions are not entirely separate: the texts of *Impudenter* and *Virtutibus* appear in *A-Wn* 883 with *Quid ultra tibi facere* and other items by Philip the Chancellor, whose poetry (whether or not musical settings survive) is frequently transmitted with the motet and conductus texts of the mid thirteenth century.[19] So definitive, however, is the separation between the Vitry motet poetry and the texts of otherwise similar motets in Ivrea, Cambrai, Trémoïlle, etc., that the fact of literary circulation may even emerge as a pointer towards attribution. Only two examples stand outside the pattern sketched here, and both of these are more properly regarded as borderline cases. First, the text of the motet *Quid scire proderit*, included by Schrade in the published *Works* but since shunned by Vitry scholarship, appears in the collections of *Magnus liber* poetry printed by Flacius and, added, on the flyleaf of a fourteenth-century Bruges manuscript.[20] Second, the texts of *Flos ortus / Celsa cedrus*, an Ivrea motet long associated with the Vitry canon, and attributed to Vitry on stylistic grounds by Daniel Leech-Wilkinson, appears in Darmstadt, MS 521, where it sits in close proximity to the triplum text of *Firmissime fidem.*[21]

The humanist materials in these and other similar anthologies travelled north of the Alps by a variety of routes. In this process, the ecclesiastical councils at Constance and Basel played an important role (familiar in another musical context), informing German tastes, and setting northern humanism firmly in the footsteps of Petrarch and his immediate disciples.[22] These gatherings

[19] For collections of *Magnus liber* poetry without music, see R. Falck, *The Notre-Dame Conductus: a Study of the Repertory*, Wissenschaftliche Abhandlungen 33 (Henryville, Ottawa and Binningen, 1981), pp. 140–52. See also sources cited in Walther, *Initia*, nos. 2254, 2607, 2763, 3470, 3799, 4349, 6487, 8391, 8394, 8401, 9038, 9150, 11448, 12510, 13814, 16158, 17915, 20563, 21142, 21206 and 21209.
[20] L. Schrade, ed., *The Roman de Fauvel: the Works of Philippe de Vitry: French Cycles of the Ordinarium Missae*, Polyphonic Music of the Fourteenth Century 1 (Monaco, 1956), pp. 104–5 (no. 13); the motet is omitted from the worklist in E. Sanders, 'Vitry, Philippe de', *The New Grove Dictionary of Music and Musicians*, ed. S. Sadie, 20 vols. (London, 1980), xx, p. 27. For sources see Table 1.
[21] D. Leech-Wilkinson, 'Related Motets from Fourteenth-Century France', *Proceedings of the Royal Musical Association*, 109 (1982–3), pp. 1–22, on p. 11.
[22] For what follows, see, among much else, W. Dotzauer, 'Deutsches Studium und deutsche Studenten an europäischen Hochschulen (Frankreich, Italien) und die nachfolgende

brought a vast influx of Italian scholars, administrators and scribes into the Germanic lands; they also inaugurated numerous longer careers for humanists in the service of northern princes anxious for the benefits that the new literary skills had already wrought in Italian chanceries. The humanistic anthologies of the mid fifteenth century still contain – alongside Petrarchan pieces – a wide range of Conciliar items, including correspondence on the burning of John Hus, and letters and addresses by Aeneas Silvius Piccolomini, the future Pope Pius II, and Poggio, both of whom spent substantial periods of time in the northern courts. But more significant perhaps for the northern reception of Vitry's motet poetry was the migration south of German scholars in this and particularly the next generation. The first emerge among the pupils of Francesco Zabarella, and the contemporaries of Pier Paolo Vergerio.[23] By the middle years of the fifteenth century German students were enrolling in their hundreds at the Italian universities, notably Bologna, Padua, Pavia and Rome, the majority in law and medicine, but a growing number to study the new literary disciplines in rhetoric and poetics. By the 1450s, northerners were well represented not only within the student body, but also among the upper echelons of university rectors and masters, where they were active in fostering the emergence of German *Nationes*.[24] Equally significant is

Tätigkeit in Stadt, Kirche und Territorium in Deutschland', *Stadt und Universität im Mittelalter und in der früheren Neuzeit*, ed. E. Maschke and J. Sydow, Veröffentlichungen des Südwestdeutschen Arbeitskreises für Stadtgeschichtsforschung 3 (Sigmaringen, 1977), pp. 112–41; Sottili, 'Wege des Humanismus', pp. 125–49; A. Sottili, 'L'università italiana e la diffusione dell'umanesimo nei paesi tedeschi', *Humanistica lovaniensia*, 20 (1971), pp. 5–22; Sottili, 'I codici . . . I', pp. 415–17; F. J. Worstbrock, 'Francesco Petrarca', *Verfasserlexikon*, VII, cols. 471–90, esp. 477–83; J. H. Overfield, *Humanism and Scholasticism in Late Medieval Germany* (Princeton, 1984), pp. 61–142; A. Karnein, 'Petrarca in Deutschland: zur Rezeption seiner lateinischen Werke im 15. und 16. Jahrhundert', *Idee, Gestalt, Geschichte: Festschrift Klaus von See*, ed. G. W. Weber (Odense, 1988), pp. 159–86. For Piccolomini, see K. Voigt, *Italienische Berichte aus dem spätmittelalterlichen Deutschland: von Francesco Petrarca zu Andrea de' Franceschi*, Kieler Historische Studien 17 (Stuttgart, 1973), pp. 77–153; F. J. Worstbrock, 'Aeneas Silvius Piccolomini (Papst Pius II.)', *Verfasserlexikon*, VII, cols. 634–69.

23 Sottili, 'I codici . . . I', p. 417, and the description of Karlsruhe, Badische Landesbibliothek, MS Aug. 48, in 'I codici . . . II', *IMU*, 11 (1968), p. 384.

24 See especially A. Sottili, 'Zur Geschichte der "Natio Germanica Ticinensis": Albrecht von Eyb, Georg Hessler und die Markgrafen von Baden an der Universität Pavia', *Zeitschrift für die Geschichte des Oberrheins*, 132 (1984), pp. 107–33, esp. pp. 109–14; Sottili, 'Tunc floruit Alamannorum natio: Doktorate deutscher Studenten in Pavia in der zweiten Hälfte des 15. Jahrhunderts', *Humanismus im Bildungswesen des 15. und 16. Jahrhunderts*, Kommission für Humanismusforschung: Mitteilung XII (Weinheim, 1984), pp. 25–44.

the strength of the student tradition, and its activities in collecting the teachings and correspondence of Italian masters. The specific-ally humanist collections that these students copied or otherwise acquired in Italy (by this time a distinct codicological genre, com-parable to the notebooks of their legal and medical counterparts) were widely circulated and recopied north of the Alps, serving often as the schoolbooks of the grammar masters and wandering scholars who clustered around the German universities, at Erfurt, Heidel-berg, Leipzig, Nuremberg and Vienna.[25] These anthologies became central to the German dissemination of Petrarch's works, to the reading of texts not otherwise available in monastic or university circles, and to the creation of an environment 'saturo di letteratura e ben cosciente delle debolezze e virtù dell'autore trecentesco'.[26]

The Milanese strand in the literary sources for Vitry's motet poetry takes on particular significance set against the position occu-pied by Pavia in the mid fifteenth-century Petrarchan tradition. Rivalling even Padua in the study of the poet's works, Pavia also took a pre-eminent role in mediating this tradition to the nascent centres of humanist learning in Germany. For the early German humanists in Italy, the quest for Petrarchiana was a primary con-cern: a distinguished line of scholars spent periods studying and teaching at Pavia. They include Albrecht von Eyb, who taught in Pavia after periods studying in Erfurt, Padua and Bologna; Niko-laus von Wyle, the translator of the literary works of Aeneas Silvius Piccolomini; Balthazar Rasinus, Lorenzo Valla's successor as the university's *scholarius*; and Rudolf Agricola, Petrarch's first German biographer (and later organist in the chapel of Ercole d'Este).[27] Pavia also emerges as a major source of Italian copies of Petrarch's works exported north of the Alps, as well as the clearing-house for innumerable smaller pieces in the Petrarchan tradition. The source of its magnetism for northern scholars is not hard to find. The Visconti library, containing the literary residue of Petrarch's period

[25] Sottili, 'Wege des Humanismus', pp. 127–8.
[26] Sottili, 'I codici . . . I', p. 416.
[27] Sottili, 'Wege des Humanismus', pp. 125–6, 128–9, and nn. 26–32; Kleineidam, *Univer-sitas studii Erfordensis*, I, p. 142; F. J. Worstbrock, in *Verfasserlexikon*, I, cols. 84–93, 180–6; VI, cols. 1016–35. For Eyb see also Sottili, 'Zur Geschichte der "Natio Germanica Ticinensis"', pp. 113ff; for Agricola see also T. E. Mommsen, 'Rudolf Agricola's Life of Petrarch', *Medieval and Renaissance Studies* (New York, 1959), pp. 236–67; L. Lockwood, *Music in Renaissance Ferrara, 1400–1505: the Creation of a Musical Centre in the Fifteenth Century* (Oxford, 1984), pp. 151–2.

in Milanese service (1351–8), was transported to Pavia in 1378, and received most of the Petrarchan treasures which had been in the hands of the Carrara family following the conquest of Padua in 1388.[28] In Pavia, Pasquino de' Capelli, Giangaleazzo's chancellor and a close associate of Salutati, played a central role in disseminating the riches of this collection, compiling a volume of the poet's complete works, acquiring a copy of the *Africa* from Petrarch's son-in-law, Francescuolo da Brossano, and arranging for works to be copied for other scholars.[29] The very availability of Petrarch's works, so closely guarded before his death, together with the stream of humanist materials flowing between Italy and France through Milan and Pavia, made these locations a natural focus for northern attentions.

Against this background, the availability of Vitry's motet poetry at Pavia in the mid fifteenth century may well be indicative of an earlier integration within the Petrarchan tradition. Supported by continuous scholarship, teaching and scribal activity, it is conceivable even that such a link might stretch back to the poet's lifetime. Certainly there is evidence for a personal connection between Vitry and Petrarch close to the latter's period in the service of the Visconti. These years embraced the completion of the first recension of the *Bucolicum carmen*, containing his celebrated debate with Vitry. It was also at Milan that he assembled from copies the parts of the *Epistole familiari* that include the letters to Vitry, the second of which, by his own testimony, he brought back with others in a bundle from France.[30] But also possible is that Vitry's motet poetry entered the humanist mainstream through the activities of the first generation of Petrarch scholars, working at Bologna, Ferrara, Milan, Pavia, Padua and Venice, in the years immediately following the poet's death: Francesco Zabarella, Donato degli Albanzani, Gugliemo da Ravenna, Giovanni Malpaghini, Pasquino de' Capelli, Giovanni Dondi, Tedaldo della Casa, Francesco Piendibeni da Montepulciano and numerous others. It was they who were

[28] Sottili, 'Wege des Humanismus', pp. 134–5, and E. Pellegrin, *La bibliothèque des Visconti et des Sforza ducs de Milan au XVe siècle*, Publications de l'Institut de Recherche et d'Histoire des Textes 5 (Paris, 1955), pp. 45–7.

[29] For Capelli see D. M. Bueno de Mesquita in *Dizionario biografico degli italiani*, XVII (Venice and Rome, 1975), pp. 727–30. For the dissemination of Petrarch's works after his death see Witt, *Hercules at the Crossroads*, pp. 184ff.

[30] See Mann, 'The Making of Petrarch's "Bucolicum carmen"', pp. 172–80; Wilkins, *Studies in the Life and Works of Petrarch*, pp. 170–1.

responsible for the wider dissemination of the works of Petrarch and others of his generation, and for nurturing a more comprehensive 'culto petrarchesco'. They also brought Vitry's literary reputation, and the fact of his literary association with Petrarch, to wider Italian attention. If Vitry's Latin verse had enjoyed a relatively limited circulation in the hands of Petrarch and his immediate disciples (as had the poet's own works), it is the scholarship of the succeeding generation that marks the clearest path to its fuller currency.

A further consequence of this activity is mirrored in the reception of Vitry's other works and those associated with his name. The distribution of copies of the motets with music – mainly earlier and mainly French – is sharply different from that of the literary sources, and that of the tradition they disclose. The copying of theoretical works with attributions to Vitry, by contrast, is almost exclusively a north Italian phenomenon, and can be seen in part as a consequence of the tradition of exegesis in his reputation and motet poetry. The overwhelming majority of the sources for these treatises date from the late fourteenth or early fifteenth century (no Italian source is earlier), and at least three are closely linked with Milanese or Florentine circles.[31] These copies account for all but one of the attributions made to Vitry of theoretical works, including those that are most direct and most easily dismissed. The sole exception is the Paris source of *Ars nova* (*F-Pn* MS lat. 7378A), whose comment that the work was 'compilata a magistro Philippo de Vitry', marks Vitry out more clearly as authority than as author.[32] Moreover, one of these attributed treatises appears in

---

[31] To those described in J. Smits van Waesberghe and P. Fischer, *The Theory of Music from the Carolingian Era up to 1400*, 2 vols., Répertoire International des Sources Musicales, B/III/1–2 (Munich and Duisburg, 1961–8), I, pp. 107–8; II, pp. 36–43, 50, 77–9, 89–91, 98–9, 100–1, 102–4, add: (i) Einsiedeln, Klosterbibliothek, MS 689, an early fifteenth-century book copied in Padua (see Kristeller, *Iter italicum*, v, p. 107; the manuscript is wrongly described as MS 638 in Smits van Waesberghe and Fischer, I, p. 75, whose account also omits the Vitry item); (ii) Florence, Biblioteca Medicea Riccardiana, MS 688 (see M. Long, 'Francesco Landini and the Florentine Cultural Élite', *Early Music History*, 3 (1983), pp. 83–99, on pp. 89–90; incomplete description in P. Böhner, 'Ein Gedicht auf die Logik Ockhams', *Franziskanische Studien*, 26 (1939), pp. 78–85, on pp. 79–80); (iii) Chicago, Newberry Library, MS 54.1, copied in Pavia (see P. E. Schreur, *Tractatus figurarum: Treatise on Noteshapes*, Greek and Latin Music Theory (Lincoln, NE, and London, 1989), pp. 31–3. See also K.-J. Sachs, *Der Contrapunctus im 14. und 15. Jahrhundert: Untersuchungen zum Terminus, zur Lehre und zu den Quellen*, Beihefte zum Archiv für Musikwissenschaft 13 (Wiesbaden, 1974), pp. 170–9.

[32] Fuller, 'A Phantom Treatise of the Fourteenth Century', pp. 26–7, 33–4.

a miscellany alongside *Petrarchiana* and other early humanistic works.[33] The entry of Vitry's reputation and motet poetry into the early tradition of humanist scholarship may thus have made him a natural target in Italy for the attribution of theoretical writings on music, particularly where scribes were widely versed in works emanating from that tradition. Conversely, the attribution of theoretical works may itself stand as further evidence for the contemporaneous circulation of Vitry's reputation and motet poetry.

The implantation of Vitry's Latin verse within later literary traditions exposes questions not only of access, but also about the range of ideologies which prompted the choice of this material, and about others that were propagated through its use. The wider literary and cultural contexts of these motet texts may in some cases have imposed quite new layers of significance. But in others they almost certainly preserve strands from earlier traditions of meaning and ideologies surrounding the musical compositions. The literary transmissions thus provide an invaluable opportunity to explore the subject of motet functions, which in the modern historiography of this genre have regularly been deemed incompatible both with the liturgy and with the ideals of *amour courtois*. Two specific cases, *Petre clemens / Lugentium siccentur* and *Colla iugo / Bona condit / Libera me*, in which the contexts for the poetry of Vitry's motets reflect on or interact with the musical traditions in these works, here invite closer scrutiny.

The court of Pope Clement VI has long been known as the setting for what is probably the latest of the surviving Vitry motets, *Petre clemens / Lugentium siccentur*.[34] It is also, as has been said, the origin of the earliest remaining literary source for Vitry's motet poetry, a collection of Clement's sermons including the *Petre clemens* texts copied in Avignon in the late 1340s. The motet texts, which appear towards the end of the volume, are immediately preceded by a longer verse celebration of Clement's rule, couched in the form of a petition for the Pope's assistance and beginning *Aperi labia mea*; they are followed by a tenor incipit, *Non est inventus similis*

---

33   Florence, Biblioteca Medicea Riccardiana, MS 688.
34   See, for example E. Pognon, 'Notes et documents du nouveau sur Philippe de Vitri et ses amis', *Humanisme et Renaissance*, 6 (1939), p. 52; Schrade, 'Philippe de Vitry', pp. 334–5, 341; Sanders, 'Vitry, Philippe de', p. 27.

illi, absent from the musical sources of the motet, and by a brief colophon, added in a different but contemporary hand, which attributes the motet clearly to Vitry and supplies a date for its composition: 'Magistri Philippus de Vitrejo in laudem Pape Clementis vj[ti] anno suo primo circa natalem domini' (literally, between 24 December 1342 and 5 January 1343).[35] This remark neatly resolves the recent discussion surrounding the date of the composition of *Petre clemens*. More important, however, it locates the poetry set in this motet within the broader context of the volume's other literary contents, which in turn serve to illuminate the function of the motet.

The main contents of this book are two sermon cycles: the first is a miscellany preached at Avignon in the 1330s among which the sermons of the future Clement VI, Pierre Roger, Archbishop of Rouen, feature prominently; the second consists almost exclusively of sermons preached by Clement immediately before his coronation and in the early years of his pontificate.[36] This latter group contains a high proportion of sermons for special occasions and other pieces delivered in consistory on political themes; of these, the most important are two preached in April 1343 and April 1346 as part of Clement VI's campaign against Louis of Bavaria, the pretender to the imperial crown. The volume also contains bulls against Louis of Bavaria, and against the flagellants, and Clement's famed reply on Rome and the empire delivered on 27 January 1343 to the ambassadors of the Roman citizens.[37] As an ensemble, therefore, this collection emerges as a general monument to Clement's early years as Pope, but more particularly as a tribute to his role in the disputed imperial election and the subjection of the empire to the Holy See.

Set in the context of these addresses, the two laudatory texts (Figure 1) on Clement VI find a clear function within the volume's programme of comment in papal-imperial affairs. Often presented as a celebration of Clement VI's coronation, or as simple eulogy,

---

[35] *A-Wn* MS 4195, fol. 157.

[36] Listed in D. Wood, *Clement VI: the Pontificate and Ideas of an Avignon Pope*, Cambridge Studies in Medieval Life and Thought, 4th series, 13 (Cambridge, 1989), pp. 209–15, and, for what follows, see pp. 31–2, 152. For Clement's sermons see also J. B. Schneyer, *Repertorium der lateinischen Sermones des Mittelalters für die Zeit von 1150–1350*, 11 vols., Beiträge zur Geschichte der Philosophie und Theologie des Mittelalters 43 (Münster, 1969–90), III, pp. 757–69.

[37] Wood, *Clement VI*, p. 212, Sermon 14; see also pp. 75–7.

Petre clemens here takes shape more clearly as a propaganda piece, designed to promulgate the message of papal diplomacy. Christmas 1342 saw the presence in Avignon of the ambassadors of the Roman citizens, sent to petition, *inter alia*, for the return of the papacy to Rome.[38] While Clement argued that practical obstacles, in particular the English wars in France, prevented this move, it is clear that a doctrinal response was also required: to view the papacy as bound to Rome invited the view that its power dwelt not in the Pope's person but in the Roman See itself, with grave consequences for papal claims to universal authority. The partisans of Louis of Bavaria had not been slow to argue that in leaving Rome the Avignon popes had forfeited the plenitude of power inherited from St Peter, and that, by failing to reside there, Clement had automatically ceased to be Pope. The diplomatic answers given to the Roman ambassadors, embracing the dictum 'ubi Papa, ibi Roma', therefore sought to detach the concept of universal papal authority from residence in Rome: the Pope's authority was universal because he was the Vicar of Christ, from whom all spiritual authority descended; Clement ruled Rome because he ruled the world, not the reverse, and he might thus live where he chose. The texts of *Petre clemens*, written in the midst of the negotiations with the Roman ambassadors, widely echo these sentiments. The independence of the papacy from the bishopric of Rome, and the universal rather than local character of papal power, are clearly expressed in phrases such as 'ergo considera quod Cephas es, sed orbi deditus' ('therefore consider that you are Cephas [i.e. head of the church], but granted to the world'), 'Vivat, vivat orbi perutilis' ('may he live, very useful to the world'), and 'stupor orbis, O tersum speculum ad formandum virtutum modulum' ('wonder of the world, O polished mirror for forming a measure of virtues').[39] Clement's role as Christ's Vicar, the sole inheritor of his power on earth, is similarly underlined: 'gloriosissimus triumphator . . . heres legitimus Ihesu Cristi' ('O most glorious triumpher . . . legitimate heir of Jesus Christ'), and, more distantly, 'radio Spiritus Clemens sextus factus divinitus' ('Clement has been made the sixth with divine approval'). And the issue of residence in Rome, which lay at the

---

[38] For what follows see Wood, pp. 43–50.
[39] For papal claims to universal authority, and the representation of Clement as the successor of St Peter, see Wood, pp. 36, 46, 80, 122, 192.

Figure 1

(a) *Petre clemens / Lugentium siccentur / Tenor. Non est inventus*

Petre clemens tam re quam nomine
cui nascenti Donantis dextera
non defuit, qui ymo cardine
et supremo beata munera
suscepisti felix, ac omnia
que reliqua celi benignitas
dare potest non defuit, pia
Pyeridum sacrarum dignitas;
harum solus precellis dotibus
harum dono cuncta gymnasia
Carmentina Pegasi pedibus
transvectus es a puericia;
aut fata nunc aut ipsa prospera
te Fortuna, melius, Spiritus
sublimavit, ergo considera
quod Cephas es, sed orbi deditus,
quod monarcha, sed servus omnium,
princeps orbis, sed orbis languidi,
servus nempe, sed delirantium,
ac ne tui tandem sint perfidi.
Arte, princeps, serva Danielicum
torque fides mundiales celis
regum divum; furorem tragicum
potens, pie, compescere velis.
Absit tuo Tyestes tempore
et Athreus, absint Thebaides
abutentes fraterno iecore;
unumque sint scissi Philipides.
Urbem vide classis per equora;
deterreat principes Thaneos
clangor tube, Turcorum pectora
decipiant augures Mempheos.
Consoletur tristis Armenia,
et elatus succumbat Ismael,
tuis unquam poterit inclitis.
Vulgi tamen modica porcio
de te saltem clangere gestio:
Vivat, vivat orbi perutilis,
cui non est inventus similis.

Lugentium siccentur oculi,
plaudant senes, exultent parvuli,
umbre mortis quoniam regio
quos tenuit splendoris visio
est exorta; radio Spiritus
Clemens sextus factus divinitus;
stupor orbis, O tersum speculum
ad formandum virtutum modulum,
tu Cirrhei Syris Apollinis
pervasisti vigor certaminis
Phitonistas heresis ubere
crapulatos solos prosternere,
ac dum flectis sermonis timpanum
corda rapis ad auris organum.
Petrus primus petrum non deseris
vices eius quia recte geris;
tu clemens es et Clemens diceris,
Pegasei qui fontis aperis
venas gratis Indis et rudibus
Athlanticis et Ethiopibus
Stiris quoque, quid in preconia
laudum mira fundat iusticia.
Non augentur memento secula,
non inane tumescunt guttula,
nec ulla laus addensere mentis
et germinet deserta Syria
et depressus resurgat Israel:
Tunc nature, gloriosissimus
triumphator, tributum solvere
non dolebis, heres legitimus
Ihesu Cristi, moriens libere;
et si desint marmor et gemula
ac metallum sculpenda funeri,
erit tandem tumulus vernula
semper fama respondens operi,
quam posteris prebebis regula
gubernandi; faveant superi.

Tenor. Non est inventus similis illi.

Peter, Clement in fact as in name, to whom at your birth the right hand of the giver was not lacking, who, fortunate, have received blessed gifts from the lowest pole and the highest, and everything which the remaining kindness of heaven can give, the holy dignity of the sacred Muses, was not lacking. You alone excel in their endowments. By their gift from boyhood, you were carried through the Carmentine [Gate in Rome] by the feet of Pegasus. Now either fate or prosperous

The motets of Philippe de Vitry

Fortune herself, better, the Spirit has elevated you. Therefore consider that you are Cephas, but granted to the world, that you are a monarch, but the servant of all, prince of the world, but an exhausted world, servant to be sure, but of raving madmen, and may they not in the end be faithless to you. By art, O prince, observe Danielic [prophecy]. Turn worldly loyalties toward the divine realm in the heavens. O powerful holy one, may you wish to restrain tragic frenzy. May Thyestes be absent in your time and Atreus, may the Theban tales in which the brothers' emotions are perverted be absent. And may the sundered sons of Philip be one. See the city of the fleet on the seas. May the clangor of the trumpet deter the princess of Zoan, may the Memphite seers deceive the hearts of the Turks. Let sad Armenia be consoled and let elated Ishmael collapse. Let deserted Syria bud and repressed Israel rise again. Then, O most glorious triumpher, legitimate heir of Jesus Christ, you will not grieve to yield the tribute of nature, dying freely. And if marble and a little gem and metal should be lacking to be wrought for your funeral, there will nonetheless always be for a tomb a faithful servant, fame, corresponding to your work, the rule of governing you will provide for those coming after. May those above favour [it].

Let the eyes of those mourning be dried, old men should clap, boys should exult, because a vision of splendour has arisen on those whom the region of the shadow of death held. By the ray of the spirit Clement has been made the sixth with divine approval; wonder of the world, O polished mirror for forming a measure of the virtues, you, the power of the struggle, have made your way through the sorceresses of the luxuriant heresy of Cirrhaean Apollo among the Syrians to lay low the forsaken drunks, and while you direct the drum of your speech you sweep hearts along to the music of the ear. Foremost Peter, you do not abandon the rock [of the church] because you guide [it] rightly in his stead. You are clement and you are called Clement, who open the veins of a Pegasean fountain [i.e. a fountain of the Muses opened by the hoof of Pegasus] to grateful Indians and rude Atlantaeans and Ethiopians, also Styrians, what praises righteousness pours into her wondrous preachings. Remember that the ages are not lengthened; they do not swell by an empty little drop; nor will praise ever be able to add any further to your merits of mind; yet I, a little part of the throng, want very much nonetheless to shout about you: 'May he live, very useful to the world, to whom the like has not been found'.

Tenor. None other like him is found.

(b) *Colla iugo / Bona condit / Egregius labor / Tenor. Libera me domine*

Colla iugo subdere	curias sectari,
quarum sunt innumere	clades, mores rari.
Potens suo vivere	debet exequari.
Aliena desere,	quadra convivari,
pane tuo vescere,	tibi dominari.
Si vis es, effugere	curis lacerari.
Malo fabam rodere	liber et letari
quam cibis affluere	servus et tristari.
Aulici sunt opere	semper adulari,
fictas laudes promere	lucraque venari,
ab implumis tollere	plumas et conari,
dominis alludere,	falsa commentari.

137

Ve quos habent pungere verba que subduntur:
Nulla fides pietasque viris qui castra secuntur.

Bona condit cetera	bonum libertatis.
Qui gazarum genera	tot thesaurisatis,
multiplici falera	vos qui faleratis,
et cum libet ubera	fercula libatis,
si vivere libera	vita nequeatis
nunquam saporifera	servi degustatis.
Vincit auri pondera	sue potestatis.
esse. Vobis funera,	servi, propinatis
mala per innumera	dum magis optatis.

Egregius labor est sub magno principe castra continuando sequi, sed sic non itur ad astra. Promittunt non dant, dicunt nec postea currant, et sic falluntur miseri qui castra secuntur.

Tenor. Libera me domine

One puts one's neck under a yoke by attending at courts, at which disasters are innumerable, good habits few. He who can should be up to living on what is his own. Leave the property of others alone; live in an open square; eat from your own bread; be your own master. If you want money, avoid being mangled by cares. I prefer to nibble a bean and rejoice as a free man than to abound with provisions and be sad as a slave. The duties of a courtier are always to flatter, to utter feigned praises, and to hunt for profits, and to try to take feathers away from the unfeathered, to play up to lords, to compose false things. Woe to those whom the words which are placed below have to sting: There is no faith or piety in men who follow camps.

The good of liberty gives zest to other things. You who lay up treasure, so many kinds of wealth, who harness yourselves with manifold ornament and when it pleases offer rich courses, if you cannot live a free life you never taste savour-bearing things as slaves. To be one's own master is better than masses of gold. You slaves, you administer death to yourselves when, among countless evils, you desire [even] more.

It is an outstanding labour to follow camps, persevering under a great prince, but one does not go thus to the stars. They [*sc.* princes] promise, they do not give; they speak and may not afterwards speed [to fulfilment], and thus the wretches are deceived who follow camps.

Tenor. Free me Lord.

I am very grateful to Dr David Howlett, editor of the *Dictionary of Medieval Latin from British Sources*, for editing and translating these texts.

very crux of the negotiations, receives a direct reference in the lines 'Petrus primus petrum non deseris, vices eius quia recta geris' ('foremost Peter, you do not abandon the rock [of the church], because you guide it rightly in his stead'). Finally, with the tenor incipit, *Non est inventus similis illi* (Eccl. 44:20), stress is again laid on the unique and representative qualities residing in the Pope's person.

These themes are similarly worked in the preceding verse in praise of Clement, the much longer *Aperi labia mea*, dismissed by Denis for its 'ταυτολογιαν, e qua nihil intelligas'.[40] A plea for papal assistance against personal enemies, these verses unfold a spectrum of literary topoi on the clerical condition, including the modesty and simplicity of the writer's life before taking the cloth, the dangers of ecclesiastical grandeur, the 'regimen ambiciosus' which led him astray, his more recent personal reform, and finally an appeal to the universal papal power, without which worldly existence is devoid of meaning: 'Recogitent qui talis secum in cordibus meditantur; quando Petrus caput ecclesie, pater omnium et janitor celi, illos repulit quos vocavit, et eos deservit quos assumpsit? quando eius vicarius pater orbis, inhumanus humanis exstitit creaturis'.[41] This undoubtedly fictional piece thus frames and amplifies the message of the motet texts, in all likelihood conceived with the same objective in mind. It also serves to focus more sharply the function of these texts within the volume's larger ideological schemes.

Without the programmatic context provided in this volume for the *Petre clemens* texts, and the clear statement on the date at which they were written, the motet might still appear as a general celebration of Clement's rule. Indeed, some have regarded it as one of the more clearly commemorative texts in the fourteenth-century motet repertory. It is true that once the immediate business of the Roman ambassadors' visit had faded into obscurity, and particularly after Charles IV was safely installed as Holy Roman Emperor (1346), the texts' praise of Clement's election and their warm anticipation of the benefits of his pontificate could be understood in a more historical light.[42] But this example nonetheless begs some questions about the interpretations customarily placed on the texts of motets (particularly celebratory motets) and about the uses to which they

[40] *Codices*, i/3, cols. 2768–9.
[41] 'Let those who recollect in such a manner meditate with themselves in [their] hearts: when Peter, the head of the church, the father of all and door-keeper of heaven, rebuffed those whom he called and abandoned those whom he took up, when his vicar, the father of the world, remained inhuman to human creatures'. A-*Wn* MS 4195, fol. 156ᵛ.
[42] For the election, see Wood, pp. 142–52.

were put. Most important, a simple, monofunctional association between motets and narrowly defined state purposes, royal and papal coronations in particular, no longer appears justifiable. It must be asked whether the primary targets of motet texts were more usually doctrinal, and whether the rationale for their performance in other contexts derived from the wider subsequent interpretations to which they were clearly susceptible.[43] Moreover, if texts could be flexibly and variously read in literary settings, was the same true of their reception in traditions of musical copying and performance? Official festivity was an important stimulus for literary and musical commemoration, but it was probably not the only performance context for a form that Grocheo described as best suited 'to the festivities of the *litterati*'.[44] It may also be that some motets survive precisely because their texts were flexible in application and thus promoted copying for use in a variety of political, ideological or commemorative settings.

The contextual issues raised by *Petre clemens* are broadened by the programmatic use made of Vitry's motet poetry in its later literary receptions. A convenient case is provided by *Colla iugo*, not only because it is the most widely disseminated of the motet poems, but also for its close relationship with moralistic writing on the virtues and vices theme in both established scholastic traditions and more recent literature. Kremsmünster MS 149 represents this connection in its most straightforward form. Here *Colla iugo* is placed at the head of a series of five poems, all known elsewhere although not in this combination, which continues with items by Walter of Châtillon and Hildebert of Tours, a meditation on death by St Bruno, and a thirteenth-century piece drawn from the *vita* of St Theophilius.[45] The worldly theme framed at the outset of this

---

[43] For another case see A. Wathey, 'The Marriage of Edward III and the Transmission of French Motets to England', *Journal of the American Musicological Society*, 45 (1992), pp. 1–29, on pp. 14–22.

[44] C. Page, *The Owl and the Nightingale: Musical Life and Ideas in France, 1100–1300* (London, 1989), p. 119; E. Rohloff, ed., *Die Quellenhandschriften zum Musiktraktat des Johannes de Grocheio* (Leipzig, 1972), p. 144.

[45] Fols. 285ᵛ–287ᵛ; 'O felix mortale genus' (Walter of Châtillon, *Proverbia Alexandreidos*, x. 433ff; a polyphonic setting of this text is in Cambridge, Gonville and Caius College, MS 803/807, fol. 1ʳ⁻ᵛ), 'Virginitatis flos est et virginis' (Hildebert of Tours; also in F-Pn MS lat. 3343, fol. 78ᵛ), 'Mortales dominus cunctos' (Bruno Carthusiensis), and 'Mater sancta dei'. See Walther, *Initia*, nos. 12632, 20475, 11284, 10768; nos. 12632 and 11284 also appear together in Aeneas Silvius Piccolomini, *De pravis mulieribus* (Paris, 1507?), fols. 10ᵛ–11.

group, in the motet text's commentary on the perils of courtly life, is thus juxtaposed with more sober reflections on the human condition, and the nature of virtue and sin. Finally, the Marian verse at the end of this group recalls the improving tale of Theophilius, who forswore all earthly advantage after the Virgin rescued him from a pact that he had sealed with the devil in order to gain high office.

The other three sources of the *Colla iugo* text present more direct, and more elaborate, commentaries on the character of courtly life. Both this text and *Bona condit* are copied in the Luder anthology, at the end of the letter of 2 May 1458, entitled *De vita curialium sacerdotum*, written by Luder to the celebrated Heidelberg theologian Johannes Ernst.[46] An important piece, ranging widely through Horace, Virgil, Ovid, Juvenal, Persius and Seneca in its choice of quoted material, this missive emerges as a political admonition to the Elector Frederick of the Palatinate, whom Ernst served as chaplain and personal tutor. Against the pleasures of life at court are set the spiritual benefits of a modest life and the pitfalls of extravagant consumption. Originally designed to speak this message to a fourteenth-century audience, the *Colla iugo* and *Bona condit* texts are here made to reflect the content of Luder's letter directly, supporting its pleas for control over clerical excess, and – more generally – the unity of the church in its abhorrence of sin. The remaining sources of *Colla iugo* teach parallel lessons. Copied in the Jena manuscript under the heading 'Der Höfling', this text immediately follows a verse on the disastrous consequences of monetary wealth, moralistic extracts from Geoffrey of Monmouth, and an elaborate piece – widely distributed from the eleventh century onwards – based on the seven deadly sins, beginning 'Septem curialitates'.[47] The juxtaposition here of *Colla iugo* with the triplum text of another Vitry motet, *Hugo, Hugo*, extends this critique of courtly excess, which is further developed in a series of verses from Bernard of Clairvaux beginning 'Si tibi pulcra domus'. In the Berlin anthology, a Heidelberg book related to that containing Luder's letters, *Colla iugo* is

---

[46]   *A-Wn* MS 3244, fols. 163ᵛ–169. For this letter see Wattenbach, 'Peter Luder', pp. 54, 80–2 (another copy appears in *A-Wn* MS 4323, fols. 71–6). A letter by Luder earlier in the volume is followed on fol. 90 by the hexameter *Egregius labor*, associated in other sources with *Colla iugo / Bona condit* (see below pp. 143–4).

[47]   Jena, Universitätsbibliothek, MS Buder 4° 104, fols. 219–25; see Bertalot, *Humanistisches Studienheft*, pp. 156–60.

again headed 'De vita curialium'; again it follows the 'Septem curialitates' piece, and stands at the head of a series of epitaphs on famous men, beginning with Boethius, Petrarch and Lorenzo Valla.[48]

As a component in programmes of this nature, *Colla iugo* evidently proved very useful, its popularity aided perhaps by the quotation in its last two lines of a distich on the same subject from Lucan's *Pharsalia*.[49] A wider context for its use can be found in the contemporary pamphleteering of the established church against ecclesiastical potentates who behaved as though they were secular lords. This was a persistent topos in late-medieval moralistic writing, but in the wake of the fifteenth-century councils the theme was taken up with a vengeance by the papacy. Pius II in particular emerges with an important voice in this movement. As Aeneas Silvius Piccolomini, he was himself responsible for a pamphlet, *De miseria curialium sacerdotium*, written at Bruck am Main in 1444, that picks up closely on the themes and possibly even on the language of *Colla iugo*.[50] A more explicit elaboration of this motet text, and of Vitry's *Hugo, Hugo*, emerges in a 119-line poem entitled *Quondam colla iugo veneris submisserat Hugo*, copied into another humanist miscellany in Bohemia in the mid fifteenth century. These verses, initially matching the metre of *Colla iugo*, narrate the ruin and exile of one Hugo, a cleric deprived of his benefice for keeping a concubine, and his bitter advice to a friend to forswear women.[51] Again there are similarities of language between the motet text and the body of the poem.

Colla iugo is the most widely distributed of the Vitry motet texts in literary copies; it is also the most widely distributed in copies

---

[48] *D-B* MS lat. 2° 49, fols. 88ᵛ–90ᵛ; see Rose, *Verzeichniss*, II/3, p. 1270.

[49] *Pharsalia*, x. 407; see also Bertalot, *Humanistisches Studienheft*, p. 158. Line 4 of this text, 'Aliena desere quadra convivari', may allude to Juvenal, *Satires*, v. 2, '. . . aliene vivere quadra'.

[50] Edited in R. Wolkan, *Der Briefwechsel des Eneas Silvius Piccolomini*, I/1, Fontes Rerum Austriacum 61 (Vienna, 1909), pp. 453–87. On this work see F. J. Worstbrock, 'Aeneas Silvius Piccolomini', *Verfasserlexikon*, VII, cols. 643–4; also P. M. Smith, *The Anti-Courtier Tradition in Sixteenth-Century French Literature*, Travaux d'Humanisme et Renaissance 84 (Geneva, 1966), pp. 22–4, 41–2.

[51] In *A-Wn* MS 4453, fol. 322; printed in J. Huemer, 'Lateinische Rhythmen des Mittelalters, II', *Wiener Studien*, 6 (1884), pp. 287–96, on pp. 293–6, and H. Walther, 'Eine misogyne Versnovelle des ausgehenden Mittelalters', *Beiträge zur Forschung: Studien aus dem Antiquariat Jacques Rosenthal*, new series, 4 (1932), pp. 37–40.

with music, surviving in a total of nine sources.[52] The flexibility and popularity of the subject matter of this text affords a convincing explanation for its widespread literary circulation. It may also account for the frequency with which the polyphonic setting was copied. From *Fauvel*, and from one or two other exceptional survivals, it is clear that motet texts with music might share meanings similar to those imputed to them in literary copies where they appear integrated in moralistic or didactic programmes. (Most music manuscripts submerge the ideological content of motet texts beneath an organisation by musical genre.) The later uses to which the *Colla iugo* texts were put suggest a variety of functions, and possibly even performance contexts, for the polyphonic setting of the motet, serving alone or within larger programmes as admonition, as approbation or more simply as general comment. They also underline the initial connection between the motet and the later-medieval virtues and vices literature. This is made clear by what appears to be an early elaboration of the motet, where the message conveyed in the upper parts is focused by the addition of a contratenor with the text *Egregius labor*.[53] This short hexameter, labelled 'contra' in *A-Wn* MS 3244 and Berlin, MS lat. 2° 49, develops the themes of *Colla iugo* and *Bona condit*, echoing the quotation from Lucan ('Nulla fides pietasque viris qui castra secuntur') in the last line of the triplum text with 'Et sic falluntur miseri qui castra secuntur'. Comparable in this respect to the contratenor part of the lost Vitry motet *Phi millies*, the *Egregius labor* verse thus serves to strengthen the motet's principal message. It also marks the existence of a four-part version of *Colla iugo*, now lost. This verse, in addition, acquired a life of its own, circulating independently of the other texts of the motet well into the sixteenth century, as part of a collection headed 'De vita sacerdotali et virginali', and in numerous adaptations, including one, 'Nocte dieque sequi, cum magno principe castra; Egregius labor est, sed sic non itur ad astra', which was twice copied into miscellanies by the brothers

---

[52] Sanders, 'Vitry, Philippe de', p. 27; M. del Carmen Gomez, 'Más códices con polifonía del siglo XIV en España', *Acta Musicologica*, 53 (1981), pp. 58–90, on pp. 85–6.

[53] Walther, *Initia*, no. 5291; H. Walther, *Proverbia sententiaeque latinitatis medii aevi: Lateinische Sprichwörter und Sentenzen des Mittelalters*, 5 vols., Carmina Medii Aevi Posterioris Latina 2 (Göttingen, 1963–7), I, p. 878, no. 7013; O. Schumann, *Lateinisches Hexameter-Lexikon: dichterisches Formelgut von Ennius bis zum Archipoeta*, 6 vols., Monumenta Germaniae Historica, Hilfsmittel 4 (Munich 1979–83), I, pp. 373–4.

Hartmann and Hermann Schedel.[54] A further resonance in the
Colla iugo texts emerges from their juxtaposition (in the Berlin and
Jena sources) with the 'Septem curialitates' piece. Beginning with
a list of seven courtly virtues, these verses continue with descriptive
lists of seven 'incurialitates', seven 'fatuitates', and seven 'turba-
tiones'. The number seven, so dominant in writings on the virtues
and vices, is also represented in the division of the fourteen-line
text of *Colla iugo*, and in the seven statements (repeated) of the
talea in its polyphonic setting. It is clear that the parallel in the
sevenfold organisation of these two texts was picked up in the
literary tradition. It also seems likely that the tradition of sevenfold
exegesis in commentaries on spiritual virtue and worldly vice was
a feature that the Vitry text was originally designed to project, and
which was duly amplified by its musical setting. Finally, a parallel
case of musical elaboration present in *Apollinis eclipsatur*, the only
fourteenth-century motet to survive in more sources than *Colla iugo*,
urges further comparative scrutiny within the surviving musical
repertories. As is well known, that piece spawned not only variant
versions with multivalent added voices, but also a long tradition
of related musician-motets. The evidence of *Egregius labor* demonstrates the first of these processes. It must be asked whether the
second also occurred, and whether we should now search among
later motets for the progeny of *Colla iugo / Bona condit*.

The individual literary histories of Vitry's motet texts remain to
be written in full. The German student anthologies, forming a
majority among the new sources for the motet poetry, are imperfectly surveyed and further copies of the motet poetry seem likely
to emerge. There is more also to be said about the relationship

---

[54] For sources of this verse see Table 1; the verse is so headed in *Signum quindecim horribilia de fine mundi et extremo judicio* (Cologne, Merlin von Werden, after 1500), and in Trier, Stadtbibliothek, MS 804. For 'Nocte dieque' (Walther, *Sprichwörter*, no. 17056, with further sources), and the Schedel books (Munich, Bayerische Staatsbibliothek, clm 460 and 650), see R. Stauber, *Die Schedelsche Bibliothek* (Freiburg im Breisgau, 1908), pp. 32, 46. Further related verses are: 'Ire, redire, sequi regum sublimia castra; Egregius status eximius, sed sic non itur ad astra' in Weimar, MS Q. 108, copied at Erfurt in the 1470s, among other sources (Walther, *Sprichwörter*, no. 12925; see also W. Wattenbach, 'Weiteres aus der Weimarer Handschrift', *Anzeiger für Kunde der deutschen Vorzeit*, 28 (1881), col. 246; Dr Fromman, 'Findlinge', *ibid.*, 21 (1874), col. 256; Kristeller, *Iter italicum*, III, pp. 463–4), 'Qui sequitur castra, non multum cogitat astra', 'Qui servit rastro, servire nequit bene castro' and 'Sunt et dicuntur miseri, qui castra sequuntur' (Walther, *Sprichwörter*, nos. 24709, 24724, 30723).

between Vitry and Petrarch, and Vitry's place in the early humanist movement, which stands alongside the evidence of the literary
transmissions of his motet texts. New archival evidence establishes
a firm connection with Louis, Duke of Bourbon, whose business at
Avignon Vitry was more than once called upon to oversee in the
years between 1326 and 1337, when Petrarch was continuously
resident there.[55] It may also point to a closer link between Vitry
and Pierre Roger, Archbishop of Rouen, in the 1330s, before his
election as Pope. Vitry made widespread use of classical quotations
in the texts of his motets, as work by David Howlett is currently
demonstrating. His learning was also acknowledged by Pierre
Bersuire, whose *Ovidus moralizatus* relates in its prologue how Vitry
had shown him 'multas bonas exposiciones, tam allegoricas quam
morales'.[56] Less well known is Vitry's appropriation of classical
imagery for his personal seals, both of which (dating from the late
1340s) portray, in different forms, the figures of Hercules and the
lion.[57] As a moral parable, this legend was a favourite among early

---

[55] Described in A. Wathey, 'European Politics and Musical Culture at the Court of
Cyprus', a paper delivered at a Congress on the Cypriot-French Repertory of the Manuscript Torino J. II. 9, Paphos, 20 March 1992; see also 'The Marriage of Edward III',
p. 12, n. 18.

[56] 'Postquam tamen ab Avinione redivissem Parisius . . . magister Philippus de Vitriaco,
vir utique excellentis ingenii, moralis philosophie, hystorie ac etiam antiquitatis zelator
precipuus et in cunctis mathematicis scienciis eruditus, dictum gallicum librum michi
tradidit, in quo procul dubio multas bonas exposiciones, tam allegoricas quam morales,
inveni' ('But after I returned from Avignon to Paris . . . master Philippe de Vitry, a
man, to be sure, of excellent intellect, an exceptional ardent lover of moral philosophy,
history, and also antiquity, and learned in all the mathematical sciences, handed to me
the aforesaid French book, in which I found without doubt many good expositions,
allegorical as well as moral'); quoted, with errors, in Samaran, 'Pierre Bersuire', pp.
342–3. Bersuire also cited Vitry as an authority, in the description of a large warlike
fish in his *Reductorium* (IX, cap. 136): '*Zytiron*, id est miles marinus: monstrum est marinum sicut dicit liber de natura rerum . . . Ab altero viro audivi semel in eodem mari
[Britannico] prope insulam ciocam parvulum piscem captum, ad formam armati militis
figuratum, casside et scuto et lorica armatum. Cuius simile audivi a venerabili viro
magistro Philippo de Vitriaco, asserente in Normandia similem militem vidisse' ('*Zytiron*,
that is marine knight: it is a marine monster, as the book *De natura rerum* says . . . .
From another man I heard once in the same sea near the isle of Cioca (?) a tiny fish
[was] taken, shaped to the form of an armed knight, armed with a helmet and shield
and breastplate. The like of which I have heard from the venerable man master Philippe
de Vitry, asserting that he had seen in Normandy a similar knight'); Petrus Berchorius
Pictaviensis, *Reductorii moralis . . . libri quatuordecim* (Venice, Gasparo Bindoni, 1589), p.
310.

[57] The known examples of Vitry's seals survive in *F-Pn* p. o. 3032 (MS fr. 29516), dossier
'Vitry' (67183): (i) attached to nos. 6 and 8, quittances issued at Paris by Vitry on 17
August 1346 and 3 January 1350, bearing the legend 'SIGILLUM SECRETI PHI[. . .]', and
portraying Hercules with a club resting on his right shoulder, the defeated lion's head

---

humanists, and its appearance here speaks volumes for Vitry's self-image. At present, German humanism in the mid fifteenth century emerges as the main guardian of Vitry's literary contribution to the early Renaissance. What is only just beginning is the wider search in fourteenth-century culture for the impact of one whom Petrarch hailed as the only true poet in France.

Royal Holloway and Bedford New College,
University of London

APPENDIX

Text sources

1. Brugge, Stadsbibliotheek (*B-BRs*), MS 258. s. xiv, parchment, 80 fols. 196×140 mm. Humbertus de Romanis, Tractatus de habundancia in sermonibus; moral extracts, etc., headed Liber de octo principalibus viciis; Petrus Alfonsus, Liber proverbiorum; compendium de confessione. *Quid scire* is added on fol. 1ʳ. Described: A. de Poorter, *Catalogue des manuscrits de la Bibliothèque publique de la ville de Bruges*, Catalogue Général des Manuscrits des Bibliothèques de Belgique (Gembloux and Paris, 1934), pp. 296–8.

2. Berlin, Staatsbibliothek Preussischer Kulturbesitz (*D-B*), MS lat. 2° 49. s. xv²⁄², paper, 236 fols. 220×110 mm. (i) Augustinus Datus, Isagogicus maior; Sallust, De coniuracione; Persius, Satires; Ovid, Heroides; History of the Trojan Wars; (ii) humanistic collectanea (not obviously later additions) interspersed among these larger texts, including: letters and addresses of Aeneas Silvius Piccolomini, Samuel Karoch of Lichtenberg and Jakob Wimpfeling; Ps. Ovid, De rustice, De philomena, De pulice and De cuculo; epitaphs on Boethius, Petrarch, Valla, Achilles, Hector and others; Latin verses, including items on the death of Frederick

under his right arm, and a shield decorated with a ram rampant in his left hand; (ii) attached to no. 12, a quittance issued by Vitry at Villeneuve-lès-Avignon on 29 September 1350, without surviving legend, bearing a lion surmounted by Hercules and David, both armed with clubs. Both seals are damaged, and the descriptions in the unprinted third volume of J. Roman, *Inventaire des sceaux de la collection des pièces originales du Cabinet des Titres à la Bibliothèque nationale*, I (Paris, 1909; vols. II and III in microfiche: Paris, Archives Nationales, 1987), III, p. 908, made when the seals' deterioration was less advanced, are therefore valuable. For the Hercules legend, see Witt, *Hercules at the Crossroads*, pp. 216–17; F. Gaeta, 'L'avventura di Ercole', *Rinascimento*, 5 (1954), pp. 227–60; T. E. Mommsen, 'Petrarch and the Story of the Choice of Hercules', *Medieval and Renaissance Studies* (New York, 1959), pp. 175–96.

von der Pfalz (1476) and the birth of Louis V (1478). Described: Rose, *Verzeichniss der lateinischen Handschriften*, II/3 (Berlin, 1905), pp. 1267–72; Kristeller, *Iter italicum*, III, pp. 472–3; Sottili, 'I codici . . . VII', *IMU*, 187 (1975), p. 17. See also W. Wattenbach, 'Aus einer Humanistenhandschrift', *Anzeiger für Kunde der deutschen Vorzeit*, 21 (1874), cols. 212–16, 244–51, 272–8, in col. 272. H. Entner, *Frühhumanismus und Schultradition in Leben und Werk des Wanderpoeten Samuel Karoch von Lichtenberg*, Veröffentlichungen des Instituts für deutsche Sprache und Literatur 39 (Berlin, 1968), pp. 81–2; C. M. Monti, 'Per la fortuna della "Questio de prole": i manoscritti', *IMU*, 28 (1985), p. 78.

3. Darmstadt, Hessische Landes- und Hochschulbibliothek (*D-DS*), MS 521. A.D. 1460–78, parchment and paper, 291 fols. Orationale, from the Cistercian Abbey of Camp, Cologne diocese, containing rhymed offices, hymns, sequences and private prayers. Described: G. Achten *et al.*, *Die lateinischen Gebetbuchhandschriften der Hessischen Landes- und Hochschulbibliothek Darmstadt* (Wiesbaden, 1972), pp. 47–64. See also Schrade, 'Philippe de Vitry', p. 353; *AH*, XXXIV, p. 45; XLII, pp. 247–8.

4. Jena, Universitätsbibliothek (*D-Ju*), MS Buder 4° 105. s. xv, paper, 230 fols. Pamphilius, De amore; Theodulus, Eclogues; letters and orations by Gasparino Barzizza, Nicolaus and Jeronimus Guarinus, Nicolaus Astesanus, Johannes de Madiis, Isotta Nogarola, Antonius Panormita, Petrarch, Johannes Pirckheimer, Balthasar Rasinus, Salutati, Valla, Vegius and others; other short pieces by Leonardo Bruni; Milanese state letters; petition of the German students at Pavia to Francesco Sforza; Genoese passport for Lorenzo Schaller. Fully described in Bertalot, *Humanistisches Studienheft*, repr. in *Studien zum italienischen und deutschen Humanismus*, 2 vols., ed. P. O. Kristeller, Storia e Letteratura: Raccolta di Studi e Testi 129 (Rome, 1975), I, pp. 83–161; Kristeller, *Iter italicum*, III, p. 411. See also F. Pontarin and C. Andreucci, 'La tradizione del carteggio di Lorenzo Valla', *IMU*, 15 (1972), pp. 188, 193, 195; L. Capra, 'Contributo a Guarino Veronese', *IMU*, 14 (1971), p. 236; D. Mazzuconi, 'Per una sistemazione dell'epistolario di Gasparino Barzizza', *IMU*, 20 (1977), pp. 201, 210.

5. Kremsmünster, Stiftbibliothek (*A-KR*), MS 149. s. xv, paper, 303 fols. Bull of Pius II, and Gregory of Heimburg, Appelatio; short poetic and dictaminal treatises, including Albertus Rosatus, Liber poetarius; Horace, De arte poetica and Epistolarium libri duo; Ps. Ovid, Epistolae heroides, De cuculo and De pulice; Persius, Satires; letters of Conrad Celtis (added fols. 258ᵛ–260ᵛ), and Latin verses. Description: unpublished manuscript

Andrew Wathey

catalogue by H. Schmid; Kristeller, *Iter italicum*, III, p. 23. See also J. Huemer, 'Iter austriacum I', *Wiener Studien*, 9 (1887), pp. 51–93: pp. 79–80.

6. Lübeck, Stadtbibliothek (*D-LÜs*), MS 152 (destroyed in 1945). s. xv, paper. Letters of Petrus Vineis, S. Johannes de Capistrano and Johannes Rockazanus, and correspondence between the universities of Erfurt and Kraków; formulary of conciliar correspondence, including items by Henry VI of England and the Emperor Sigismund; letters and orations of Leonardo Bruni and Poggio. See W. Wattenbach, 'Notizien aus Handschriften der Stadtbibliothek zu Lübeck', *Beilage zum Archiv für Kunde österreichischer Geschichtsquellen*, 1 (1851), pp. 382–4; Entner, *Frühhumanismus und Schultradition*, p. 86; L. Bertalot, *Initia humanistica latina*, I, p. xlvii.

7. Paris, Bibliothèque Nationale (*F-Pn*), MS lat. 3343. s. xv, paper, 173 fols. Miscellany of verses, sentences, and extracts from longer works totalling 1193 separate items, including the 'ballades mythologiques' between Jean de le Motte, Philippe de Vitry and Jean Campion. Fully described in *Bibliothèque nationale: catalogue général des manuscrits latins V (nos. 3278 à 3535)* (Paris, 1966), pp. 236–48. See also E. Sanders, 'Vitry, Philippe de', *The New Grove Dictionary*, xx, p. 27; E. Pognon, 'Ballades mythologiques de Jean de le Mote, Philippe de Vitri, Jean Campion', *Humanisme et Renaissance*, 5 (1938), pp. 385–417.

8. Trier, Stadtbibliothek (*D-TRs*), MS 804. s. xvi in., paper, 279 fols. 102 × 140 mm. Elucidarium religionis; extracts from St Bernard; large miscellany of verses and sentences, in Latin and German, on moral subjects; epitaphs by Aeneas Silvius Piccolomini and others, and other short pieces. From St Matthias, Trier. Described: G. Kentenich, *Die ascetischen Handschriften der Stadtbibliothek zu Trier: beschreibendes Verzeichnis VI* (Trier, 1910), pp. 129–33.

9. Vienna, Österreichische Nationalbibliothek (*A-Wn*), MS 883. s. xiv/xv, parchment, 164 fols. Everard of Béthune, Labyrinthus; Theodulus, Eclogues; verses and sentencia on the virtues and vices, De clericis et militis amore, and other moral and ethical subjects, and other short pieces; hymns to the Virgin, on worldly vanities and corruption, and to the saints. Described: Denis, *Codices manuscripti theologici bibliothecae palatinae vindobonensis latini aliarumque occidentalis linguarum*, 2 vols. in 6 (Vienna 1793–1802), I/2, cols. 2309–23; *Tabulae codicum manu scriptorum praeter graecos et orientales in bibliotheca palatina vindobonensi asservatorum*, 11 vols. (Vienna, 1864–1912), I, pp. 148–50. See also J. Huemer, 'Lateinische Rhythmen

des Mittelalters, II', *Wiener Studien*, 5 (1883), pp. 144–53: pp. 150–3; *ibid.*, 6 (1884), pp. 287–96: pp. 287–92.

10. Vienna, Österreichische Nationalbibliothek (*A-Wn*), MS 3219. s. xv, paper, 302 fols. Boethius, De consolatione philosophiae cum commentario; Geoffroi de Vinsauf, Carmen de statu curia romane; Everard of Béthune, Labyrinthus; Pier Paolo Vergerio, De ingenuis moribus; short tracts and poetry by Henricus de Hassia, Johannes de Garlandia, Theobald de Senis, Hugh of St Victor and others, and miscellaneous Latin verses by Josephus Brivius Mediolanensis, and on the virtues and vices. Described: S. Endlicher, *Catalogus codicum philologicorum latinorum bibliothecae palatinae vindobonensis* (Vienna, 1836), pp. 268–72; *Tabulae codicum*, II, pp. 236–7.

11. Vienna, Österreichische Nationalbibliothek (*A-Wn*), MS 3244. s. xv, paper, 331 fols. Grammatical tracts and epigrams; letters by Peter Luder (for which this book is the main source), Arringinus, Gasparino Barzizza, Cardinal Bessarion, Leonardo Bruni, Petrus Antonius Finariensis, Matthias von Kemnat, Merkel Kulmann, Paolo Maffei, Johannes Mendel, Petrarch, Aeneas Silvius Piccolomini, Poggio, Serafino de Urbino, Johann Wildenherz and others; Gregory of Heimburg, Appelatio, and an address to Filipo-Maria Sforza. Described: *Tabulae codicum*, II, pp. 241–3; see also W. Wattenbach, 'Geistliche Scherze', *Anzeiger für Künde der deutschen Vorzeit*, 15 (1868), cols. 325–6; W. Wattenbach, 'Peter Luder: der erste humanistische Lehrer in Heidelberg', *Zeitschrift für die Geschichte des Oberrheins*, 22 (1869), pp. 33–127; Sottili, 'I codici . . . VII', *IMU*, 18 (1975), p. 17. D. Mazzuconi, 'Stefano Fieschi da Soncino: un allievo di Gasparino Barzizza', *IMU*, 24 (1981), p. 277.

12. Vienna, Österreichische Nationalbibliothek (*A-Wn*), MS 4195. s. xiv, parchment, 161 fols. Sermons, addresses delivered in consistory, and other political pieces, in particular against Louis of Bavaria, by Pierre Roger, Archbishop of Rouen, elected Pope Clement VI in 1342. Described: Denis, *Codices*, I/3, cols. 2756–72; *Tabulae codicum*, III, p. 198.

13. Wolfenbüttel, Herzog August Bibliothek (*D-W*), MS Helmst. 525. s. xiv/xv, paper, 69 fols. 220×160 mm. Digest of civil and canon law *tituli*; short legal tracts and extracts, including the Brevis notitia of Petrus Guillelmus Sanderi, and a vocabulary. *Egregius labor* and other verses added s. xv$^{2/2}$ on fol. 69. Described: O. von Heinemann, *Die Handschriften der herzoglichen Bibliothek zu Wolfenbüttel*, II (Wolfenbüttel, 1886), pp. 15–16.

14. Wolfenbüttel, Herzog August Bibliothek (*D-W*), MS Helmst. 608. s. xv (A.D. 1471), paper, 234 fols. 215×160 mm. Notes and extracts from Boethius; Thomas Brabanti, Liber de disciplina scolarium; Seneca, Epistolae; Everard of Béthune, Labyrinthus; Maximianus, Comedies; letters and Bulls of Popes Calixtus III and Pius II; letters of Henricus de Hassia, St Bernard and Henricus de Ro.; miscellany of Leonine hexameters. Owned by Henricus Osnaburgensis. Described: Heinemann, II, pp. 71–3.

EVELYN S. WELCH

SIGHT, SOUND AND CEREMONY IN THE CHAPEL OF GALEAZZO MARIA SFORZA

Bernardino Corio's late fifteenth-century history of Milan covers the city's past from its foundations to the collapse of the Sforza dynasty.[1] Following the historiographic traditions established by Leonardo Bruni, its essential outlines are founded on careful use of sources and, for more recent events, contemporary memories and impressions. It is, however, also characterised by judicious revisionism and anecdotal invention. The careful reader always needs to ask why digressions have been included and what hidden points are being made. It is therefore well worth inquiring why Corio, a member of Duke Galeazzo Maria Sforza's court, chose to link his master's assassination on 26 December 1476 with a passage on his chapel choir and musical taste.

Literary conventions demanded warnings of impending disaster and Corio provided a series of portents leading up to the fateful day. There were the traditional signs: falling stars, flying crows, unexplained fires and an atypical desire on Galeazzo Maria's part to see his children. But the clearest evidence of a death foretold was the duke's own order that his chapel singers should put on mourning garments and insert a section from the Office for the Dead into the daily mass: *Maria mater gratiae, mater misericordiae.* Whether genuine or not, this bizarre anecdote permitted a short description of Galeazzo Maria's musical enthusiasms: 'The duke took great delight in song, for which he kept about thirty northern singers, honourably paid, and among whom there was one called

---

[1] B. Corio, *Storia di Milano*, ed. E. De Magri (Milan, 1857; repr. Milan, 1975). On history writing in Milan see G. Ianziti, *Humanistic Historiography under the Sforzas: Politics and Propaganda in Fifteenth-Century Milan* (Oxford, 1988).

Evelyn S. Welch

Cordiero, to whom he gave a salary of 100 ducats a month. And the ornaments in his chapel were such that they could be valued at 100,000 ducats.'² Corio pointedly ended this description of the Sforza chapel with the seemingly unconnected information that during the Christmas festivities of 1476, 'all the duke's feudatories and courtiers had come from his dominions to Milan to await his arrival, and all were malcontent since he had not made any payments'.³ In Corio's conjunction, the contrast between the enormous riches heaped on the singer, Jean Cordier, and the relative disenfranchisement of the Milanese aristocracy had its effect at the end of the month. With the support of a significant section of the city's Ghibelline nobility, three of Galeazzo Maria's courtiers stabbed the duke to death in the church of S. Stefano.

Was the duke's fondness for music responsible, even indirectly, for his murder? Scholars have long recognised the importance of his short-lived court chapel.⁴ Yet it has received surprisingly little detailed attention in its own right, remaining as a backdrop to the excellent studies devoted to the fifteenth-century court chapels of Ferrara and Naples. The duke himself has been perceived primarily as a poor counterpart of Ferrante of Aragon, Ercole d'Este and Pope Sixtus IV.⁵ It is now time to reverse the comparison and examine Galeazzo Maria's own reasons for establishing one of the

² Corio, *Storio di Milano*, III, p. 301: 'Il duca si dilittava molto col canto, pel quale tenea circa trenta cantori oltremontani, da esso onorevolmente stipendiati, e tra gli altri, uno ne avea chiamato Cordiero, al quale dava per stipendio cento ducati al mese. Avea tanti ornamenti di cappella che erano del valore di centomila ducati; nella festa dell'apostolo ordinò che fossero vestiti a lutto, e poi impose loro che tutti i giorni in avvenire cantassero nella messa questo versetto tolto dall'ufficio dei morti: *Maria mater gratiae, mater misericordiae.*'

³ *Ibid.*, III, p. 301: 'Per l'arrivo del duca a Milano erano accorsi tutti i suoi feudatari e cortigiani del dominio, e tutti erano malcontenti perchè non avea dispensati denari.'

⁴ The most recent survey is that of W. F. Prizer, 'Music at the Court of the Sforza: the Birth and Death of a Musical Center', *Musica Disciplina*, 43 (1989), pp. 141–93, which contains important new documents and summarises the current bibliography. For Galeazzo Maria's court see G. Lubkin, 'The Court of Galeazzo Maria Sforza, Fifth Duke of Milan, 1466–1476' (Ph.D. dissertation, University of California at Berkeley, 1982; revised version, as *A Renaissance Court*, Berkeley and Los Angeles, 1993; forthcoming).

⁵ On Ferrara and Naples see the now standard works, L. Lockwood, *Music in Renaissance Ferrara, 1400–1505: the Creation of a Musical Centre in the Fifteenth Century* (Oxford, 1984) and A. Atlas, *Music at the Aragonese Court of Naples* (Cambridge, 1985). The only author to make an extended comparison, albeit negative, between Galeazzo Maria and Ercole d'Este is Lewis Lockwood, 'Strategies of Music Patronage in the Fifteenth Century: the Cappella of Ercole I d'Este', *Music in Medieval and Early Modern Europe*, ed. I. Fenlon (Cambridge, 1981), pp. 227–48.

greatest collections of singers and composers of the period, and the political implications of his patronage.

The simultaneous creation of polyphonic court chapels in Italy in the 1470s has usually been explained in terms of princely rivalry. Much of the relevant correspondence accuses Galeazzo Maria and his ambassadors of preventing singers from arriving at their posts or of suborning musicians contracted elsewhere. The diplomatic stakes could be high, creating tensions between major Italian and non-Italian powers. In 1475, for example, the Duke of Burgundy, Charles the Bold, was forced to intervene in the dispute between King Ferrante of Naples and Galeazzo Maria over Jean Cordier's employment.[6] Yet such arguments reveal less about the individual ambitions of particular patrons than they do about the limited availability of the finest singers. Like precious gems or classical coins, renowned musicians were prestige objects which rulers fought to obtain. But competitive or acquisitive instincts do not fully explain the sums which Galeazzo Maria was willing to invest in his chapel. *Magnificentia* had many aspects; yet the Duke of Milan was singularly uninterested in antiquities, made no effort to obtain well-known painters or sculptors, and, having dismissed the humanists resident at his father's court, commissioned little prose or poetry in either Latin or the vernacular.[7] Music was the only area in which he could claim international renown for the quality and sophistication of his patronage. Why?

His early education offers only a partial explanation for this specialised interest. At the age of six Galeazzo Maria found his life transformed when his father, Francesco Sforza, accepted the surrender of Milan's republican government in 1450. No longer the son of a stateless *condottiere*, the boy, now the Count of Pavia, was heir to one of Italy's most powerful dominions. Every care was taken over his upbringing. With a personal retinue of almost forty men (who were ordered to keep him under continual surveillance)

---

[6] R. J. Walsh, 'Music and Quattrocento Diplomacy: the Singer Jean Cordier between Milan, Naples and Burgundy in 1475', *Archiv für Kulturgeschichte*, 60 (1978), pp. 439–42.

[7] On Galeazzo Maria Sforza's artistic patronage see E. S. Welch, 'Secular Fresco Painting at the Court of Galeazzo Maria Sforza, 1466–1476' (Ph.D. dissertation, University of London, 1987); 'Galeazzo Maria Sforza and the Castello di Pavia, 1469', *Art Bulletin*, 71 (1989), pp. 351–75; and 'The Image of a Fifteenth-Century Court: Secular Frescoes for the Castello di Porta Giovia, Milan', *Journal of the Warburg and Courtauld Institutes*, 53 (1990), pp. 163–84.

and the best tutor in Milan, no moment or opportunity was lost in his training.[8] While his younger brothers and sisters were permitted a degree of freedom, Galeazzo Maria was expected to undergo extensive preparations for his inheritance. This included musicianship,[9] and even if he never achieved the standards of Ercole d'Este, Galeazzo Maria emerged with some crucial skills. A well-known letter of 1452 from his tutor reported that the eight-year-old boy had just begun Latin but was still learning French songs with 'great pleasure' and that his riding was improving daily.[10] He also learned to play the organ, becoming a keen collector of instruments in later life.[11]

Such training had many merits. Songs were an obvious means of teaching a foreign language and even tiny children could put on performances for distinguished guests. Another letter, from 1450, describes a display by the five-year-old Ippolita Maria Sforza before the French ambassador:

Yesterday, around the 22nd hour, the ambassador of the King of France, the magnificent lord Baylis de Senis arrived. Wishing to execute the orders which your lordship had written to me, I sent our son, Count Galeazzo Maria, to meet him two miles out accompanied by all my gentlemen with four trumpets . . . who accompanied [the ambassador] to the castle . . . after lunch he came to visit me. And I, having been advised, arranged to meet him with the most magnificent lady my mother at the head of the hall, and with my ladies and many others of this territory, all well arranged, and with my children next to me, I most pleasantly received him. Having taken him into the beautifully prepared hall, I had him sit down between my mother and myself. And as he was speaking of many pleasurable matters [cose da piacere], I had our children and the other youths and ladies perform a number of dances. And then he had his perform some, which were most attractive. And thus we carried on

---

[8] An extensive manual for the Count of Pavia's early care was prepared by his household supervisor and his doctor, Cristoforo da Soncino. See Paris, Bibliothèque Nationale, ital. 1585, fols. 117–26.

[9] A. Cappelli, 'Guiniforte Barzizza, maestro di Galeazzo Maria Sforza', *Archivio Storico Lombardo*, 3rd ser., 2 (anno 21) (1894), pp. 399–442. For a comparative discussion of the Este children's education see Lockwood, *Music in Renaissance Ferrara*, p. 125; examples of other Sforza children's musical skills are mentioned by E. Lowinsky, 'Ascanio Sforza's Life: a Key to Josquin's Biography and an Aid to the Chronology of his Works', in *Josquin des Prez: Proceedings of the . . . Festival-Conference, New York 1971*, ed. E. Lowinsky and B. J. Blackburn (London, 1976), p. 45.

[10] Cappelli, 'Guiniforte Barzizza', p. 405.

[11] C. Sartori, 'Organs, Organ Builders and Organists in Milan: New and Unpublished Documents', *Musical Quarterly*, 43 (1957), pp. 57–67. His younger brother, Ottaviano, was taught to play the clavichord.

until the hour for dinner, and I also had our daughter Ippolita sing him a few pretty songs. Then he and I went to supper. Having dined, that is he in his room and I in mine, we returned to the said hall, where more and more similar dances, most lovely, were performed with the greatest pleasure of the said Monsignore who, considering their young age, marvelled at the excellent dancing and singing of our children.[12]

Such performances impressed guests at home. Cultivating the ability to listen with discernment proved equally important when travelling abroad. The count's early state visits were all punctuated with musical events. As an adolescent in Venice in 1455, he was, among other amusements, treated to the singing of an English woman. His tutors and courtiers reported that:

Today the *signoria* sent, according to its custom, many most notable gentlemen to pick up your son, the illustrious Count Galeazzo, and accompany him to the Darsena, where first they showed him all those galleys, rope-making and the other artefacts they make. Secondly, in order to give him greater delight and pleasure, they had some birds boiled up according to the custom here. Thirdly, they conducted him and the rest of us into the room of the Arsenale where they had arranged an elegant luncheon of confections of many different types. And to ensure that he had even greater pleasure, they arranged for the arrival of some most notable singers, among whom there was a young English woman who sang so sweetly and pleasantly that it seemed not a human voice, but divine. Then, with the arrival of evening, they accompanied us to the house with great honour and kindness, striving continuously, besides the company they offered, to give us all those pleasures which were possible.[13]

[12] Paris, Bibliothèque Nationale, ital. 1585, fol. 175, 21 December 1450; Bianca Maria Sforza to Francesco Sforza: 'Hieri circa ale xxii hore giungendo qua il magnifico monsignore Bayli de Sanis, ambassiatore de la maesta del Re de Franza, vogliando io exequire quanto la illustrissima vostra signoria m'avea scripto gli manday incontro per il spacio de dua miglia il fiolo nostro conte Galeazmaria con tuti li miei gentilhomini bene in puncto con quatro trombeti ... Quali l'accompagnavano fino a qui in castello ... dopo collatione segondo gli piaque se misse venire advisitarme. Et io advisata me gli face incontra con la magnifica madona mia madre fino in capo dela salla et con le mie done e molte altre di questa terra bene in puncto. Et amane essendo etiam preso de me li mei fioli allegrissimamente lo recevete. Et conductolo in salla molto bene etiam parata lo fece assetare tra la magnifica madona mia madre et mi. Et lui ragionando de molte cose da piacere fece fare più danze per li notri fioli et per le altre done et gioveni. Et anche gline fo deli suoi che ne feceno de molte pellegrine. Et facto così fino hora de cena et cantate etiam alcune belle cancione per la fiola nostra Ipolita. Esso et io andassemo a cena. Et cenati, cioè ipso ala camera suso, io ala mia, ritornassemo in la dita salla dove se feceno più e più simile danze molto belle et cum grandissimo piacere del prefato monsignore meravigliandose luy del ben ballare et cantare deli fioli notri per rispecto del suo piccolo tempo.'
[13] Paris, Bibliothèque Nationale, ital. 1587, fol. 90, 21 November 1455; Guarnerio Castiglione, Lancilloto del Maino, Guido Visconti, Pietro da Pusterla, Scaramuccia Balbo, Petro da Galarate to Francesco Sforza: 'In questa zornata la illustrissima signoria ha

Such delights were designed to appeal to a young guest and are recorded wherever Galeazzo Maria travelled in his youth. The ballad performance in 1459 by Cosimo de Medici's professional *improvisatori* which took place when the Count of Pavia arrived in the villa at Careggi have been widely reported.[14] But a more informal type of performance also took place within the household, as a letter by Galeazzo Maria to his father reveals:

> I went to visit the magnificent Cosimo who had one of his son Piero's daughters play a pipe organ, which was a lovely thing to hear. But he did the same thing every day after I arrived, and he also arranged for some of his singers to sing. This gave us singular pleasure; but a much greater pleasure was the familiarity extended to me, in arranging for me to stay with the women, where I am. By this act, he has shown me that he wishes me well as a good servant. Then having heard these instrumental pieces and songs, in which master Hector, who was always present and sang and had one of his sons play an accompaniment, I went for my pleasure through the city with master Sigismondo and him.[15]

The examples could be multiplied. Providing pleasure, *piacere*, was an essential item in fifteenth-century state visits; whether at home or abroad, music was an expected part of this entertainment. Sforza *feste* were characterised by 'balli et canti'. Players were

mandato secundo il suo costume molti notabilissimi zentilhomini ad levare lo illustrissimo conte Galeazo vostro figliolo et l'hanno accompagnato ad la Darsena over prima gli hanno monstrato tutte quelle galee, cordarie et artificii che gli fano. Secundo per darli mazor delecto et piacere gli hanno facto abollotare de li olcelli secundo l'usanza de qua. Tertio hano facto conducto ne la camera del arsenato con nuy altri tutti et li hanno facto fare una solenne colatione de cofecti de più maynere. Et che e havuto molto mazore piacere hano facto venire li alcuni notabilissimi cantatori, fra li quali gli era una damisela anglese che cantava tanto dolcemente et suavamente che pareva una voce non humana ma divina. Poy venuta la sera l'hanno accompagnato a casa con grandissimo honore et amorevoleza, studiandose continuamente oltra la compagnia gli fanno de dargli tutti quelle piacere siano possibile.'

[14]   The letter was first published in B. Buser, *Die Beziehungen der Mediceer zu Frankreich während der Jahre 1434–1494* (Leipzig, 1879), p. 324, and is discussed at length in N. Pirrotta, 'Musica e orientamenti culturali nell'Italia del Quattrocento', *Musica tra Medioevo e Rinascimento* (Turin, 1984), pp. 213–49.

[15]   Paris, Bibliothèque Nationale, ital. 1588, fol. 225, 19 April 1459; Galeazzo Maria to Francesco Sforza: 'Manday al visitare el Magnifico Cosimo quale fece sonare una figliola di Piero suo figliolo uno organo de cane che era una zentil cosa da audire. La quale cosa pero l'ha facto ogni dì dopo ch'io sono qui et fece anchora cantare per alcuni soy cantatori non senza singulare piacere tute queste cose, ma molto magiore e l'usare la domesticheza con mi che egli fa in fare stare con le donne sue dove io sto. Pero che per tal acto me significa che 'l mi voglia bene da bon servo. Or olditi questi soni et canti, ali quali el signore messer Hector anchora luy era sempre presente et canto et fece sonare uno suo figliolo di compagnia, con el signore mesere Sigismondo et luy sono andato a solazo per la città.'

invited to perform while guests dined or during the evening after the party had returned from a long day's hunting.[16] By the mid-Quattrocento, an ability to enjoy, understand and perform music was a necessary element of any aristocratic child's education. This was particularly true for marriageable young girls, for whom the ability to sing and dance brought decorous opportunities for public display. Bona of Savoy, for example, danced a moresca for the Sforza ambassador in order to show her fine physique; that of Dorotea Gonzaga (suspected of an inherited back disorder) was demonstrated by her dancing in a thin gown.[17] While similar male performances were rarely commented upon in such detail, older men also shared these popular musical enthusiasms. The burdens of state did not prevent the Sforza's chief secretary, Cicco Simonetta, from collecting the music of Lorenzo Giustinian.[18] Yet it is significant that in his letter requesting not only the songs but also an adolescent singer and lute player for his household, Simonetta made it clear that the boy and the music were not for his personal pleasure. They were destined for his children's education.[19] Learning and listening to secular music was still perceived as an adjunct to youth, not as an appropriate occupation for an elder statesman.

In procuring a lutenist for his household this secretary, an immigrant from Calabria, was imitating the educational and social

---

[16] In 1464, for example, Francesco Sforza dined with Jacopo Piccinino while musicians played. See A. Luzio and R. Renier, 'Filelfo e l'umanesimo alla corte dei Gonzaga', *Giornale Storico della Letteratura Italiana*, 16 (1890), pp. 58–9.

[17] On Dorotea see L. Beltrami, 'L'annullamento del contratto di matrimonio fra Galeazzo Maria Sforza e Dorotea Gonzaga (1463)', *Archivio Storico Lombardo*, 2nd ser., 6 (anno 16) (1889), pp. 126–32. Even after she married, the adolescent Ippolita Maria was invited by her father-in-law, the King of Naples, to dance privately for honoured guests. See E. Motta, 'Musici alla corte degli Sforza: ricerche e documenti milanesi', *Archivio Storico Lombardo*, 2nd ser., 4 (anno 14) (1887), p. 62.

[18] Motta, 'Musici alla corte', pp. 554–5. That Simonetta's search was successful is documented in an inventory of his books published by C. Magenta, *I Visconti e gli Sforza nel castello di Pavia e loro attinenze con la Certosa e la storia cittadina* (Milan, 1883), ii, pp. 346–7: 'Papie, die xxiiii Augusti 1476. Lista deli libri lassati in casa a Pavia del magnifico domino Cicho: repositi in la camera de le asse verso la strata dove el se veste el prefato domino Cicho, li quali libri sono reposti per Leonardo de Gluxiano, cancellero del prefato domino Cicho nel capsono grande novo . . . Liber unus canzionum Simonis de Sena et de sonetti de Burgiel. Item libro uno de canzone a laude de Iesu et de la nostra Dona sua madre et altre canzone de messer Leonardo Iustiniano.'

[19] He was particularly anxious (perhaps because he feared that the Venetians would attempt to insert a spy in his home) that the Sforza ambassador should 'not mention that you wish these things for my sake, but for some other friend of yours'.

expectations of the Milanese court.[20] But in emphasising the ubiquity of the culture to which Simonetta aspired it is possible to overstress its importance. Good horsemanship and an understanding of the finer points of falconry were as important as an ability to sing or play the lute. Music was only one part of an aristocratic child's education; for a future prince it had to take second place to more 'serious' matters. This was particularly problematic in Milan. If Galeazzo Maria's abilities as a hunter or lover of music were never in doubt, his interest in Latin and the examples of antiquity was always questionable. It became a cliché that the count was reluctant to read classical literature, and as he entered adolescence the *piacere* that he so enjoyed was increasingly viewed as an impediment to his preparation for rulership. The conflict is best documented during the count's trip to Ferrara in 1457. On that journey, as is well known, the young boy asked for French romances to read on the hot summer journey, 'to give pleasure to the assembled company'.[21] The request was couched, however, in such a way as to suggest that he would also read his Latin texts. At thirteen, Galeazzo Maria was no longer a child and, as a little tract his father prepared for him pointed out, it was time to put aside childish ways and take up serious matters.[22] The dispute over how much Latin Galeazzo Maria was required to read over the summer raged in correspondence between Milan and Ferrara, with his tutor, Guiniforte Barzizza, complaining that his charge, aided and abetted by Borso d'Este, would not scan his daily passages.[23] To the deep disapproval of the humanist and his parents he preferred the pleasures of hunting, dining and dancing. Barzizza noted with annoyance that Borso d'Este was spending all his time indulging Galeazzo Maria's youthful desires and that the time given over to *piacere* prevented the Ferrarese leader from attending to state matters and, indeed, caused him to lose all dignity.[24]

[20] The account book kept by Simonetta's treasurer, which contains no references to musicians, instruments or musical manuscripts, does indicate many of the other expenses incurred in maintaining a household befitting one of the most powerful men at the Milanese court. See P. G. Pisoni, ed., *Un libro-cassa per Cicco Simonetta (1478–1479) e altre note del tesoriere Leonardo da Giussano* (Germignaga, 1981).

[21] Cappelli, 'Guiniforte Barzizza', p. 406.

[22] D. Orano, *I suggerimenti di buon vivere dettati da Francesco Sforza pel figliolo Galeazzo Maria* (Rome, 1910).

[23] Cappelli, 'Guiniforte Barzizza', p. 410.

[24] *Ibid.*, p. 410: 'Questo ill.mo signore duca tutto el suo tempo spende in dargli el modo de avere piacere et pare ad ognuno così de suoy como de nostri la sua signoria havere

The arguments continued as Galeazzo Maria grew older. In 1459 his uncle Lancilloto del Maino noted with satisfaction that the count had left a dancing party in Dorotea Gonzaga's honour to meet an ambassador (he also noted with similar pleasure the young man's ability to get his hand down the front of Dorotea's dress).[25] But that year Galeazzo Maria's behaviour in Florence gave rise to concern, with the Mantuan ambassador reporting Francesco's fears that 'Count Galeazzo . . . doesn't seem to have grown up yet'. [26] Six years later matters had still not improved and the duke refused to allow his son to visit either the Gonzaga or Este courts, saying that Galeazzo Maria's inclinations to *piacere*, particularly that of hunting birds, were interfering with his future role: 'It was necessary for [Galeazzo Maria] to leave the birds alone and to devote himself to, and be of assistance in, important matters in order to learn the style and the practice of rulership and governing.'[27] Sforza's despair at his son's seeming immaturity was conveyed in one of the last letters he wrote before his death in March 1466: 'Galeazzo, I want you from now on to apply your

non solo interlasciato ogni sua facenda et di stato et d'ogni cosa, ma scordatosi anchora ogni sua dignità, gravità consueta et inveterata et factosi uno altro homo, adaptandosi ad piaceri giovenili in tutto et a quelli ponendo l'ingegno et lo pensiero'.

[25] Paris, Bibliothèque Nationale, ital. 1588, fol. 197, 26 November 1458; Lancilloto del Maino to Francesco Sforza: '. . . hogi dopo el disnare la ill.ma madona vostra consorte ha facto fare una festa dal canto dove è allogiato la ill.ma madona marchesana alla quale gli sono state molte done cremonese et li si e ballato alla polita con singulare piacere fin sera da tutti se non da lo ill.mo conte Galiaz quale intenendo che l'ambassiatori del duca di Bossina giongeva qui hogi havendo pero ballato prima uno pezo circa xxi hora se partite da decta festa per andarli incontra . . . facendogli in vero sempre digna et grata accoglianza como anche di continuo el si studio di fare alla ill.ma madonna Dorotea sua la quale pur el si avede che 'l non sia guardato aviso la ex. vostra chel non li perde tempo ad basarla et manegiarla molto bene conducendola qualche volte per la cantono sel puo et metendoli la mano de molte volte per la scolatura de la socha recerchando più inante che 'l puo con tal modo che 'l mi fa molto bene intendere che sella fusse in età che non bisognaria che m. Guiniforte insignasse quelle lettere, portandosi pero in ogni cosa benissimo et talmente che quando el se trova da la prefata ill.ma madona marchesana non si lassa porto vincere de cortesia.'

[26] Mantua, Archivio di Stato, Archivio Gonzaga, busta 1620, 1 May 1459; Vincenzo Scalone to Ludovico Gonzaga.

[27] Mantua, Archivio di Stato, Archivio Gonzaga, busta 1620, 13 June 1463; Vincenzo Scalone to Ludovico Gonzaga: '. . . era de bisogno che 'l disponess lassare li ucelli per darse e essere assistente alle cose de importantia per pigliare el modo e la pratica de sapersi regere e gubernare . . . Fino gli fara uno singulare apiacere se come da si la vostra signoria se move ad amonirle che 'l si vogli hora mai delectare de non perdere tempo a darsi alle cose de importantia et essere assiduo ad intenderla cum quello megliore modo gli parera cum farli intendere che questa, la via de farsi e de sapersi gubernare e che gli dara condictione presso de ciascuno e segundo le apetiti suoi de ucelli e de altre apiacere e mancare de questo gli potera col tempo fare danno e vergogna'.

brain and your mind to military matters and to what makes a soldier . . . I want you from now on to put aside boys' concerns and turn to those of men . . .'[28]

Although not specifically singled out for comment, music and dancing, as well as hunting, seem to have been included in the pleasures Galeazzo Maria was expected to place to one side. For rulers of the mid-Quattrocento the decorum of musical entertainment was clear: it could not be allowed to distract from more weighty matters. The humanist Panormita had commented approvingly that King Alfonso of Aragon 'sometimes dismissed his trumpeters in order to concentrate on his reading of Livy, and . . . occasionally became so absorbed in his reading that he seemed not to hear the music of flutes and the sounds of dancers around him'.[29] Galeazzo Maria's desire to present a newly matured image after his father's death in 1466 did not extend this far; but in the early years he was willing to concentrate on military and diplomatic responsibilities. Thus, the transition from Francesco, a soldier with little formal education, to the new, carefully trained duke initially brought little change to Milan's cultural patronage. Even when he deposed his mother from joint rule in late 1467, there was considerable continuity in their patterns of musical employment. Francesco and Bianca Maria had already made considerable changes during their sixteen-year reign. The previous duke, Filippo Maria Visconti, had, according to his somewhat astonished contemporary biographer, been totally indifferent to *spettacoli* and had refused to hire musicians.[30] In introducing a steady succession of performers, including the famous Pietrobono himself, to whom they sent their

---

28 Paris, Bibliothèque Nationale, ital. 1591, fol. 260, 3 February 1466: 'Galeaz, vogli de qui inanzi mettero l'animo e lo cervello a queste cose de soldo e ad intendere la natura deli solditi li quali sonno de natura de cercare quello sia el suo utile e non le cose de homo e provedere al inconvenienti e ale malitie deli malcomposta et non volere expectare che ogni volte hoy siamo quelli che debiamo provedere ali desordini e mancamenti che si commettono per quelli li quale te haveano dati in cura e governo.' The letter was written in response to Galeazzo Maria's behaviour during the War of the Public Weal in France. See P. Ghinzoni, 'Spedizione sforzesca in Francia (1465–1466)', *Archivio Storico Lombardo*, 2nd ser., 7 (anno 17) (1890), pp. 314–54.
29 Paraphrased in J. Bentley, *Politics and Culture in Renaissance Naples* (Princeton, 1987), pp. 72–3.
30 P. C. Decembrio, *Vita di Filippo Maria Visconti*, trans. and ed. E. Bartolini (Milan, 1983), p. 113: 'trascurò talemente gli accorgimenti per tener viva la fantasia e ricreare lo spirito da non curarsi nè d'andar a vedere istrioni nè d'assistere a spettacoli di mimo nè di tenere musici a corte'.

own protégés for training,[31] Francesco and Bianca Maria had returned the Milanese court to the intellectual and social mainstream. In general, however, they maintained a modestly-sized group of instrumentalists and singers whose primary function was secular entertainment, the 'cose da piacere' with which they had enticed the French ambassador in 1450.[32] The cathedral choir, numbering around seven singers, could be called upon for important ceremonial occasions and the court itself contained men well versed in musical matters.[33] With some advance notice, an impressive display could be put on by joining these amateur and professional musicians with those of neighbouring courts. The continuing ad hoc arrangement of such occasions emerges from a letter of 15 June 1468 when Vincenzo de' Medici (a member of the important Lombard as opposed to Florentine clan of the same name) wrote to Galeazzo Maria concerning the duke's forthcoming wedding to Bona of Savoy.

In talking of the arrival of the most illustrious and excellent lady your wife, I seem, with reverence, to have understood that your lordship has made and is making provisions for many virtuous persons, such as citizens and courtiers and others of whatever rank, as is worthy and accustomed. But I don't believe that your lordship has had time, being occupied in so many diverse things, to consider my role. Therefore I thought I would suggest that your lordship deign to use me in some way as one who has always been brought up and has exercised his profession in the court in many things, above all in singing. Now I have found a good singing companion called Lanceloto dala Croce, a gentleman of worth. He and I are almost of the same age and well matched in our singing, and perhaps, indeed without any perhaps, we will shame the young ones, as you will see when we are put to the test. Again, as the French are arriving, they will see and understand that in Lombardy there are those who know how to sing songs in their language just as well as them and better. Your lordship is well informed and knows how many virtues God on high has endowed me with. Do not forget me in this festival as I will bring it honour.[34]

---

[31] Motta, 'Musici alla corte', p. 53, and Lockwood, *Music in Renaissance Ferrara*, p. 100.

[32] A partial list of members of Francesco's court in Paris, Bibliothèque Nationale, ital. 1586, fol. 2, 1452, includes Barbante, *sonatore de viola*, and Antonello, *sonatore de liguto*.

[33] F. Fano, *La cappella musicale del duomo di Milano* (Milan, 1956).

[34] Milan, Archivio di Stato, Carteggio Sforzesco 884, 15 June 1468; Vincenzo de Medici to Galeazzo Maria Sforza: 'Mi pare intendere cum debita reverentia parlando in questa venuta dela illustrissima et excellentissima madona vostra consorte la signoria vostra havere fato e fa provisione de più virtuose persone come e de citadini, cortesani et d'altri in qualunque grado come è ben debita e digna cosa. Ma de me pare non habi ricordo

While Vincenzo's fate is unknown, Galeazzo Maria did borrow musicians in order to put on a convincing performance of some magnificence for his bride and her French followers. The Marquis of Monferrato's trumpeters and an English soprano were, for example, called in for the ceremonies.[35] These difficulties may have convinced him of the need for a more permanent group of performers. A few months after Bona's arrival the Sforza ambassador in Naples engaged two singers from Alfonso of Aragon's chapel, Raynerio de Precigneyo and the Frenchman Antonio Ponzo.[36] This does not, however, indicate any major expansion. The duke was perfectly happy to let yet another singer, Filipeto Romeo, leave Milan.[37] Only in 1469, after the death of his mother and the birth of a son, was Galeazzo Maria able to break free of previous inhibitions. At the age of twenty-five he finally consigned the school books still in his personal possession (including a 'librazolo in vulgare de balli et canti' and the 'librazolo de diversi soneti facti per Donato Cagnola musico ducale') to the library in the castle at Pavia before embarking on a period of extraordinary grand gestures.[38]

These ranged from painting the city walls of Vigevano in the Sforza colours of red and white, through redecorating the castles of Pavia and Milan, beginning new fortresses and palaces, repaving the urban centre of Milan, and commissioning large-scale medallion portraits of his wife and himself in pure gold, to – perhaps most startling to his contemporaries – opening negotiations for the title of King of Lombardy.[39] Much of his attention, however, was

la signoria vostra como credo occupata la mente sua in più e più diverse cose. Pur me parso di fare qualche aviso ala prelibata signoria vostra se voglia dignare di farmi ancho adoperare in qualche cosa como quelo chi sono sempre alevato e praticato ne le corte et operato in più cose e maxime nel cantare. Nam ho trovato uno compagno bono cantore chiamato Lanceloto dala Croce, zentilhomo e da bene loquale et io siamo quasi de una etate et bene conformi ne la nostro cantare e forsi, e senza forsi farissimo vergogna a li giovani como essendo ala prova assai se cognoscere. Anchora venendo de li francesi como credo vegnerano haverano ad intendere et cognoscere in lombardia essere chi saperano così ben cantare cantione de li loro linguagi como loro e meglio. La signoria vostra è molto bene informata et sa assai de quante virtute me ha dotato l'altrissimo dio. E pero non me voglia dimenticare in questa festa ch'io li faro honore.'

35 Motta, 'Musici alla corte', pp. 299–300.
36 *Ibid.*, pp. 529–32.
37 *Ibid.*, p. 298.
38 For the inventory of Galeazzo Maria's books see E. Pellegrin, *La bibliothèque des Visconti et des Sforza, ducs de Milan, au XVe siècle* (Paris, 1955), pp. 328–52.
39 On this period see Welch, 'Secular Fresco Painting', chapter 4 and the associated documentary appendix.

focused on the reorganisation of his personal retinue, which quad-rupled in the 1470s. But it was still another year before music came to the fore. With their experience of the Neapolitan royal chapel, Raynerio and Antonio Ponzo might have been expected to be influential in convincing Galeazzo Maria that such regal aspira-tions required regal music. But in late 1470 there was still no suggestion of a court choir and sacred music was not yet a priority. When, after an aborted attempt to travel to either France[40] or Rome, the young duke and his wife proceeded to Florence under the guise of a vow to Ss Annunziata, they took a small number of singers. Passing through Emilia Romagna and Tuscany the ret-inue, numbering in the hundreds, awed the locals with their lavish gold and silver brocades.[41] Although a substantial group of trum-peters was used on the trip, there were only four unnamed *cantori*, the same number recorded in Francesco Sforza's court, suggesting that early efforts to locate musicians had been limited.[42] Indeed the list of participants in the abortive French trip hints that it may have been difficult to muster even these four. While every other court position was filled, the spaces for singers on the administra-tive lists included only Raynerio's name, leaving blank lines for his, as yet unknown, companions.[43] Thus even if the duke had had long-term plans for a major chapel, he had still not acted upon them.

When he did, however, the innovations were startling in their scope. Between 1471 and 1472, the choir of four became one of almost thirty. This decision, as Lewis Lockwood has pointed out, was taken at the same time as the Duke of Ferrara, Ercole d'Este, put his plans for a new court chapel into motion. It is unlikely, if

[40] Documents from early 1471 suggest that the first plan was to visit the King of France; Milan, Archivio di Stato, Missive 95.

[41] On the Florentine trip see R. Fubini, 'In margine all'edizione delle "Lettere" di Lorenzo de' Medici: la visita a Firenze del Duca di Milano nel 1471', *Lorenzo de' Medici: studi*, ed. G. C. Garfagnini (Florence, 1992), pp. 168–77.

[42] Milan, Archivio di Stato, Carteggio Sforzesco 898: 'Lista de l'andata del nostro illustris-simo signore a Fiorenza facta adi xxi zenaro 1471'. The document lists approximately 166 individuals including two *magistri da balla*, a jeweller, and four *cantori*, six *piffari* and twenty *trombetti*. When the Florentine trip was finalised further disaster struck, as Galeazzo Maria had thrown his own *piffari* and *tromboni* in prison and was reduced to borrowing the Marquis of Mantua's players for the occasion. See Motta, 'Musici alla corte', p. 47.

[43] Paris, Bibliothèque Nationale, ital. 1592, fol. 52. The list recorded the same number of six *piffari* and twenty *trombetti* as the documents concerning the trip to Florence.

not impossible, that having made no move to establish sacred music within his court for over five years, Galeazzo Maria chose purely by coincidence to establish a chapel just before Ercole began recruiting singers himself. Milanese soldiers and informants had been camped on the Mantuan borders during the period of the Ferrarese succession, and although no documentation survives, Sforza spies within the Este court may well have reported on the new musical plans. But while the connection is clear, the relationship between the two initiatives may be more complex than straightforward competition. As a mature, internationally respected figure, Ercole gave licence to the younger, much less well-established Galeazzo Maria. With the nascent Ferrarese choir as his example, the Duke of Milan could follow his own instincts and transfer music from the traditional category of court entertainment to the realm of a serious state interest; *cose da piacere* could now become *cose di stato*.

The Milanese chapel's establishment was closely connected to other changes underway in the Sforza court. Many events once reserved for semi-private enjoyment had become increasingly public in their presentation and importance. The large-scale performance of sacred and secular music at the Milanese court joined a series of new ceremonies already underway, such as the processions of the feast of St George and the Christmas ceremony of the Yule Log. These annual festivals and other celebratory events such as baptisms and betrothals were designed to ensure that independent vassals and difficult members of the Lombard aristocracy would be drawn to the Sforza centres of Pavia and Milan.[44] After 1469 feudatories had to attend Galeazzo Maria's court on major feast days such as Christmas and Easter in order to maintain their standing and privileges. Foreign dignitaries and ambassadors would also be invited to attend. In this way each group would, despite the Sforza dynasty's lack of legal title to the duchy of Milan, ritually acknowledge the family's standing. It was, indeed, just this imposition in Christmas 1476 which provided the chance for Galeazzo Maria's assassination.

The duke was murdered while attending mass but piety, the traditional formula for expressing an interest in sacred music,

[44]   G. Lubkin, 'Christmas at the Court of Milan: 1466–1476', *Florence and Milan: Comparisons and Relations* (Florence, 1989), pp. 257–70.

played a relatively small role on these occasions. Galeazzo Maria was perfectly aware of the need to appear in the guise of a Christian prince, founding at least one monastery and several chapels. Nevertheless, the language of secular pleasure dominated discussions concerning the new choir. When writing to the Bishop of Novara on 29 January 1473, for example, he made the association clear: chapels were being founded because song gave him more delight than any other pleasure.[45] Like Ercole d'Este and the King of Naples, the Duke of Milan would be regularly observed while attending mass. But in following and improving on these examples, he could enjoy what was otherwise a tedious state duty.

To those close to the court, this attitude lacked decorum. In describing the duke's newly acquired habit of listening to Lenten preachers, the Mantuan ambassador could barely restrain himself:

This time I have little to write to your lordship as I have not heard anything new from any side. This illustrious lord [Galeazzo Maria Sforza] attends to his confessions and sermons. He has arranged for preaching in the castle every day since Sunday; he calls for preachers, now one, now another, from those who are preaching in this land and has had many new confessors come. And, during one sermon, he spoke with me and asked me whether your lordship would confess and take communion this Easter. I replied, yes, and that it was your custom to take communion at Easter. He then asked me if you would leave off women this time. I replied no, because as you had none there were none to leave off. His lordship laughed and said, 'the Marquis [Ludovico Gonzaga] has many more sins than I do . . . Undoubtedly I am a bit pompous, but that is no great sin in a lord. I am not proud. I have only the sin of sensuality [luxuria], and that I have in all perfection. I have adopted it in all the types and forms that one can have, but I have no other sins, certainly I have few.' My lord, if I had had the authority I would have hit His Excellency for having made me such an appalling confession.[46]

---

[45] Motta, 'Musici alla corte', p. 310: 'Havendo nuy d'alcuni tempi in quà pigliato delectione de musica et de canto più che de veruno altro piacere, havemo dato opera de havere cantori per fare una capella, et fin da mò havemo conducto bon numero de cantori ultramontani et da diversi paesi et cominzata una celebre et digna capella.'

[46] Mantua, Archivio di Stato, Archivio Gonzaga, busta 1624, 15 April 1473; Zacharia da Pisa to Ludovico Gonzaga: 'Questa volta io non ho che scrivere a vostra signoria per non intendersi alchuna cosa di nuova d'alchun canto. Questo ill.mo signore attende a le confessione e ale prediche. Fa predichare in castello ogni dì da domenicha in qua e fa venire quando uno predicatore e quando un'altro di questi che predicano in questa terra e fa venire molti confessori nuovi. E rasonando meco, stando ala predica, me adimandoe se vostra signoria si confesseva e comunicheria questa pasqua. Lo dissi che sì, e che l'era sua usanza di comunicarsi ala pasqua, quale me adimandoe se la lasseria star le femine questa volta. Io respuosi che non per che non gli accade hauerle lassare non havendo ne alchuna. Sua signoria rise e disse "il Marchese ha molto più peccati

Galeazzo Maria's attitude that pomp was no sin in a great lord reached its logical conclusion in his court chapel. No effort and little expense were spared on its recruitment and construction. On 15 October 1471, six months after his return from Florence and two months after he got back from an extended hunting trip in the *montavano*, the duke wrote to King Edward of England explaining that Raynerio 'musico nostro' and his courtier Aloysio would be arriving to search out new singers.[47] Near-death in November did not lessen his determination, nor did it slow down his incessant acquisition of other Italian rulers' musicians.[48] Although Galeazzo Maria continued to seek musicians from Naples, Savoy, closer and more vulnerable to Sforza pressure, quickly became his favourite poaching ground. A close connection between the Savoyard chapel and its new Milanese counterpart can be demonstrated in a variety of ways. In December 1471 he asked Yolanda of Savoy to send her entire choir to meet him in Novara, a request repeated on two occasions the following year when he specified she need send only the 'adult singers and not the little ones'.[49] That same year he acquired the duchess's choirmaster, the tenor Antonio Guinati, and made the well-known request for the song 'Robineto notato su l'ayre de Rosabella'.[50] Yolanda's irritation at this auditioning at her expense is clear from her comments two years later that, while she did not blame the duke, her singers had left her without licence and were required to return.[51] This did not, however, stop Galeazzo Maria from demanding the loan of her organ-maker in 1474.[52]

The continual search for singers from 1471 until 1476 is extens-

---

de mi. Certo, certo che peccati ho io, ne ho pochissimi. Io non ho de l'altrue ne meglio quello di persona. Indebitamente sonno pomposo un pocho, non è gran peccato in un signore. Non sonno superbo. Io ho solamente il peccato de la luxuria e quello ho in tuta perfectione. Perchè lo ho adaptato in tutti quelli modi e forme chesi posse fare, siché altri peccati non ho io. Certo ne ho pochi." Signore mio, se io havessi havuta l'autorita io haveva assolto sua excellentia havendomi fato cosi capelleta confessione.'

[47] Motta, 'Musici alla corte', p. 301.
[48] On Galeazzo Maria's near-death and will see G. Lubkin and S. Eiche, 'The Mausoleum Plan of Galeazzo Maria Sforza', *Mitteilungen des Kunsthistorischen Institutes in Florenz*, 32 (1988), pp. 547–53.
[49] Motta, 'Musici alla corte', p. 302: 'li cantori grandi et non li picolini'.
[50] On the Savoyard chapel see M. T. Bouquet, 'La cappella musicale dei duchi di Savoia, dal 1450 al 1500', *Rivista Italiana di Musicologia*, 3 (1968), pp. 233–85 and 'La cappella musicale dei duchi di Savoia', *Rivista Italiana di Musicologia*, 5 (1970), pp. 3–36. On 'Rosabella' see N. Pirrotta, 'Ricercare e variazioni su *O rosa bella*', *Musica tra Medioevo e Rinascimento* (Turin, 1984), pp. 195–212.
[51] Motta, 'Musici alla corte', p. 303.
[52] *Ibid.*, p. 290.

ively documented in the magisterial nineteenth-century study of Emilio Motta. Galeazzo Maria scooped up the available musicians within Milan itself, and by promising high wages threatened the stability of the Aragonese and Estense choirs. Italy alone could not provide the necessary talent. France was a favourite source, and in 1472 and again in 1473 Gaspar van Weerbeke returned to his native Flanders to preach the benefits of a move to Milan. Galeazzo Maria's broadcasting of the fact that he wished, as he put it, to 'breathe new life into music in Italy' (*suscitare la musica in Italia*) by establishing chapels throughout his dominions had rapid effects. Even rulers and ambassadors who had not had the privilege of listening to his choir remarked upon it. It quickly became public knowledge that the introduction of a good singer or a piece of music would ensure Galeazzo Maria's gratitude.[53] The Mantuan ambassador, Zaccaria da Pisa, acted as an informal adviser and procurement officer; ecclesiastics like the Bishop of Como, Branda Castiglione, began recommending artists. In introducing the French singer Tomaso Leporis, the bishop, a close political ally of the Sforza, was careful to flatter the duke, noting that 'every day the news that your lordship wishes to found a notable and worthy chapel is spreading'.[54]

The result was that by 1474 Galeazzo Maria's choir contained, on either full or temporary contracts, some of the most renowned names of music history, including Loyset Compère, Josquin Desprez, Alexander Agricola and Jean Cordier. Motta published several lists of these singers to which a further document from the end of Galeazzo Maria's lifetime can now be added. The lists were not, however, originally compiled for musicological purposes. The rapidly increasing court required a large chancery, and these papers formed an integral part of the Sforza court's financial and administrative bureaucracy. The 1474 register of singers, for example, was included in Cicco Simonetta's notebooks as one of many documents concerning the court's expansion and related

---

[53] In 1473 Galeazzo Maria was sent the order of King Alfonso's victory mass which was carefully recorded in Cicco Simonetta's diary. See A. Natale, ed., *I diarii di Cicco Simonetta* (Milan, 1962), pp. 16–17. In 1474 Alexander Agricola wrote to recommend the compositions of a German organist in Ferrara, Bernardo Todesco. See Sartori, 'Organs, Organ Builders', p. 64 and Lockwood, 'Strategies of Music Patronage', p. 236.

[54] Motta, 'Musici alla corte', p. 305: 'divulgandose ogni dì più la fama che v. s. vole fare una notabile et degnissima Cappella'.

salary payments.[55] Lists of singers from 1475 have been extracted from the names of ducal householders who were given special outfits for the feast of St George and from other salary records.[56] The last, previously unpublished, list of 1476, which includes thirty-three singers and three organists, is a register of those members of the court who would receive stabling when they travelled with the duke in 1476 (see Appendix).

Removing this information from its bureaucratic context disguises the fact that the information was rarely exclusively concerned with either music or the chapel itself. The singers formed part of a much larger vision of court spectacle, whereby sound, vision and ceremonial reverence combined to ensure both the duke's private pleasure and dramatic public performances. Singling out singers' names does a disservice to an understanding of this more general role and conceals the fact that Galeazzo Maria's decision to expand his choir did not take place in isolation. In 1472–3 Galeazzo Maria embarked on an unprecedented expansion of all of his courtiers. Just as Weerbeke was sent out to find additional tenors and sopranos in Flanders, so too did other officials leave Milan for their homelands to encourage their compatriots to move to the Sforza court. In October 1472, for example, one of the duke's under-chamberlains arrived from Naples with twelve young Neapolitans to serve as *camerieri del signore*.[57] Young men of good family, preferably tall and good-looking, were sought in Cremona, Bologna, Piacenza and Milan itself. This was not just a display of luxurious indulgence. Lacking a legitimate title, Galeazzo Maria hoped to integrate potential opponents into his court, and considerable political skill went into the choice of new courtiers. Despite the financial strains which had imposed cut-backs the previous year, the 1476 list of those 'appointed to follow the court of our illustrious prince and excellent signore to whom accommodation must be given' suggests that Galeazzo Maria's retinue must have been remarkably impressive.[58]

[55] Natale, *I diarii*, pp. 128–9.
[56] G. Porro, 'Lettere di Galeazzo Maria Sforza, duca di Milano', *Archivio Storico Lombardo*, 5 (1878), p. 27.
[57] On this expansion see Lubkin, 'The Court of Galeazzo Maria'.
[58] On the financial burden the court expansion imposed see F. Leverotti, 'Scritture finanziarie dell'età sforzesca', *Squarci d'Archivio sforzesco* (Como, 1981), pp. 121–37 and 'La crisi finanziaria del ducato di Milano alla fine del Quattrocento', *Milano nell'età di Ludovico il Moro* (Milan, 1983), pp. 585–632.

Even this document, however, represents only a small fraction of those with court connections. In order to save money, many courtiers were non-resident. The travelling court, therefore, consisted of those members whose presence was considered worth paying for. Putting the singers into context the document reveals that Galeazzo Maria moved with ten professional hand-ball players, five barbers, forty dog-handlers and thirty staff to supervise the hunts and the hawks. His summary of expenses for the year in question indicates that the same sum, 5000 ducats, was spent on both his singers and his dog-handlers.[59] The list's compilers were quite straightforward in their assessment of an individual's worth, measuring status purely in terms of the number of horses he was permitted to stable at ducal expense. Thus the duke's younger brothers were each allowed thirty-two, while the most senior *cameriere da camera*, Francesco de Petrasanta, had to make do with twelve. The leading *cameriere da guardacamera*, Giovanni Francesco Pallavicino, and the singer Pietro da Holi or Daule were permitted four horses each; the under-chamberlains had no allowance at all. This document suggests that Daule's standing surpassed that of his fellow singers, who were paired according to criteria which are still unclear and given a mutual stabling allowance. Even Jean Cordier, the most highly paid member of the choir, was expected to share seven horses with a singer named Rolando, while the choir leader, Antonio Guinati, and his friend Bovis had four horses between them. The most famous composer of Galeazzo Maria's chapel, Josquin Desprez, did particularly badly, sharing a single pair of horses with Michael of Tours. Scholars have correctly noted that, as singers often relied on benefices, Josquin's low salary did not necessarily indicate a lower estimation of his talents.[60] But in this impartial indicator, Josquin was still down at the bottom of the list at a time when he was already producing music for the court.[61]

Instead it was Pietro Daule and Antonio Guinati, now relatively

[59] G. Porro, 'Preventivo delle spese pel ducato di Milano nel 1476', *Archivio Storico Lombardo*, 5 (1878), pp. 130–4.

[60] E. Lowinsky, 'Ascanio Sforza's Life', p. 37. On Josquin in Milan see also C. Sartori, 'Josquin des Pres, cantore del duomo di Milano, 1459–1472', *Annales Musicologiques*, 4 (1956), pp. 55–83.

[61] In 1475 Josquin was given 20 quinterns of paper 'per un libro ch'esso ha da fare per la nostra capella'. See Porro, 'Lettere di Galeazzo Maria', p. 251. It is perhaps significant that when Ercole was considering singers from the Milanese chapel after Galeazzo

unknown, who prospered. Although the former's position in 1476 as *cameriere da guardacamera* represents a demotion it is still superior to that of most other members of the court. Four years earlier, as a *cameriere da camera* – one of the duke's inner circle of associates – he had been even more elevated. A list of expensive garments given to the twenty-two chamberlains in 1472 carefully noted his dual status as courtier and musician. While the other *camerieri da camera* were given half-length gold brocade garments, Pietro Daule received 'A long gown of smooth red velvet, lined with fox fur . . . which should be made in the French fashion, and five tunics of smooth crimson velvet also in the French style, and these are in addition to the garments which he has been given along with the other singers'.[62]

Guinati, usually referred to as L'Abbé, was never given a courtier's status but, as choirmaster, wielded considerable power. His voice obviously pleased the duke, for when Galeazzo Maria made his request for the 'Robineto/Rosabella' combination he specified that the words should be those normally used by Guinati.[63] Guinati's organisational skills were also at a premium.[64] He did not always join the choir when the duke demanded its presence, but he was responsible for selecting and sending the required singers.[65] With a degree in law, and a long history of service in the Savoyard chapel, Guinati was able to take advantage of the wealth and patronage his position offered.[66] His brother, originally a bombardier (he continued to offer advice on canonry to Galeazzo Maria), soon

Maria's death he specifed that the recruits were to have no stabling rights. See Lockwood, 'Strategies of Music Patronage', p. 246.

[62] Milan, Archivio di Stato, Carteggio Sforzesco 909; Pietro da Oli: 'Turcha de veluto piano morello longa et fodrata de volpe quam per fille de martore laqual sia facto alo foza franzosa et zuppone de veluto piano cremexino similiter ala franzose et aqueste oltre le altre vestimente gli hano esse facto como ali altri cantatori.' He had also profited in the initial years from the fief of Morbio near Como in 1473, and houses in Como and in Milan. In 1475 he still enjoyed a superior status to the other singers receiving, like most of the duke's favoured courtiers, a monthly stabling allowance for three horses. The only other singers awarded this privilege were Jean Cordier and Antonio Guinati, who were allowed two horses apiece. See C. Morbio, *Storie dei municipi italiani illustrate con documenti inediti*, vi: *Codice visconteo-sforzesco* (Milan, 1846), p. 442.

[63] Motta, 'Musici alla corte', p. 303: 'havendo bona advertentia ad fargli mettere quelle parole medesime dice el prefato Abbate quanto canta Robineto'.

[64] On Guinati's role in Yolanda of Savoy's choir see Bouquet, 'La cappella musicale' (1968), p. 281.

[65] It was Guinati, for example, who was told to organise a prospective trip to Rome in 1474. See Motta, 'Musici alla corte', p. 316.

[66] *Ibid.*, pp. 515–18.

joined the choir and he also was able to bring at least one close associate from Savoy, Pietro Alardi, known as Bovis.[67] The latter had been an important member of Yolanda's choir and was heavily promoted at the expense of earlier arrivals.[68] As Guinati and Bovis's powers increased the two singers who had arrived from Naples in 1469 felt particularly hard done by. In 1473 Raynerio, whose comparatively low salary had been stopped, sent three Spanish songs, 'scripti et notati', to the duke, complaining that malicious tongues, particularly those of the choirmaster and Bovis, had been working against him. The letter, published by Motta in 1887, is worth republishing in full both for its evidence of Galeazzo Maria's continued fascination with secular music and for the details of the choir's internal intrigues:

Along with the present letter, I am sending you three Spanish songs which I am sure will be good and sweet. If you enjoy them I will send you others, and if there if you find anything lacking or faulty in the said songs, your excellency should not blame me, who have written and notated them. Have them sung sweetly, *sotto voce* and slowly, then I am sure they will please you.

I should also advise your illustrious lordship that I am very badly out of pocket. I do not have a penny to spend and I find myself with debts; I have no means of satisfying and paying my creditors if not through your help. My debts amount to about 46 ducats. And I have to satisfy them at all costs by the feast of St Martin next November. I wish to appear a man of worth, my lord, and to pay that which I owe and to maintain faith and credit as any worthy man should do, so that your lordship need not be ashamed of my deeds. Only one thing saddens me greatly, my lord, for after the many pleasures and services which I have done for master l'Abbé [Guinati] and master Bovis, they wish at present to do me harm in return for this goodness. Praise God and let his will be done in all. Our Lord God forgive them, for they have no excuse. But I am certain and have no doubt that our Lord God is just and patient and will show the truth in all things. The evil tongues have done me enough harm, and I am certain that they have had my provision taken away, and they do nothing every day with your lordship but assault your ears with evil tales of me . . . God forgive them, for certainly, my lord, it is not the act of a virtuous and good man to speak badly of anyone. But I am comforted by one fact, that they and I have a good schoolteacher. When one thinks well, illustrious lord, there has never been a time when envy has not reigned among equals. If we all had the intellect and understanding to know our common good, we would live together honestly as

[67] *Ibid.*, pp. 528–9.
[68] On Bovis see Bouquet, 'La cappella musicale' (1968), p. 255.

good men, and eat the bread of your lordship in peace and with happiness. But it seems to me that we go seeking more bread than grain; I believe that when we have looked everywhere, we will not find any bread more flavoursome than that of your lordship. But this cursed envy destroys everything.

I do not believe, nor can I believe, that master l'Abbé and master Bovis could be so cruel and iniquitous against me, that they wish to kill me in this way. I would sooner have the fever for an entire year, than have even thought of doing them the smallest displeasure, even to the lowest of their servants. And if I have offended them in some way I humbly ask for a good pardon, and if I have failed in some way I offer myself up to any reproof which would please them and, please God, to your lordship to whom I humbly and continually commend myself.[69]

With this fascinating description of the in-fighting taking place

---

[69] Motta, 'Musici alla corte', pp. 530–1: 'Io vi mando tre canti spagnoli in nela presente interclusi, li quali certamente credo serani boni et dolci. Se ve piacerano ve ne mandarò deli altri, et si alcuno mancamento et discorectione se trovasse in dicti canti, vostra excellentia non lo voglia imputare a me che li ho scripti et notati; faciateli cantare dolcemente et sotto voce, et ben pianamente, che son certo ve piacerano.
Insuper avisando vostra Ill.ma signoria che sto molto male de la borsa che non ho un denaro ad spendere et si me ritrovo con debiti, et si non cho lo modo de satisffare et pagare alo presente ali mey creditori si non mediante lo soccurso vostro; ho de debiti circa quaranta e sei ducati in tutto. E necessario che li paghi in omni modo a questa festa di San Martino che serà quisto novembre prossimo che vene. Voglio parere homo da bene, Ill.mo signore, satisfare et pagare a chi deve havere da me et conservare la fede et lo credito, como ogni uno da bene deve fare, et etiamdio acciò che la signoria vostra non habia reprehensione da li facti mey. De una cosa me condole molto Ill.mo signore de tanti piaceri et serviti che ho facti a messer l'abbè et a messere Bovis, et che alo presente me voleno rendere mal per bene. Laux deo et fiat voluntas sua in omnibus, nostro signore dio le voglie perdonare, che non hanno ragione. Ma son certo et non dubito niente che nostro signore Dio è iusto e paziente, et si fa la verita in ogni cosa. Le male lengue me hanno facto delo male assay, che so certamente me hano facto levare la mia provisione, et non fano altro ogni dì con la signoria vostra, si non martellare et boffare in le orecchie vostre et dire mal de my, et del segondo et del terzo: dio le vogle perdonare che certamente signore non hè acto de homo virtuoso et da bene de dire mal de nesuno. Ma di una cosa me conforto, che my e loro habiamo da fare con un bon maestro de scola: quando penso ben ill.mo signore non fo may ne sarà che inter pares non regnasset invidia. Si nuy tutti havessimo intellecto et discretione da cognoscere lo nostro ben commune, viveriamo honestamente come homini da bene, et mangiariamo lo pane de la vostra signoria in pace et con allegressa, ma me pare andamo cercando mello pano che de grano: credo che quando haveremo ben cercato per tutto, non ne trovaremo pane più saporito che quello de la signoria vostra. Ma questa maledecta invidia guasta ogni cosa. Io non credo pur ne possa credere signore che messere l'Abbà et messer Bovis siano tanti crudeli ne iniqui verso da me, che me volesseno così amassare: più presto voria havere la febre per tutto un anno, che havere solamente pensato de lor fare uno minimo despiacere, ne al minimo de la loro compagnia. Et si pur li havessi offensati in cose alcune, io le demande humilmente bona perdonanza, et si ho fallato in cosa alcuna me offero ad ogni correctione che piacerà a loro et etiam dio ala signoria vostra ala quale humilmente et de continuo me ricomando. Papie iii Julii 1473. De vostra illustrissima signoria humile et obediente servitore che in gratia de a quella humilmente se ricomanda Rainero cantarino.'

in the Milanese choir, Raynerio's letter suggests that the struggle for position and prominence was as acute among the musicians as it was among other gentlemen of the court. While Weerbeke and Tomaso Leporis may have had the tasks of selecting singers from abroad, Guinati and his Savoyard compatriots controlled their promotion in Milan. Along with Pietro Daule, their access to the duke and his duchess (who was, of course, originally from Savoy herself) gave them considerable powers.[70] Guinati personally benefited from Milanese citizenship, two houses in Milan, water rights (which he sublet to another singer) and an extraordinary three-year concession for the exploitation of the duchy's mineral rights.[71] These were the rewards for personally supervising both the singers and the preparation of Galeazzo Maria's secular and sacred choir manuscripts. This may have involved the purchase of choirbooks for the duke's new observant monastery of S. Maria degli Angeli outside Abbiategrasso[72] and certainly included the 1472 acquisition of four volumes of French and Spanish songs (which cost 40 ducats in total) and a songbook which Pietro Daule had personally purchased from the Duchess of Savoy.[73] Another undated note from around the same time reveals that at least some of these items were being manufactured for Galeazzo Maria's private chamber: 'libro uno de canzone spagnole et franzose per tenire in camera'.[74]

While the expansion of sacred music had clearly not diminished

---

[70] The problems caused by the demand for patronage and secure income for singers was not just reserved for religious benefices as this letter reveals: Paris, Bibliothèque Nationale, ital. 1585, fol. 178; Supplica to Galeazzo Maria: 'Illustrissimo Signore. Havendo la vostra i.s. per sua gratia concesso al vostro fidelissimo servito magistro Antonio de lombardi franxoxo la cura del relogio del campanile de sancto Gotardo de Milano et expedire le lettere opportune pare che la prefata v.i.s. ad contemplatione de li vostri cantori quali postponeno la utilitate et honore de v.i.s. e risguardando ali suoy apetiti o liciti o inliciti voglia revocare decte lettere et concedere la dicta cura ad uno Antonio Balbo quale non ha afare comparatione de sufficientia con esso magistro Antonio franxoso.'

[71] Motta, 'Musici alla corte', pp. 516–17. He quickly took advantage of these rights, and it is tempting to think that his brother's metallurgic skills were put to use.

[72] The books are listed in Natale, *I diarii*, p. 19.

[73] C. d'Adda, *Libreria viscontea et sforzesca del Castello di Pavia* (Milan, 1875), p. 134: 'Spexa de contanti per il paramenti de la Cappella del nostro Ill.mo Signore. 1472: Per libri iiii da canzone Franzese et Spagnole ... d. 40. Item per lo libro mandato a tore d. Petro da Oli da la Ill. ma Madama de Savoya secundo il mercato ha dicto domino Petro ... d. 40'.

[74] *Ibid.*, p. 128. That Galeazzo Maria had some ability to understand Spanish as well as French may be indicated by his request for 'un libro che tracta delle cazze in lingua spagnola' in 1469. See d'Adda, *Libreria viscontea*, appendix, p. 57.

Galeazzo Maria's interest in the chanson, Guinati's main concern in 1472 and 1473 revolved around the new chapel being constructed in the duke's Milanese residence, the Castello di Porta Giovia. The choirmaster was responsible for providing cloth for the priests' robes, lecterns and four extremely expensive Graduals.[75] From the documentation it emerges that the lettering was done 'ala parexina' and that each book had an illuminated frontispiece and elaborate bindings. Although none of the Graduals survive, two other sumptuous religious texts from the same period, the 'Great Hours of Galeazzo Maria Sforza'[76] and an Italian New Testament,[77] indicate the scale of investment involved in these commissions. With gilt borders, and two large-scale miniatures on almost every page by the painter Cristoforo dei Predis, the latter was a highly prized object. It is impossible to determine the extent of Guinati's responsibility for any of the artistic decisions concerning the chapel and its furnishings. In March 1473 he purchased a *pace*, the image kissed during the mass, and made arrangements for its redesign. The metal plate would be incised with a scene of the Resurrection, the theme that dominated the frescoed chapel ceiling.[78]

In this instance, Guinati may have been passing on ducal instructions, rather than acting independently. Artistic and architectural matters were generally the jealously guarded province of the supervisor of ducal works, another ex-bombardier, Bartolomeo Gadio da Cremona, who with his colleague, the Florentine architect Benedetto Ferrini, produced three new palace chapels in Pavia and Milan between 1469 and 1473. How Galeazzo Maria was seen listening to the music seems to have been as important as what he

---

[75] *Ibid.*, p. 133.
[76] *The Astor Collection of Illuminated Manuscripts*, Sotheby's sale catalogue, 21 June 1988, pp. 48–54.
[77] *Il codice Varia 124 della Biblioteca Reale di Torino miniato da Cristoforo de Predis (Milan, 1476)*, ed. A. Vitale-Brovarone (Turin, 1987).
[78] Milan, Archivio di Stato, Autografi 231, fasc. 4, 3 March 1473; Francesco Pagano to Galeazzo Maria Sforza: 'Hogi me ha ritrovato l'Abé cantore per parte de la illustrissima signoria vostra el quale ma dito che gli dia per parte di quella prelibata ducati 80 per pagamento de una pace quale dice ha veduta vostra excellentia et cossi me he dato dicta pace quammodo che io gli facesse lo resurrectto secondo il dissegno quale ha veduto vostra celsitudine. Illustrissimo signore, me son miravegliato parendome non habia inteso e non di mancho ho tolta la suprascripta pace del modo del denaro ne specta a me ne gli ho modo. Prego vostra illustrissima signore me avisa quanto ho affare sopra zio. Vero è che 'l merchato è bono.'

heard. The Visconti castle in Pavia already had a large double-vaulted chapel on the ground floor. In 1469, however, during an extensive scheme of redecoration, the duke took the opportunity to designate the single-vaulted room which led from the great hall into his private apartments (a space which had previously served as his father's courtiers' dining-room) as a second chapel, the *cappella di camera*.[79] Only the *camerieri da camera* had permission to enter the ducal suite regularly, and the physical distinction between the upper and lower chapels, mirrored in the later construction in Milan, may have contributed to the division of Sforza singers into *cantori di cappella* and *cantori di camera*.[80]

The transformations in the Milanese and Pavian chapels were not designed to offer fine acoustics. They were undertaken to ensure that the visual impact of Galeazzo Maria's choir was as splendid as its sound. Signorial magnificence would touch both senses simultaneously. By 1471 Galeazzo Maria had decided to place an elaborate carved polyptych housing the Visconti's most precious sacred relics in the upper chapel at Pavia. The sum of 2000 ducats was assigned to complete the work, half of which was taken up by the carved woodwork. Three of Milan's most prominent painters – Vincenzo Foppa, Bonifacio Bembo and the portraitist Zanetto Bugatto – were given the commission to paint 200 saints on the doors, a job which occupied their attention from 1473 to 1476. During that period Galeazzo Maria was equally preoccupied with his Milanese chapels. The architects had just finished work on a second chapel in the Sforza castle and were already planning a third for the newly extended south wing. The most important of these was, once again, that sited on the *piano nobile* leading into the duke's private apartments. The use of a chapel as an entry point into a signorial suite was not Galeazzo Maria's innovation. He himself had been received by Cosimo de' Medici in the as yet unfrescoed palace chapel of Via Larga in 1459.[81] But he had noted how unsuitable the small private space was for large crowds and how quickly the group had had to vacate the room. He would not

---

[79] Welch, 'Galeazzo Maria Sforza', pp. 352–74.

[80] The notion that this was a social division as much as a practical one is reinforced by the fact that the dog-handlers were also divided into *canateri da camera* and other ranks on the 1476 list.

[81] R. Hatfield, 'Cosimo de' Medici and the Chapel of his Palace', *Cosimo 'il Vecchio' de' Medici, 1389–1464*, ed. F. Ames-Lewis (Oxford, 1991), pp. 221–44.

repeat the mistake. His new chapels were dramatically enlarged. Unlike their Medici or Montefeltro counterparts, these Milanese rooms were not spaces for private prayer and contemplation but areas of public performance. Even when the throngs invited for special feasts could not get into the lower chapel they could watch from the adjacent *camera delle columbine* (so called because of the dove motif with which it was decorated) through a large grated window.[82]

This chapel still survives today and gives some impression of the effect the duke intended to convey. Its lower walls, now left bare, were probably covered in tapestries or brocade. The upper section is still covered with large figures of saints standing against a background of raised gold gesso. The lunettes carried an image of the Annunciation along with Galeazzo Maria's arms, monograms and *imprese*, while the ceiling, completed by the artist Stefano dei Fedelis, was filled with two separate scenes from the Resurrection. More than four artists were involved in the decoration, which had to be done rapidly and to a tight budget. Nonetheless, the lavish use of azure and gold tends to blur the stylistic distinctions, creating an overall sense of grandeur at a reasonable cost.[83]

The Milanese castle's upper chapel, which led into Galeazzo Maria's private suite, has disappeared. The documentation suggests that access to this space was more restricted, and that the room was split by a *tramezzo* wall, a pattern the ducal supervisor of works suggested should be imitated in Pavia using a 'transverse wall like that in Milan with a door in the centre and a window on each side, through which those in the chapel might be able to follow the Mass and also see the altarpiece'.[84] A door connected the chapel to the bedroom used by either the duke or his most distinguished guests. It was particularly appropriate that its first occupant after the chapel's completion was Cardinal Pietro Riario, the nephew of the other great fifteenth-century musical patron, Pope Sixtus IV. On 12 September 1473 the Mantuan ambassador, Zaccaria da Pisa, gave a full description of the visit:

In the castle courtyard all the trumpets of his lordship were arrayed, and

---

[82]   G. Marangoni, 'La cappella di Galeazzo Maria nel castello sforzesco', *Bollettino d'Arte*, 1 (1921), p. 176.

[83]   On the chapel's decoration see Welch, 'Secular Fresco Painting', pp. 180–4.

[84]   C. Ffoulkes and R. Maiocchi, *Vincenzo Foppa* (London, 1904), p. 94.

playing they accompanied him inside; they went up on horseback to the hall where, dismounting, they went towards the rooms where your lordship had stayed. At the head of this hall there was a chapel, newly built above the other one below. Gathered here were all the chapel singers [cantori di cappella], who immediately began singing the *Te Deum laudamus*. The chapel was completely adorned with brocade cloths, and the ceiling above was painted, the altar in the middle with the usual ornaments and so too the rest of the ornaments of the chapel. From this chapel one enters the room where your lordship had stayed without returning to the hall since at the side of the chapel, to the left, a double door has been built which serves as two exits. One leads into the above-mentioned room, the other into another room on the left which is above our lord's room below – the one which is panelled . . . They are all beautifully decorated and in his [Pietro Riario's] there is a set of white-gold brocade hangings and the walls around are covered with tapestries as are all the rest of the rooms.[85]

Riario was undoubtedly impressed by both the visual and aural wealth displayed for his benefit. His own ninety-three-strong retinue included two musicians, and some of his time in Pavia was spent admiring and listening to the instruments of the famed organmaker Isaac Argyropoulos.[86] It is again undoubtedly no coincidence that Galeazzo Maria put on a dramatic presentation of choral skill in the same year that Sixtus IV began recruiting singers for the Sistine chapel. Indeed, the duke hoped to take his choir to Rome the following year to impress Della Rovere personally. But

[85] Mantua, Archivio di Stato, Archivio Gonzaga, busta 1624, 12 September 1473; Zaccaria da Pisa to Ludovico Gonzaga: 'Io so in quanta expectatione sta la vostra signoria per intendere del giongere qui del reverendissimo Monsignore Cardinal di San Sisto . . . si gionse ala piazza del castello, erano apparechiati tutti li trombetti del signore e sonando fui acompagnato in castello . . . e montati sopra la terraza così a cavallo se andoe suso in sala ove smontati se aviarono verso la camera dove allogioe vostra signoria. E prima in capo dela sala era una capella, fatta di nuovo, sopra a quella che è di sotto nela quale erano tutti li cantori di cappella, li quali tutta via cantavano Te Deum Laudamus. La capella era tutta adornata de panni di razzo, el cielo di sopra depincto, l'altare in mezo con gli ornamenti usati e così tutto il resto del ornamento d'essa capella per la quale si entra nella camera dove allogiava vostra signoria senza entrare altramente nella sala perchè nel canton dela capella a man sinistra è fatto una bussola la qual serve a duy ussi deli quali l'uno entra in detta camera e l'altro ne l'altra camera de mano sinistra la quale è sopra ala camera del signore la quale è di sotto fodrato di asse. E vien a tenere quella e l'altra camera che glie appresso e poy quelle altre quatro camere che tenne vostra signoria che vengono essere sey in tutto. Tutte sonno benissimo apparate. Ne la sua glie il paramento di brocato d'oro biancho e le mure d'intorno coperte di razzi come prima e così l'altre camere subsequentamente.'

[86] The list of the cardinal's personal entourage included 'uno sonatore per monsignore' while a Gaspare *sonatore* formed part of the general company. See Natale, *I diarii*, pp. 50–3. On the organs see Motta, 'Musici alla corte', pp. 288–9.

music was not the primary reason for these exchanges; it provided a highly effective backdrop to serious diplomacy. Galeazzo Maria had already forged a strong alliance with the Savonese pope; by the end of the 1473 visit Riario's brother, Girolamo, was the new owner of the contested city of Imola with Caterina Sforza as his newly betrothed fiancée. The singers, therefore, were only one part, albeit a very important one, of the court scenery, which assured the pope's representatives of the high value of a Milanese alliance. The publicly strengthened tie to the papacy, in turn, convinced doubting Sforza courtiers, citizens and feudatories that any internal opposition would be fruitless.

In his final assessment of Galeazzo Maria's reign, Bernardino Corio described him as 'above all, most liberal, eager for glory and to be feared. He held it dear that one could say with truth that his court was one of the most splendid in the universe. He was most magnificent in his trappings and in his lifestyle and in his court was above all most splendid'.[87]

The concentration on the court and personal display has often been seen by modern scholars as a sign of the weakness and vanity which led to his death.[88] But, as Riccardo Fubini has shown, the assassination was not the isolated act of impetuous youths outraged at Galeazzo Maria's excesses.[89] It seems rather to have been a well-coordinated attempt undertaken by resentful members of the Milanese nobility. For a group once accustomed to real political influence, the sight, sounds and ceremonies devised by the duke had worked all too well. The rituals of court life were replacing the possibilities of genuine power. Confined by Galeazzo Maria to rigidly defined court roles, starved of the privileges and funds they had come to accept as their due, the families who sponsored the plot hoped to regain their influence under a more compliant regime. Galeazzo Maria's singers alone did not, therefore, draw him to his death. But when, in 1477, Bona of Savoy dismissed many

[87] Corio, *Storia di Milano*, III, p. 314: 'Fu oltramodo liberalissimo, cupido di gloria e d'essere temuto. Avea caro che si potesse dire con verità che la sua corte era una delle più splendide dell'universo; era magnificentissimo di suppellettili e nel suo vivere e nella sua corte fu oltre modo splendidissimo.'

[88] Lockwood ('Strategies of Music Patronage'), for example, wrote: 'to call him impetuous, extravagant and vain would be bland understatement'.

[89] R. Fubini, 'L'assassinio di Galeazzo Maria Sforza nelle sue circonstanze politiche', *Lorenzo de' Medici: lettere* (Florence, 1977–90), II, pp. 523–35.

of the choir members and refused to complete the vast polyptych in the Pavian chapel she was doing much more than saving money. If music had become a symbol of Galeazzo Maria's signorial ambitions, its reduction was a sign that the new regent had recognised the limitations of magnificence.

Warburg Institute, University of London

APPENDIX

Milan, Archive di Stato, Archivio Sforzesco 932

1476
Lista de li deputati a cavalcare dreto ala Corte del nostro Illustrissimo Principe et Excellentissimo Signore aliquali se ha a dare alogiamento:

El nostro Ill.mo P. et Ex.mo Sig.re	ca.li	
Lo Ill.o Duca de Barro	ca.li	xxx ii
Lo Ill.o. Sig.re Ludovico	ca.li	xxx ii
d. Petro de Gallara	ca.li	x
d. Orpheo	ca.li	x
d. Jo. iacobo da treultio	ca.li	vii
d. Guidoantonio arcimboldo	ca.li	vii
d. Jo. antonio cotta	ca.li	vii
Jo. petro del Bergamino	ca.li	vii
El R.mo Mon.re. di piacenza	ca.li	x
d. lo Abbate de sancto sevino	ca.li	iii
d. lo Abbate de quartagiola	ca.li	
Fra Francisco	ca.li	
Mag.ro Giohanne de marliano	ca.li	iii
Mag.ro Lazaro	ca.li	iii
el conte Galeato bevilaqua	ca.li	vi
Mag.ro Ambrosio de binasco	ca.li	iii
el Spiciaro	ca.li	

Juliano de Varese	ca.li	vi
Cosma de Briosco	ca.li	iiii
Pizeto	ca.li	iiii

Camereri de camera

d. Francisco de petrasancta	ca.li	x ii
d. Antonio carazo	ca.li	x
d. Georgio del careto	ca.li	vi
d. Karlino Varesino	ca.li	vi
d. Antonieto de presentia	ca.li	iiii
d. Hyeronimo de Becharia	ca.li	iiii
d. Petro de birago	ca.li	vi
d. Baptista e Andrea selassenato	ca.li	vi
d. Baptista de parma	ca.li	vi
Francesco di strozzi	ca.li	viii
Nicolo de cortona	ca.li	vi
Bartolomeo de locarne	ca.li	iiii
Jo. petro crivello	ca.li	viii
Covelle de sancto severino	ca.li	v
Alessandro de castiglione	ca.li	viii
Jo. Baptista del conte	ca.li	viii
Castellino vesconte	ca.li	v
Berlingere caldoro	ca.li	vi
Alesio de durazio	ca.li	ii
d. Gasparo nano spagnolo	ca.li	iii
d. Alfonso spagnolo	ca.li	iii
Gasparro Vesconte	ca.li	iiii

Camereri da guardacamera

d. Jo. francisco pallavicino	ca.li	iiii
Petro de oly	ca.li	iiii
Marchino de Abia	ca.li	vi
Johanne de Verona	ca.li	iiii
Roberto vesconte	ca.li	iiii
El Bruscho	ca.li	iiii
Nicolo maleta	ca.li	ii
Jo. luchino crivello	ca.li	ii
Jacobino del castelatio	ca.li	ii
Aluysino de cornagliano	ca.li	ii
Francisco de olza	ca.li	ii
Jacometo del mayno	ca.li	ii

Jacobino de caponago	ca.li	ii
Baldesaro choyro	ca.li	ii
Brecella	ca.li	ii
El fazardo	ca.li	ii
Bernardino del misalia	ca.li	iii

Sotto camereri
Fidelle
Goffino
Nasino
Hyeronimo da Sena
Baptisino barbavara
Zentille
Morelleto
Danielle da palii
Euxebio da lode
Francisco de cotignola
Alesandro da cremona
Faxano

Uschieri ducali
Francisco choyro
Ciorino

La ducale canzelaria

El Mag.co d. Cicho	ca.li	x ii
d. Jo. iacobo suo figliolo	ca.li	iii
Marcho troto	ca.li	iii
Alesandro coletta	ca.li	iiii
Filipo ferussino	ca.li	iii
Francisco Rizio	ca.li	ii
Tomasio da Hexio e Nicolo toschano	ca.li	iii
d. Antiquario	ca.li	ii
Francisco da Tolentino	ca.lo	i
Jo. petro comino	ca.lo	i
Jo. Petro de caxale offitiale deli cavalarii	ca.li	ii
cavallarii	ca.li	x

Uschieri dela canzelaria

Ruspino	ca.li	ii
Francino	ca.lo	i

d. Fabricio	ca.li	vii
d. Gabriello pagliaro	ca.li	vii
Cavallarii del ss.to	ca.li	x
d. Jacobo alfero	ca.li	vi
Johanne de novate	ca.li	iiii
Bernardino da treultio	ca.li	
S. Gasparo ghilimberto	ca.li	
Scriptore		

Cantatori

d. lo Abbe e d. Bovis	ca.li	iiii
d. Cordiere e d. Rollando	ca.li	vii
Brant e d. Gulielmo	ca.li	iii
d. Henricho et Elloy	ca.li	iii
Gaspare e damiello	ca.li	iiii
Avignono e Guinet	ca.li	ii
Ruglerio e Cornellio	ca.li	iii
Peroto e Perotino	ca.li	iii
Pruglii e Ottinet	ca.li	ii
Jannes e Gillet	ca.li	iii
d. Antonio el proposito de Sancta tegia	ca.li	ii
Cardin e Aluyseto	ca.li	iii
Michel de torsa e Juschin	ca.li	ii
Antonio ponzo [e] d. Raynere	ca.li	ii
Jannes e Marcho	ca.li	iii
Jannes franan [e] Jannes barbero	ca.li	iiii

Sonatori da orghani

Fra matheo garza		
Jo. andrea da cerusa		
Georgio da Viana		
El mag.ro di perfumi	ca.li	ii
Mag.ro Zanino da rellori		
mag.ro Francisco bombardero		
Malpagha stambechinero	ca.lo	i
Boniforte stambechinero	ca.lo	i

Giochatori da balla

Corazina	ca.li	ii
el mayfredo		
Nicollo		

El Bresano
Rizo
Chito grande
El florenzoto
Juliano trombeta
Sacho trombeta   ca.lo   i
Gulielmo   ca.lo   i

Barberi
Mag.ro bono
Mag.ro aonario
Travaglino
Tomasio piacentino
Barbero Mato

Credenzeri
Antonio de vicomercato
El cavalere
Ambrosio

Sotto credenzeri
Matheo
Rossino
Jacometo
Ambroseto

Spenditori e dispensatori
d. Aluysio de petrasancta   ca.li   ii
Matheo dal castelatio
Bartholomeo
Nicolo del cirexa
Jo. antonio de castello sancto
Zohane
Andrea bosso
Ardizone

Sartori
Cazardo
Mag.ro Antoniolo
El calzante
Paulino calzolane

Sig.re buffone

Apperegiatori da salla
Furiano mag.ro de salla   ca.li   ii
Cristoforo
Apoloniario
Petro

Soto apperegiatori
Georgino
Marchiano

Fornari
Georgio
Jo. antonio

Bechari
Tomasio
Andriolo fasolo

Canevari
Domenico
Petro

Polarolli
Baptista
Moreto

Cochi
Nicolo da meda
Mag.ro Tomasio
Mag.ro petro
Mag.ro hyeronimo
Mag.ro Gulielmo
Mag.ro Bartho

Soto cochi
Bonadies
Guido
Bono

Scotini
Romagnollo
Scarpagiodi
Guerino
Gulielmo

Stalla ducalle

Per la persona del nostro Ill.mo p. et ex.mo sig.re	ca.li	L
El conte Borella	ca.li	vi
Spagnollo	ca.li	ii
Jo. antonio barbaresco spenditore		
Sucollino soto spenditore		
Mag.ro Rolando marescalcho	ca.li	ii
Mag.ro Gotardo sellaro		
Matheo dala mandolla		
Mag.ro maffeo barbero		
Victore dispensere cibario		
Jo. maria dispensere del feno e de biada		
Mag.ro Johanne cocho		
martino aparegiatore		
Jacobo da cremona cavalcatore		
Thenchone cavalcatore		
mulateri da stalla	ca.li	x
mulateri da camera	m.	iiii
cavagli da fatione	ca.li	lxxx

El Vesconte sopra li infrascripti
   ducali regazi
Reversino de fontanella
Karlo da seragnio
Clemente de pavia
V. Nocente de mantoa
Tadeo da pisa
Jo. antonio da milano
Petro zohane de cayno
Io. matheo da lode
V. ludovico de parma
Scarioto
Saffeto
Evangelista
Jacobo da corte
Jacobo da monza

Ludovicho del guasto
Batayno
Francisco de Birago
Bernardino de piacentia
Jo. antonio de vigevano
Bartolomeo todeschino

Galupi di quali sono etiam alcuni usellatori
Jo. antonio Uselatore
Venturino
Bataglino
Barbeta Uselatore
Diana Uselatore
Biancho Uselatore
Tachino Uselatore
Roberto Uselatore
Turcheto Uselatore
Antonio de Valentino
Pixanello
Bichino

Cristoforo da milano sopra li infrascripti caretoni et mulateri	ca.lo	i
Cecharello mulatero	m.	ii
Augustino	m.	ii
Cristoforo mezatesta	m.	i
Aluysio mulatero	m.	ii
Furgusino	m.	ii
Antonio del conte	m.	ii
Girardo	m.	ii
Jeronimo	m.	i
Steffano da milano	m.	ii
Johanne de Romanengo	m.	ii
Lenzo	m.	ii
Bagio	ca.lo	i
Petro dela Bella	m.	

Caretoni		
Francesco	ca.li	iiii
Adam	ca.li	iiii
Vicentio	ca.li	iiii
Johanne todescho	ca.li	iiii

Malvava	ca.li	iiii
Morello	ca.li	iiii
Gorino	ca.li	iiii
Bossino	ca.li	iiii
Fontana	ca.li	iiii
Johanne maio	ca.li	iiii
Leonardo	ca.li	iiii
Petro todescho	ca.li	iiii
Zentilhomo	ca.li	iiii
Johannepetro cocho	ca.lo	i
Pizino sopra le legna	ca.lo	i
Magistro francho maresino		
Calcho		
Borera		
Beltramino	ca.li	v
Gieronovexe		
Cornexano		
d. Karlo da cremona computa		
carete due per portare pane e cani	ca.li	xii
Canateri da brachi del nostro Ill.mo Signore		
Cristophoro de bolla	ca.lo	i
Lanzalloto de bolla	ca.lo	i
Canateri da camera		
Antonio de Buste	ca.lo	i
Gulielmoto	ca.li	ii
Betrame de ligurno	ca.lo	i
Morello da rognano	ca.lo	i
Gulielmino		
Canateri da Livreri a cavallo		
Antonio de belolo	ca.lo	i
Bernardo da milano	ca.lo	i
Righino	ca.lo	i
Donato da moreto	ca.lo	i
Francesco da sexto	ca.lo	i
Nicolino	ca.lo	i
Ambrosio dabia	ca.lo	i
Nicolla	ca.lo	i
Barbiglio	ca.lo	i

187

Jacobo dabia	ca.lo	i
Cristoforo de Vigevano	ca.lo	i
Antonio da milano	ca.lo	i
Gulielmo	ca.lo	i
Iamentro da rognano	ca.lo	i
Antonio da mixinti	ca.lo	i
Johanne antonio da milano	ca.lo	i
Baptista	ca.lo	i
Bartolomeo	ca.lo	i

Canateri a pede
Corero
Capelleto da casora
Comello da ligneno

Canateri da sansi
Stanghelino
El priore
Mazaloste
El prioreto
Mag.ro Stanghero
Simone todescho
Lazarino
Barone
Martelino
Chitolla
Granzino de cusago
Johanne da proltrino

Cazadori per provedere ale caze
Mazono de Cusago
Ambroseto da Moreto
Andriollo da Corsicho
Sancto da Moreto
Cristoforo da Corsicho
Simone da Corsicho
Antonio da Bexana

Uselatori ducali

Jacobo de mag.ro Nicolo greco	ca.li	ii
Jacomello	ca.li	ii
Hestor	ca.li	ii

Lazarino	ca.li	ii
Bochazino	ca.li	ii
Fioramonte	ca.li	ii
Pillato	ca.li	ii
Beltrame Capello	ca.lo	i

Uselatori che vene dreto ala Invernata

Rizo	ca.li	ii
Donato	ca.li	ii
Tadeo	ca.li	ii
Johanne greco	ca.li	ii
Mag.ro Leone	ca.li	ii
Georgio greco	ca.li	ii
Georgio de larte	ca.li	ii
Georgio albanese	ca.li	ii
Carleto	ca.li	ii
Jane	ca.li	ii
Augustino	ca.lo	i

Uselatori dela Ill.ma madona duchessa

Guido e Andoardo	ca.li	iii

Uselatori de [sic]

Perino e Francisco de Nicolo de Rizo	ca.li	iii

Stafferi ducali

Johanne grande		
Cristoforo de buste	ca.li	ii
San Cristoforo		
Sforza da castellione		
Jacobino crivello		
Giemigniano de pontremolo		
Stefano da cremona		
Gallo boza		
Bartolla lita		
Ambrosio porro		
Domenico de castrono		
Antonio de catelione		
Baptistino de Gavi		
Cexaro de traieta		
Johanne antonio porro		
Donato basso		

Gigante da ferara
Bartolomeo pegoraro
Johanne de Riva
Bernardino dela tarcheta
Francisco de Rippa
Andrea dalza
Pedroleone
Todeschino
Bernardino de Varese
Gasparo de Romanengo

Rosso capitane dela guardia	ca.li	ii
Item provisionati a pede		

Balestreri a cavallo

Gaspeto e Silvestro	ca.li	xxvii
Conte	ca.li	xxvii
Gregheto		
Simone	ca.li	xxvii
Covelle		
Parmesano	ca.li	xxvii
d. Jo. angello de florentia	ca.li	viii
d. Jo. baptista de cotignola	ca.li	iii
Cristoforo de Bolla	ca.li	v

Lista dela Ill.ma et ex.ma madona duchessa computa cavalli xiii del ill.mo signore ottaviano et compute carete mulli et ogni altra cosa e in summa	ca.li	Clxx
Lista computatis omnibus extracto fora perino, francesco et el Biancho uselatore	ca.li	xL

E in summa

fachini viii

REVIEWS

Bonnie J. Blackburn, Edward E. Lowinsky, Clement
A. Miller, *A Correspondence of Renaissance Musicians*. Oxford,
Oxford University Press, 1991, xliv+1067 pp.

In 1941 Knud Jeppesen published an article on a correspondence
between early sixteenth-century Italian theorists, preserved mainly
in the Vatican library.[1] He included an inventory of the letters,
summarised their contents, provided concordances to eighteenth-
and nineteenth-century copies of the letters, and gave a colourful
description of the main participants of the correspondence. It was
immediately apparent that this was a unique document which presented a wealth of information on some of the most important and
controversial issues in Renaissance music and theory, issues not
often discussed in theoretical treatises. Unfortunately, it was not
easy of access and often difficult to read. When Padre Martini
commissioned a copy of most of the letters from a certain Luigi
Antonio Sabbatini in 1774, the latter wrote, in explaining his delay:
'the copyist I had chosen to do the copying came to me this morning in a fright to tell me that he can't do anything with it because
it's all written in gothic and irregular and full of music and he
hasn't the courage to do it'.[2] It must therefore come as a tremen-
dous relief for us, if not for Sabbatini's copyist, that these letters
are finally available in a modern edition which is not only reliable,
but in every respect exemplary. The project was initiated in 1952
by Edward E. Lowinsky, who was assisted from 1973 by Bonnie J.
Blackburn and Clement A. Miller. Lowinsky died in 1985, having
approved the transcription and edition of a little more than half

[1] 'Eine musiktheoretische Korrespondenz des frühen Cinquecento', *Acta Musicologica*, 13
(1941), pp. 3–39.
[2] *A Correspondence of Renaissance Musicians*, p. 36.

the letters. His widow, Bonnie Blackburn, deserves most of the credit for the completion of the project: not only did she transcribe, edit, translate and annotate the texts, but she also wrote all but one chapter of a substantial introduction, added a biographical dictionary and a discussion of problematic terms, and tracked down the sources of frequent quotations and allusions, often not indicated as such in the letters. In addition, Blackburn did extensive research on the writings, compositions and biographies of virtually everyone involved in the correspondence and managed to unearth much new information in the process. In general, it may be said of the main editor that she is not one to take short cuts: if there was a lead to be pursued, the reader may rest assured that Blackburn has tried to follow it, not infrequently bringing back a substantial catch. The result must surely be counted among the most impressive achievements of Renaissance musicology of recent years. Generations of scholars will be grateful to Blackburn, Lowinsky and Miller for allowing us to eavesdrop on the ferocious quarrels of early sixteenth-century music theorists with so much ease.

The correspondence consists of 110 letters written between 1517 and 1543, mostly by Giovanni Spataro in Bologna (fifty-four letters), Giovanni del Lago in Venice (twenty-six letters), and Pietro Aaron in Venice and, from 1536, in Bergamo (nine letters). In addition, there are two letters by Giovanni Maria Lanfranco and a small number by minor musicians. The two protagonists (or, rather, antagonists) of the correspondence, Spataro and Del Lago, planned (though never managed) to publish their own letters, and it is ironic that Spataro's letters came down to us only thanks to his adversary, who certainly would not have wished to make them public but could not bring himself to throw them away. Had it not been for Del Lago (to say nothing of Blackburn, Lowinsky and Miller), Spataro would have been remembered mainly as a music theorist obsessed with breve equality,[3] and Del Lago himself as the author of a very minor treatise entitled *Breve introduttione di musica misurata*.[4]

The central figure in the correspondence, Giovanni Spataro,

[3] He wrote a long treatise entitled *Tractato di musica di Giovanni Spataro musico bolognese nel quale si tracta de la perfectione de la sesqualtera producta in la musica mensurata exercitate* (Venice, 1531).
[4] Venice, 1540.

emerges as a man with interesting observations to make on both tonal and notational systems and as a singularly unsympathetic character, a perfect match for the utterly unsavoury Del Lago. Spataro's speciality is to flatter his correspondent in one letter in the hope of obtaining assistance with the publication of his book, only to heap insults on him in the next once these hopes have proved futile. He is quite unable to accept criticism. When Del Lago dares to take him at his word and criticise his manuscript, Spataro reacts as follows:

> You say you are making preparations for printing my treatise. It seems to me I have fallen into a trap, as I always feared, for I find in you more prattle than action: you wait two, three, and four months, then you write to me with your infantile doubts and you argue in a way that reveals not only your small knowledge, but your intention to learn under the veil of 'disputation', just to drag things out. So do me a favour and return my treatises; my works are too humble for your exalted mediation and would bring you little honour. For you are the great scholar of Venice and to inflate your reputation you go around saying I have sent you my treatises for correction. I won't send you even one page of my *Appostille*; it pains me to death that I sent you anything at all. I shall complain to Marc'Antonio Cavazzoni, whom I consulted about you first, and this I did not without reason; I already had an inkling of your conduct. Don't expect any more letters from me on your puerile arguments; there is no profit in corresponding with you, who are ignorance personified.[5]

While Spataro could hardly be considered a model of scholarly *savoir faire*, his suspicions and accusations were by no means baseless. Del Lago delighted in 'testing' others and teasing information and opinion out of them. In his own copies of the letters sent to Spataro, one may find postscripts like: 'I asked Spataro for the resolution of the two tenors to test him.'[6] His letters are full of false modesty and shameless flattery:

> I pray you, for the love you bear me, to ask your Bolognese musicians on my behalf to resolve these two tenors for me, which I cannot sing with the other parts, because I do not understand them well. Your musicians are so learned and accomplished, in theory as well as practice, it will be no trouble for them, nor for you, the foremost musician of our time.[7]

---

[5] *A Correspondence*, p. 412. All quotations are from the condensed English translations of the letters.
[6] *A Correspondence*, p. 663.
[7] *A Correspondence*, p. 662.

Thanks to Dr Blackburn's archival research, we now have a full picture of Del Lago's less than brilliant ecclesiastical career. It would be no less difficult than futile to decide whether Del Lago's professional frustrations were responsible for the flaws in his character, or the reverse. Scholars have already been puzzled when finding an answer to a question in a letter dated earlier than the letter in which the question has been posed. But no one before Blackburn suspected to what extent Del Lago 'edited' his letters as he prepared them for publication (for which he had hopes as late as 1542). Half of the twenty-two letters intended for publication are fictitious or have borrowed elements. Five others seem to have been revised, Del Lago making sure that his most serious errors had been corrected. Dr Blackburn is surely right in pointing out that had these letters been published as intended by Del Lago, and had Spataro's letters to Del Lago been lost, the latter rather than the former would have been remembered today as a learned, if pedantic, theorist. But Del Lago never published his *Epistole* – for one thing, because he did not have enough money, for another, because Spataro and Aaron, who would have noticed many of the revisions, fictitious dates, borrowings etc., were still alive in the early 1540s. But possibly the most important reason is that by the time Del Lago wanted to publish these letters, musicians were simply no longer interested in most of the questions discussed. (The one exception, is, of course, the topic of the chromatic and enharmonic genera.) The correspondence would have excited much more interest in the late fifteenth or very early sixteenth century.

Blackburn's detective work makes for lively reading, and she shows a wonderful sense of humour in uncovering Del Lago's deceptions. Yet, like all authors, Blackburn and Lowinsky, though on the whole remarkably judicious, are not completely impartial. To a greater extent than the evidence warrants, they see Spataro as the hero and Del Lago as the villain of their story. This can sometimes lead to a misinterpretation, as will be shown below.

Two people as unpleasant as Spataro and Del Lago could not possibly remain on good terms for long. They needed an intermediary to whom Spataro could write his letters when he was no longer on speaking terms with Del Lago. This role was filled by Pietro Aaron, who is the best-known of the theorists involved in the correspondence. Aaron was a prolific writer, six of whose treatises are known today. But our picture of him is also altered through the correspondence. Without it, we would not have known the full extent to which he revised his theories under the influence of Giovanni Spataro. Thus, for instance, in his early treatises, *Libri tres de institutione harmonica* of 1516 and *Thoscanello de la musica* of 1523, he advocated minim equivalence, while in the late 1530s he became an advocate of breve equality. Similarly, he had used only flat signs when explaining the theory of mutations in his *Trattato della natura et cognitione di tutti gli tuoni di canto figurato* of 1525, but, again under Spataro's influence, published a new pamphlet in 1531 (without a title) which included thirty mutations on each position and made use of sharps.[8] Aaron comes across as a far more sympathetic character than either of his correspondents; he had a great gift for friendship and was generally liked. Certainly his are the only letters in the correspondence that are intentionally entertaining, since they are full of gossip, such as, for example, that Giovanni Maria Lanfranco 'has fled Verona, . . . losing his good name and all his belongings, his house ransacked, because he violated a boy – or so they say'.[9]

It is of considerable interest that, as the correspondence clearly shows, by this time the distance between a great composer, best exemplified by the constantly mentioned and universally admired Adrian Willaert, and a theorist seemed unbridgeable. Not only do most of our correspondents seem afraid of approaching him (the one exception being Del Lago, who, strangely enough, appears to have been a good friend of the composer), they are fully aware of the fact that a thorough grounding in theory will not make them into great composers. To quote Spataro: 'Rules are good for the beginner but will not make a good composer, for good composers are born, just as are poets. The gift of heaven is almost more important than the rules, for good composers, through natural

---

[8]   Even though Spataro expressly allowed Aaron to publish his now lost chart under his (Aaron's) name, I believe Lowinsky may be rash to conclude from this that Spataro was the author of Aaron's pamphlet (*A Correspondence*, pp. 438–9). It is more likely that Aaron simply revised the chart himself when he received Spataro's letter. In his congratulatory letter of 24 October 1531 (pp. 433–8), Spataro never mentioned that he himself wrote the pamphlet, as he would surely have done, given his vanity, were he the author. The letter sounds more like that of a theorist who is happy that a colleague has finally come round to his point of view.

[9]   *A Correspondence*, p. 956.

instinct and a certain graceful manner, which can hardly be taught, sometimes find expressions that no rule allows.'[10] We find here an early expression of a clear shift from a theorist who considered himself at least equal, if not superior, to the composer, to one who acknowledges the composer's superiority. Only half a century earlier, Johannes Tinctoris had not flinched from criticising famous composers like Busnoys and Okeghem for their faulty use of mensuration signs.[11] Now Spataro, when discussing ligatures, quotes the Italian saying 'Practice is as good as a law' and continues: 'even if the earliest musicians observed Prosdocimo's rule, later musicians, up to our time, have not; one finds many compositions by the most eminent composers, older and more recent, that ignore that unsupported rule'.[12]

Of the main topics discussed in the correspondence, perhaps the most controversial, and the one that has attracted the most attention from modern scholars, is that of *musica ficta*. Edward Lowinsky,[13] Lewis Lockwood[14] and, most recently and most exhaustively, Karol Berger[15] have thoroughly combed the correspondence for information on this subject. Other topics discussed are the chromatic and enharmonic genera (detailed annotations are provided by Lowinsky and Blackburn) and the art of composition, of which Blackburn presents a lucid discussion in a separate chapter of the introduction. In this context, we find the earliest known description (by Spataro) of a *cartella* or *abacus* (that is, arithmetic) slate which he used to sketch compositions. It is possible that Spataro was not the first one to make use of the slate.[16] The earliest known description of the slate is found in an *algorismus* written by the music theorist Prosdocimus de Beldemandis in 1410.[17] It is not inconceivable that the Paduan musicians in his circle made use of this writing tool (which he called *lapis*).

[10] *A Correspondence*, pp. 364–5.
[11] See, for example, his discussion in *Proportionale musices*, in *Opera theoretica*, ed. A. Seay, Corpus Scriptorum de Musica 22 ([Rome], 1975–8), IIa, pp. 14 and 49–50.
[12] *A Correspondence*, p. 599.
[13] See the detailed bibliography given at the end of *A Correspondence*.
[14] 'A Sample Problem of *Musica ficta*: Willaert's *Pater noster*', in *Studies in Music History: Essays for Oliver Strunk*, ed. H. Powers (Princeton, 1968), pp. 161–82.
[15] *Musica Ficta: Theories of Accidental Inflections in Vocal Polyphony from Marchetta da Padova to Gioseffo Zarlino* (Cambridge, 1987).
[16] See also J. Chailley, '*Tabula compositoriae*', *Acta Musicologica*, 51 (1979), 51–4. Chailley describes a slate from the early sixteenth century found in France.
[17] D. E. Smith, *Rara arithmetica* (Boston, 1908), p. 13.

The subject that takes up by far the most space in the correspondence, and which has received relatively little attention among
modern scholars, including the editors of the volume under discussion, is rhythmic notation. In the introduction Clement Miller
focuses his attention on only one among many rhythmic topics that
exercised our theorists, namely the breve equality (that is, the
equal duration of breves under the perfect and imperfect times)
advocated by Spataro and, under his influence, also by the late
Aaron. But the editors' low regard for Del Lago somewhat mars
Miller's discussion. He is aware of the statements that place Del
Lago among the advocates of minim equality (which gives minims
under perfect and imperfect times and prolations equal duration
and, consequently, makes perfect breves and semibreves longer
than the imperfect ones). But he also discusses two passages which
are supposed to place Del Lago in the equal-breve camp and concludes therefore that the theorist was confused about the subject.
Unfortunately, Miller's discussion of the two passages is not convincing. In the first statement (p. 801) Del Lago places the breve
at the centre of the mensural system, which for Miller is enough
to make him an advocate of breve equality. However, many fourteenth-century Italian theorists describe a central breve in which
perfect time is a third shorter than imperfect.[18] The second quotation given by Miller to show Del Lago's alleged support of breve
equality actually proves the opposite:

But if at the beginning of some part of some work there is this sign: C,
and then later this one: O, which has the same tactus as C although the
breve is perfect, I say that now the proportion which will be signed
immediately after the second sign can draw its tactus from the first as
well as from the second sign, because both signs are similar and equal in
tactus, but different in value.[19]

All theorists place in O and C the tactus on the semibreve, but for
the advocates of breve equality the tactus under O has to be a third

---

[18]   See my *Mensuration and Proportion Signs: Origins and Evolution* (Oxford, 1993), pp. 56–7
    and 81–2.
[19]   'Ma se nel principio di ciascuna particola di ciascuno canto fusse segnato questo segno
    C, et poi in processu questo O, el quale non è diverso quantum ad mensuram di questo
    C, se non in quanto alla perfectione della breve, dico che allhora la proportione, la
    quale sarà segnata immediate appresso al secundo segno, porrà torre la sua misura così
    dal primo segno come dal secundo, perché tutti a duoi i segni sono simili et equali in
    misura, ma diversi di valore.' *A Correspondence*, p. 806.

faster than under C, since the perfect time stands in a *sesqualtera* relationship to the imperfect time. Since Del Lago explicitly states that the tactus under O and C is of the same length, he belongs clearly in the equal-minim camp. In short, Del Lago was not confused but, here as also in his discussion of other aspects of the notational system, a follower of the theories of Johannes Tinctoris and Franchinus Gaffurius.

Similarly, Del Lago is misunderstood in Blackburn's commentary on perfection and imperfection under the *sesqualtera*.[20] Again, the theorist is not confused, but rather follows Tinctoris' and Gaffurius' teaching that after any proportion sign the original mensuration has to be preserved, that is, for instance, that notes under the *sesqualtera* following binary mensurations will remain binary. His adversary Spataro held the opposite opinion and wanted the *sesqualtera* proportion to make the notes truly perfect.[21]

A number of other mensural topics raised in the correspondence deserve more attention than they had received in the introduction. Let me mention a few. The letters provide a wealth of new information on *modus cum tempore* signs, O2, O3, C2, and O3, as well as O2, O3, etc. These signs were used to indicate mode and time, once diminished if one number followed the geometric sign, twice diminished if two numbers followed. The problem with these signs (unfortunately not explained in Blackburn's otherwise excellent commentary, pp. 545–7) is that fifteenth- and sixteenth-century theorists interpreted them in two different ways: O2, for instance, could signal either perfect minor mode and imperfect time, or imperfect minor mode and perfect time. In the first case (and this is the most common interpretation), the geometric sign indicated mode and the number time; in the second, the geometric sign indicated time and the number mode. Tinctoris objected to the use of these signs for two reasons: first, they diminish without using either a stroke or a fraction, and secondly, in the first interpretation the circle, normally reserved for *tempus*, indicates mode.[22] It is interesting that by the late fifteenth and early sixteenth century many theorists describe both interpretations, as do our correspondents.

[20] *A Correspondence*, pp. 755–6 and 753.
[21] See my *Mensuration and Proportion Signs*, pp. 187–95.
[22] For a detailed discussion of the *modus cum tempore* signs see my *Mensuration and Proportion Signs*, pp. 20–3 and 148–59; see in particular pp. 153–4.

Musicians seem to have been confused as to what these signs really meant.

When theorists of the period talked about cut circle, they often alluded to the fact that the stroke was drawn through the middle of the circle and therefore everything was performed *ad mediam*.[23] In other words, they drew a parallel between the graphic representation of the sign and its performance. Spataro describes a stroke on the left or right side of the circle in a letter of autumn 1532 to Pietro Aaron (it should have really been addressed to Del Lago but Spataro could not bring himself to address Del Lago directly): 'But if he wants to revive ancient practice, he misunderstood it, for my teacher said that older musicians used to write ₵ or ₵ (with the stroke at the side) to indicate a faster tempo than O. Therefore, ₵ should indicate an even faster tempo and not ₵ again diminished.'[24] This opens the intriguing possibility that the stroke was placed intentionally on the left or right side of the circle, to indicate a slight acceleration of tempo, as compared to ₵ where either the note values or the tactus were always diminished by half.[25]

Another recurring topic, and one of equal interest to our correspondents as it is to scholars today, is that of proportions. Spataro wrote several masses in the 1470s and 80s in which he explored complex temporal and acoustical proportions. We are fortunate indeed to find in his letters detailed commentaries, since these allow us to see to what extent methods used in commercial arithmetic, in particular the Rule of Three, were applied to music. Commercial arithmetic was enjoying increasing popularity in the fifteenth century. Boys who were taught at private or municipal lay schools were first taught to read and write. Then, from the age of ten to fourteen, they would attend *abacus* schools. There, after having covered the basic arithmetical operations, they learned how to solve word problems based on the Rule of Three. The Rule of Three can be summarised as follows: we have four different numbers of which we know three and want to know the fourth, the first standing in the same proportional relationship to the third as the second to the fourth. To give an example: we know that 3 lb of

---

[23] See my *Mensuration and Proportion Signs*, pp. 120–48.
[24] *A Correspondence*, p. 535.
[25] See, for example, *A Correspondence*, p. 225.

meat cost £10, and we would like to compute how much 7 lb cost. In order to find the correct answer (£$23\frac{1}{3}$), anyone versed in the commercial arithmetic of the period might write the numbers as follows (the line shows which numbers to multiply):

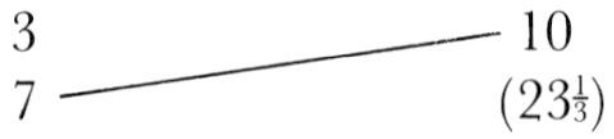

Ten would first be multiplied by seven (=70) and then be divided by three (=$23\frac{1}{3}$). Figure 1 shows the most common way of notating the relationship between the numbers in the Renaissance. 3 stands to 7 in the same relationship as 10 to $23\frac{1}{3}$. The product of the first and the last number (70) is the same as that of the second and third number – in other words, the numbers stand in the geometrical proportion.[26]

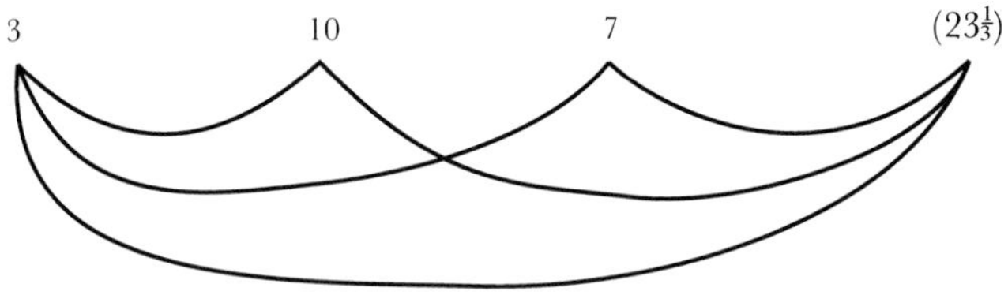

Figure 1

The following quote from a letter of Spataro to Del Lago (written on 20 July 1520) applies the rule to rhythmic proportions in which 1/18 is related to 21/2:[27] 'Under $\frac{21}{2}$ you figure out the value of the perfect long rest by counting minims. If twenty-one minims under $\frac{21}{2}$ have the value of two minims under $\frac{1}{18}$, how many minims under $\frac{1}{18}$ are equivalent to the eighteen minims of the perfect long rest under $\frac{22}{2}$? And in order to find the pure truth, we shall put these numbers, namely 21, 2, 18, and then we shall multiply 18 by 2, or 2 by 18, which equals 36. And then we shall divide the product, that is 36, by 21, which makes $1\frac{5}{7}$.'[28]

[26] See J. Tropfke, *Geschichte der Elementarmathematik* (4th edn, Berlin, 1980), p. 328.

[27] The proportions which occur in Spataro's *Missa Da pacem* are: 9:2, 6:3, 1:18, 21:2, 6:1, 3:7. The piece is lost.

[28] *A Correspondence*, pp. 221 and 225. For a detailed discussion of the relationship between the Rule of Three and rhythmic proportions, see also my *Mensuration and Proportion Signs*, pp. 198–210.

When we apply the Rule of Three to rhythmic proportions we want to know (a) how many notes of a particular value (for example, minims) after the proportion sign replace how many notes of the same value before it; and (b) the number of the shortest notes within a perfection after the proportion sign. Since the proportion sign ($\frac{21}{2}$) has the form of a fraction, the answer to the first question is known, but the answer to the second is not. We will know the number of notes compared, but we will need to find out the number of the shortest note values included within a perfection, usually the minim. Spataro's example will result in Figure 2.

21   18   2   ($1\frac{5}{7}$)

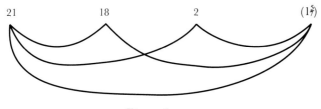

Figure 2

Even though Tinctoris must already have applied the Rule of Three in his *Proportionale musices* of 1473–4,[29] I believe that Spataro's is the earliest discussion which explicitly applies to music the techniques and wordings found in fifteenth-century *abacus* treatises. In other words, while the university-educated Tinctoris must have known and used the Rule of Three, he was somehow reluctant to use the techniques taught at *abacus* schools in a learned treatise. Spataro, on the other hand, never attended a university, but probably learned the trade of a swordmaker.[30] Thus, he would probably have attended one of the *abacus* schools, where children were forced to solve word problems based on the Rule of Three. And he described his method of computation in a less formal mode of communication, a letter rather than a learned treatise.

Spataro's masses may be considered a characteristic musical outgrowth of the late fifteenth-century preoccupation with proportions. Almost anyone with a modicum of education delighted in solving word problems; merchants and bankers had to exchange one Italian currency for another, lawyers tried to settle complicated

[29]   See *Mensuration and Proportion Signs*, pp. 205–7.
[30]   *A Correspondence*, p. 52.

inheritance cases, and artists were refining their use of perspective, all by using the Rule of Three.[31] Similarly, musicians devised sophisticated canons and applied acoustical and rhythmic proportions wherever they could. The fifteenth-century fascination with proportions and the Rule of Three seems to me at least as relevant a cultural context for Tinctoris' and Gaffurius' treatises on proportions and for Spataro's masses as Boethian number theory, which by that time no longer inspired new developments in mathematics.[32]

And what of the 'architectural' or durational proportions, that is, the proportions that according to some present-day scholars obtain between the lengths of individual sections of some musical works? It has long been known that Renaissance music theorists are silent on the matter, but for proponents of durational analysis this has never been taken to signal that composers did not use them to give their works a satisfyingly harmonious outward shape. However, our collection of letters is not a formal theoretical treatise. It is, rather, a uniquely informal document, revealing a number of musicians and theorists of the period passionately discussing the most lively and controversial issues of their art, with proportions featured very prominently among those. Surely, if 'architectural' proportions were ever applied in composition of the period, we would be likely to encounter at least a hint that they were so used. But there is none. And would not Spataro's proportional masses be just the kind of music where one would expect them to be applied? A theorist who used every imaginable intervallic and rhythmic proportion would certainly have tried to use durational proportions too, if this were done. But he doesn't. All this, I believe, should raise serious doubts among musicologists whether durational proportions were ever used in practice.[33] Moreover, we

[31] For a fascinating description of the influence of commercial arithmetic on painting, see M. Baxandall, *Painting and Experience in Fifteenth-Century Italy* (Oxford, 1972), pp. 86ff.
[32] See, in particular, Hermann Hankel, *Zur Geschichte der Mathematik im Altertum und Mittelalter* (Leipzig, 1874; repr. Hildesheim, 1965), p. 353, and Smith, *Rara arithmetica*, pp. 81–2.
[33] For an excellent discussion of the Golden Section and Fibonacci Series, see W. Keil, 'Gibt es den Goldenen Schnitt in der Musik des 15. bis 19. Jahrhunderts? – Eine kritische Untersuchung rezenter Forschungen', *Augsburger Jahrbuch für Musikwissenschaft* (1991), pp. 7–70. Keil concludes that there is no reason to believe that either the Golden Section or the Fibonacci Series was ever used in music before Bartók.

should remember that all our evidence for the use of 'architectural' proportions has been, not surprisingly, derived from treatises on architecture or painting. When Alberti discussed architectural proportions, he drew a parallel with musical intervals, but never mentioned durational proportions in music.[34] Literary theorists were almost equally vague on the subject. All one finds are general references to 'the value of order, harmony, and proportion'.[35] Clearly, scepticism is in order.

Anna Maria Busse Berger
University of California at Davis

CHRISTOPHER PAGE, *The Summa Musice: a Thirteenth-Century Manual for Singers*. Cambridge, Cambridge University Press, 1991, xvii+275 pp.

The *Summa musice* addresses a comprehensive range of topics appropriate to a course of basic instruction in the theory and practice of plainsong. It opens with a discussion of the 'invention' of music, its utilitarian value and its divisions, before moving on to the author's central focus: music in the worship of the church. This includes a brief sketch of the history of notation followed by a presentation of the fundamental principles of medieval theory: solmisation syllables, the musical hand, intervals, modality, the multiple functions of *claves*, psalmody, faults in singing, and rules for composition. The treatise closes with a chapter on polyphony and a supplementary chapter – probably a later addition – on the mystical number symbolism of music. The treatise is cast in the form of a *prosimetrum*, a combination of prose and poetry in dactylic hexameter couplets like the *De consolatione philosophiae* of Boethius and the *De nuptiis Philologiae et Mercurii* of Martianus Capella, both of which were surely known to its author. Among music treatises the *Tractatus musicae scientiae* of Gobelinus and the St Emmeram Anonymous of

---

[34] R. Wittkower, *Architectural Principles in the Age of Humanism* (London, 1988), p. 97.
[35] R. G. Peterson, 'Critical Calculations: Measure and Symmetry in Literature', *PMLA*, 91 (1976), pp. 371ff.

1279 share this form, but the latter also incorporates an additional layer of interlinear glosses.[1]

Christopher Page presents this new edition of the *Summa musice* with introductory chapters on authorship and date, a discussion of its 'scope and character', and a brief review of the sources used by the author. Notes to the Latin edition identify and usually quote specific passages in these sources and offer parallel readings from other music treatises, particularly the *De musica* of John (of Afflighem) to which the *Summa* is most often indebted. Some of this matter is duplicated in the notes to the English translation, but these notes provide additional material and commentary. An index of chants lists the pieces mentioned in the treatise and indicates where they may be found in modern books and published facsimiles. (Most of this seems to have been drawn from the Bryden–Hughes *Index of Gregorian Chant*.) The editor adds to each entry a helpful note explaining the context in which the chant is cited.[2] Aside from an *index auctorum* no other indices are provided, thus rendering access to concepts and terms in the text more difficult than it might otherwise be. Probably the most surprising aspect of the publication is the separation of the Latin text and English translation in two sections of the book instead of on facing pages. This hinders the ease with which the English text can be consulted, unfortunately so, because the reader will often need its assistance in mastering this difficult text. Each line (not sentence) of the Latin text is numbered sequentially, and the translation is arranged in paragraphs headed by the numbers of the lines being translated. Comparisons between text and translation would have been facilitated if the paragraph divisions between the prose text and its translation had been made to correspond. In fact they do not, as can be observed in the prologue, where two long Latin paragraphs are subdivided into four shorter English ones.

---

[1] See the new edition with translation and commentary by J. Yudkin, *De musica mensurata: the Anonymous of St. Emmeram* (Bloomington, IN, 1990). On *prosimetra* see E. R. Curtius, *European Literature and the Latin Middle Ages*, trans. W. Trask (New York, 1953), pp. 109, 151. Gobelinus' treatise has been edited by H. Müller, 'Der Tractatus musicae scientiae des Gobelinus Person (1358–1421)', *Kirchenmusikalisches Jahrbuch*, 20 (1907), pp. 177–96.

[2] Only a few chants could not be traced, but these could surely have been found if relevant manuscript sources from the presumed region of origin had been consulted. I have not attempted this, but the unidentified chant listed as 'Fabrice' is most probably the celebrated *neuma* added to the responsory *Descendit*, mentioned elsewhere in the treatise (2165) as a chant with a special *nota* added to the repetition of the respond. See T. F. Kelly, 'Neuma Triplex', *Acta Musicologica*, 60 (1988), pp. 1–30.

The *Summa musice* survives in a single manuscript source, several centuries removed from its presumed date of origin. The manuscript containing the *Summa* and several works either by or attributed to Johannes de Muris (*c.* 1300–*c.* 1350) came into the hands of Martin Gerbert as he was preparing his monumental edition of music treatises. Gerbert acquired the manuscript through an intermediary in Paris, and he edited several of the treatises it contained in the third volume of the Scriptores. There the *Summa musice* heads Gerbert's collection of 'tractatus de musica' by de Muris.[3] The manuscript was assembled about the year 1400 from earlier sources, and it is conceivable that this late Parisian copy of the *Summa musice* was based on a unique extant source, possibly even the original manuscript. The model had already undergone interpolation, however. Page identified sixteen lines in chapter 20 as extraneous to the original conception, and he regards the final chapter ('Integumentum musice') as a later addition.

The manuscript presents the two components of the treatise in a manner that creates maximum contrast between the running prose text and the associated *metra*. The latter stand out in a bold Gothic textura hand in black ink, while the prose is written in paler ink by a fluent, though not particularly calligraphic, Gothic cursive hand. The poem occupies the left-hand sides of the pages, surrounded by the longer prose text which takes over the entire width of the page when necessary to keep the two versions approximately parallel. The prose text continues in the margin beside the *metrum* of the previous chapter. Page demonstrates how the early fifteenth-century scribe moved back and forth between entering the prose text and the *metrum*, presumably duplicating the format and rubrics of his model exactly. The new edition incorporates the occasional marginal rubrics (most frequently *nota*, but also *questio*, *solutio*, *objectio* and *dubitatio*) found in the manuscript but omitted by Gerbert.

In appearance the manuscript would seem to be one of those in which a central text (in this case the poem) is explicated by

[3] M. Gerbert, *Scriptores ecclesiastici de musica sacra*, 3 vols. (St Blaise, 1784), iii, pp. 189–248. The contents of the manuscript (St Paul im Lavanttal 264/4) are listed in U. Michels, *Johannes de Muris Notitia artis musicae*, Corpus Scriptorum de Musica 17, pp. 31–4. I am grateful to Dr J. Plante of the Hill Monastic Manuscript Library and Fr L. Kull of the Benediktinerstift St Paul for placing a microfilm copy of the treatise at my disposal.

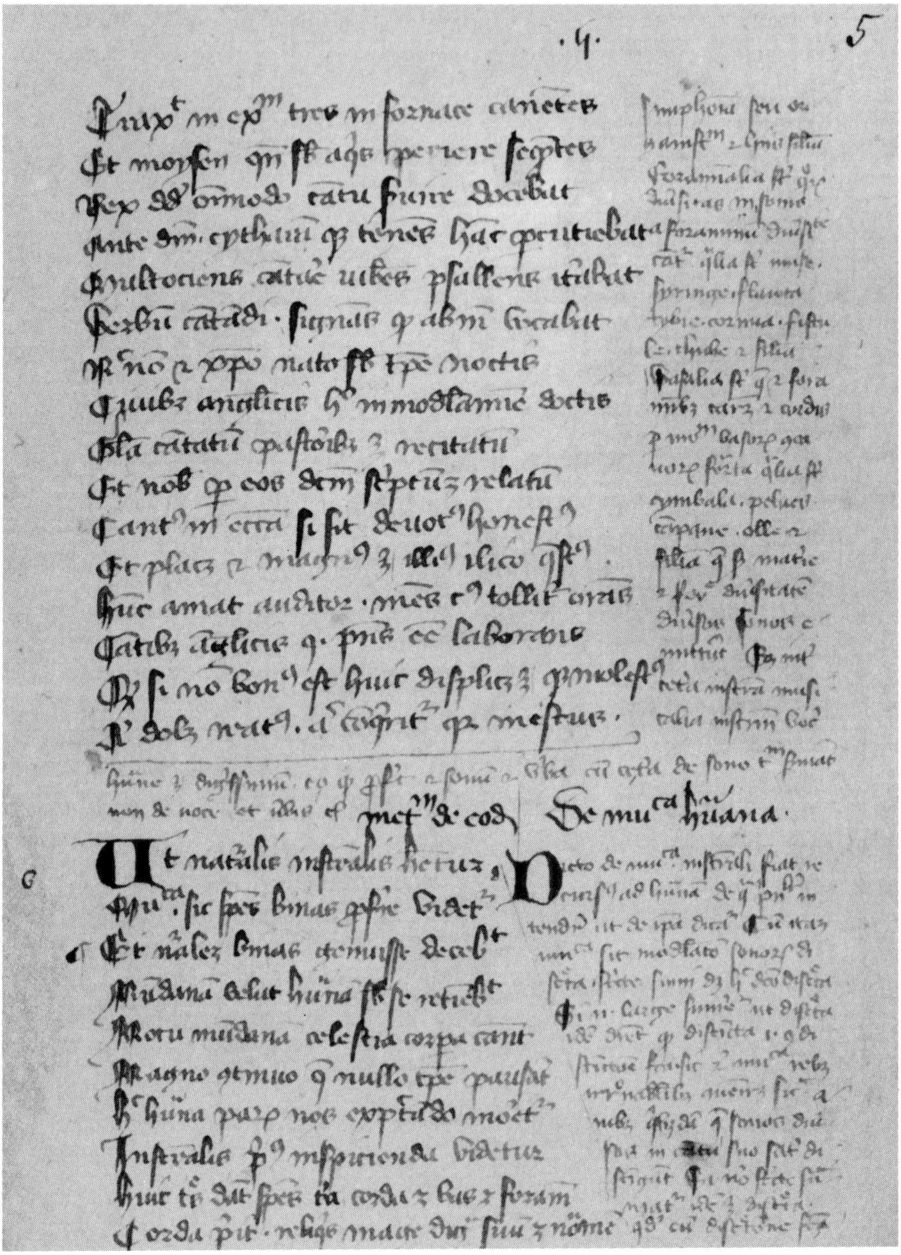

Figure 1 St Paul im Lavanttal, MS 264/4, fol. 5ʳ (*Summa musice*): the end of the *metrum* of chapter 3 and the beginning of the *metrum* of chapter 4. The right margin contains the end of chapter 4 and the beginning of chapter 5.

interpretative glosses. Actually, the two components are coordinated, the poetic text (introduced by the rubric 'metrum de eodem') serving as a support and memory aid, albeit sometimes a bafflingly obscure one, for mastering the teaching presented in the prose text.[4] The two are not entirely congruent, however, since the instruction of the prose text is more or less abbreviated in the poetic summary.

With this new edition of the *Summa musice* Christopher Page offers a text vastly improved over that printed by Gerbert in the eighteenth century. This is no small achievement, and Page modestly alludes to the difficulties of deciphering the manuscript and its many abbreviations.[5] Gerbert provided some of the groundwork that facilitated the preparation for this successor edition, but Page notes that he has emended Gerbert's text in about a thousand places, often by resolving abbreviations more accurately. In the case of recurrent connective words the meaning of the text is not markedly altered, but many of the corrections offer substantially new and clearer readings. Fewer corrections were required in the poetic sections of the treatise, since the text is easier to transcribe and the constraints of syllable count and quantity in dactylic hexameter acted as a control. Some errors had crept into the poetry, however. In line 281 of the *metrum* Page replaced Gerbert's 'brevem' with the correct 'virum', thus making sense of the author's triptych of childhood, youth and old age.[6] In line 500 the difficult 'cantum animi verbis docet' is replaced by the clearer 'cantum cum verbis docet' ('[human music] teaches song with words'). A similar difficulty is resolved when, speaking of the clefs (*claves*), the author admonishes that they be kept in mind ('sit memor harum', 1226), a reading that is more satisfactory than Gerbert's 'sit melior harum'. In the treatise's description of *diaphonia basilica* (improvised

---

[4]   The poetic versions of the introduction and chapters 1, 9 and 14 are preceded by the rubric 'metrum eiusdem' (43, 187, 891, 1351); the title is omitted after chapter 10 (984). References to Page's edition will be indicated by line numbers; page numbers refer to the translation or the commentary. (At divisions between prose and verse the line numbers are occasionally misplaced.)

[5]   Gerbert alluded to the problems in the introduction to his edition, and he asked for understanding that some words had to be assumed 'per coniecturam quidem aut ex contextu'. A modern edition of the *Summa musice* with commentary and (Russian) translation is being prepared by Dr Andrey V. Pilgun of Moscow.

[6]   Unfortunately, by confusing the noun 'canis' (dog) with the adjective 'canus' (grey-haired), the translation ('Music . . . exhilarates the infant and the youth, be they human or canine', p. 56) obscures this image.

207

singing over a drone) the new reading 'pars altera circuit apte' (2367) is certainly more evocative than Gerbert's 'pars altera concinit apte'.

When one turns to the prose version of the treatise, on the other hand, the number of emended passages which clarify previously incomprehensible sentences is considerable. Page interprets correctly the sign for *gamma*, a symbol that Gerbert consistently misconstrued as *C*. The correct resolution of an abbreviation identifies Gerbert's enigmatic 'poeta' as 'Petrus Riga' (158) and allows Page to identify a line from Riga's poem *Aurora*. 'Orpheo Trecensi' (174) comes closer to Orpheus' mythical Thracian origins than does Gerbert's 'Cretensi'. Though 'spirituales' (404–5) better evokes the music of the spheres than does 'speciales', it does not resolve all the problems with this particular passage, as Page himself admits (p. 61). One can easily imagine how replacing Gerbert's 'a verbis' with the correct 'avibus' (461) alters the meaning not a little.

A pair of corrections in close proximity can clarify critical definitions in the treatise: 'Cum itaque decemnovem sunt articuli digitorum, ut palpe [Gerbert: palpare] vel frontes vel summitates eorum, quod pro eodem accipio, articuli [Gerbert: artificialiter] esse dicantur'.[7] Some of Gerbert's conjectures were quite reasonable: 'Quidquid impedit finem artis *illud maiore* iure debet ab arte removeri', but the italicised phrase turns out to be the single word 'illuminare' (1017). The replacement of 'assumptarum' by 'affirmationem' clarifies the author's allusion to the second figure of the syllogism (1024) and situates the passage in the context of medieval logic. It is amazing that the same graphic configuration can produce 'antiphona: Omnibus Deum timentibus' (Gerbert) and 'antiphonis omnibus de Trinitate' (1767–8) or 'diversa contemplabuntur' (Gerbert) and 'diversis tropis utuntur' (1788). This list could be continued with hundreds of other examples of greater or lesser importance, but these few examples should demonstrate just how significant is the appearance of this reliable text of an important manual of chant theory from the Middle Ages. With such a problematical source, however, it might be unwise to abandon all refer-

---

[7] 696–8: 'When [since?] there are nineteen junctures of the fingers (the tips, ends or summits, which I take to be the same) they may be called connectives' (p. 72). On the 'connectives' see below.

ence to the manuscript in favour of the readings provided by the Page edition.

Ever since Gerbert's attribution of the *Summa musice* to Johannes de Muris was shown to be unfounded, it has been assumed that the identity of its author could not be determined.[8] Page believes that he has identified the author, and this identification leads (in part at least) to new conclusions about the date of the treatise. He places the writing of the treatise at the beginning of the thirteenth century, nearly 100 years earlier than previously thought. He also claims that the author is not anonymous but mentions himself three times in the course of his work. Page's evidence for the latter view rests on the fact that the authority of a certain 'Perseus' is twice called upon to support assertions made in the treatise. Once the subject concerns word order in Latin (615). In another passage a dictum of Perseus is introduced to excuse those who, for various reasons not under their control, cannot sing chant properly, the principle being that 'a fault arising from nature is not to be mocked'.[9]

As the capstone of his argument in favour of Perseus' authorship, Page points to the end of the *metrum* which summarises chapter 22, where he finds 'an authorial "signature" in which Perseus (and now someone of whom we have heard nothing so far) draw attention to themselves by putting their own special *signa*, surely their names, into the poetry' (p. 4). The lines in question read:

> Scriptores etiam libris quandoque metrorum
> Affigunt etenim signum speciale decorum.
> Perseus et Petrus hoc observare docentur,
> Qui versus ornare suos per signa videntur.[10]

The case does not strike me as particularly persuasive, even though Page makes the point that some medieval authors spoke of themselves in the third person. Neither of the passages in which Perseus

---

[8]   U. Michels, *Die Musiktraktate des Johannes de Muris*, Beihefte zum Archiv für Musikwissenschaft 8 (Wiesbaden, 1970), pp. 116–17.

[9]   (1) 'Dicit enim Perseus quod quidam, imperitie sue solatium querentes, fortuitas estimant partium orationis positiones et contra ordinem non posse peccare, quod dicere stultum est et potest probari' (615–18). (2) 'Propter quod Perseus docet "Naturale vicium/Non est deridendum"' (1987–9).

[10] 2220–3. 'Sometimes writers of poems also fix a special, gracious mark in books. Perseus and Petrus are taught to observe this, for they adorn their verses with their tokens' (p. 121). One might suggest 'suitable, appropriate' for 'decorum' and, given the generally literal rendition favoured by Page, 'videntur' could have been reflected in the translation.

is cited as an authority has anything to do with music, a strange state of affairs if he wishes to present himself as an expert in musical matters. One might expect, moreover, that the enigmatic 'signature' observation would occur closer to what is supposedly the original conclusion of the treatise (the *metrum* to chapter 24), rather than several chapters earlier. The passage quoted above (not without its own obscurities) has no parallel in the preceding prose text that might have been helpful in interpreting *signa* or in determining why Perseus and Petrus had to be 'taught' to use them.

Page applies this principle a second time to a hypothesis about the authorship of the concluding chapter (25) and *metrum*, which he regards as an addition to the original treatise. Commenting on the line 'Annicius dicit quod delectabile summum/Est deus . . .' (2625), Page observes that 'the identity of this Annicius is unknown. He is possibly the author of this chapter' (p. 134, n. 141). I think that it is even more likely that the author is here paraphrasing Anicius Manlius Torquatus Severinus Boethius. The exact wording of the *metrum* occurs neither in *De consolatione philosophiae* nor in the theological tractates, but the phrase might be an echo of Boethius' discussion of the *summum bonum* in the third book of the *Consolatio*.[11] Given that the reference appears in the hexameter paraphrase, a certain freedom of allusion is to be expected. Perhaps the neglect to make this fairly obvious identification was merely a matter of editorial oversight, but I think that it reveals the weakness of the reasoning used to establish the 'authorship' of a shadowy figure known only as Perseus.

Nevertheless, Page's conviction that Perseus was the author of the *Summa musice* is one of the keys to his re-dating of the treatise. A search of archival documents from the region in which the treatise is presumed to have originated (South Germany, the Tirol, St Gall) for an ecclesiastic with this unusual name uncovered a likely candidate: a deacon active at the cathedral of Würzburg between 1182 and 1215/17.[12] This seemed to confirm the date of *c.* 1200 for

---

[11] *Philosophiae consolatio* 3.10, ed. L. Bieler, Corpus Christianorum: Series Latina 94 (2nd edn, 1984), pp. 52–4. (Cf. the medieval theological dictum that 'bonum est quod omnia appetunt'.)
[12] This region was chosen because it is the one in which the manuscripts of the *Musica* of John (of Afflighem?), a treatise on which the *Summa musice* depends, are most strongly represented. See M. Huglo, 'L'auteur du traité de musique dédié à Fulgence d'Afflighem', *Revue Belge de Musicologie*, 31 (1977), pp. 5–19. John's work also influenced

210

the main body of the treatise (chapters 1–24). Page believes with good reason that the final chapter ('Integumentum musice') was written later. Since it mentions the mendicant orders, founded in the early thirteenth century, and the Templars, disbanded in 1312, the date at which it was added to the *Summa musice* must fall between these two points. Perhaps anxious to keep both portions of the treatise in close chronological proximity, Page identified the reference to a certain 'Ordo fratrum cum gladio' (2527–8) with the Germanic Swordbrothers (*Schwertbrüder*). Since they were merged with the Teutonic knights in 1237, the argument is that the final chapter must have been added before that date. Page simply dismisses the possibility, which seems far more likely to me, that this is a reference to the illustrious military Order of Santiago, called 'of the sword' because of its distinctive emblem.[13] Since this Order survived into the twentieth century, its mention in the *Summa musice* is of little value for assigning a date to the final chapter of the treatise.

While most of the contents of the treatise are not inconsistent with a dating early in the thirteenth century, the mere fact that an individual named Perseus, about whom nothing more is known, was alive at this time constitutes a fragile basis for establishing a chronology. A later (*c.* 1300) date is not inconsistent with the renewed interest in chant theory that characterised the last half of the thirteenth century and the opening decades of the fourteenth. A series of important treatises began with Johannes de Garlandia (*c.* 1240) and continued with the works of Lambertus (*Tractatus de musica*, 1240–50), Amerus (*Practica artis musice*, 1271), Hélie Salomon (*Scientia artis musice*, 1274), Jerome of Moravia (*Tractatus*, after 1272), Engelbert of Admont (*De musica, c.* 1300), Johannes de Grocheo (*De musica, c.* 1300), Walter Odington (*Summa de speculatione musice, c.* 1300), Marchetto (*Lucidarium*, 1317–18), and Jacques de Liège (*Speculum musice, c.* 1330). The commonly accepted dating of

---

Johannes Aegidius de Zamora (*Ars musica*, ed. M. Robert-Tissot, Corpus Scriptorum de Musica 20), who wrote in Spain.

[13] D. W. Lomax, 'Santiago', *Dizionario degli istituti di perfezione*, ed. G. Rocca (Rome, 1974–), VIII, cols. 783–92. See especially the illustration of a title page from an edition of the order's rule which displays the characteristic cross in the form of a sword. In modern Spain the same emblem adorns the top of an almond cake known as *tarta de Santiago*.

the *Summa musice* towards the end of the thirteenth century fits very well into a period when this development came to a climax.

The way in which Page addresses the problems would seem to undermine his proposed dating of *c.* 1200. Twice the *Summa musice* mentions a certain 'Salomon' in the company of such luminaries of medieval music theory as Guido of Arezzo and Odo (28, 1157). On the first occasion Hermannus Contractus is associated with them. The only music theorist known by this name is Hélie (or Elias) Salomon, author of the *Scientia artis musice*, a chant treatise that can be securely dated 1274. Although Page hints at the possibility that this reference might be an interpolation and claims that 'there is a prima-facie case for identifying the Salomon of lines 28 and 1157 with Elias Salomon' (p. 9), he never follows up either of these points. Nor does he explain why any theorist living in Germany would summon the authority of the obscure Hélie Salomon to add weight to his teaching. While there are a few parallels between the *Summa* and the *Scientia* (one of them occurring a few lines after Salomon is mentioned), there is no evidence that the *Summa musice* underwent any revision or interpolation based on the *Scientia artis musice*.[14] There is, however, another candidate who might have merited association with monastic authors as a music theorist: Salomon, monk of St Gall, pupil of Notker and later Bishop of Constance.[15] His claim to be included rests on admittedly slim foundations: his compilation of glosses devotes considerable space to music in the form of citations from the writings of Cassiodorus and Isidore.

The teaching of the *Summa musice* generally follows the conventional paths established earlier in the Middle Ages for works of this genre, but it develops certain topics more fully and proposes several new concepts. A short introductory chapter divides music into 'natural' and 'instrumental', the former including the music

---

[14] The author's statement near the beginning of the *Summa* that he will seek his reward from God, 'et pro isto quantulocumque labore nec a fame susurro nec alieno quoque marsupio remunerari vel spero vel posco' (33–5), bears only an incidental affinity to Hélie's denunciation of singers who look for worldly recognition and monetary rewards 'forte ad illicitos usus convertendae et in marsupiis recludendae' (*Scientia*, preface; Gerbert, *Scriptores*, III, p. 17b).

[15] See A. Schubiger, *Die Sängerschule St. Gallens vom 8. bis 12. Jahrhundert* (Einsiedeln, 1858), p. 34; G. Pietzsch, *Die Musik im Erziehungs- und Bildungsideal des ausgehenden Altertums und frühen Mittelalter*, Mittelalterliche Studien zur Geschichte der Musiktheorie im Mittelalter (Halle, 1932), pp. 88–90.

of the heavenly bodies and human music, a subject that receives no further elaboration. The *artificialia instrumenta* fall into three groups: *chordalia, foraminalia* and *vasalia*. The human voice, although classified 'inter cetera instrumenta musicalia', is considered 'dignissimum', since it embraces both sound and words.[16] The chapter on notation (6) not only describes the neumes but also suggests how some are to be interpreted. It would appear that the author comes from a region where liquescent neumes, the quilisma and the pressus were important nuances of the notational system. He treats the musical (sc. Guidonian) hand thoroughly, explaining every *articulus* together with the constellation of letter name and solmisation syllables proper to each location. The novice singer is counselled to learn chants by heart, but the assistance of a musical instrument – advised also by Hucbald – can be of use for beginners and those with unpleasant voices. The treatise's extensive discussion of modality and the tonal system of chant includes a novel method for discriminating between authentic and plagal by means of *claves discretivae*: the number of notes above or below which determines the mode in cases of doubt. The author maintains definite opinions about the aesthetics of chant composition and the faults that should be avoided by composers. The chapter on polyphony furnishes unique classifications of what seems to be a mostly improvised practice.

The author of the *Summa musice* is not content merely to describe the traditional techniques and principles of plainsong. He has original concepts to promote, creative elaborations of familiar concepts to explain and abuses to denounce. Probably his most individual contribution is the aforementioned system of *claves discretivae*. The four *claves*, one for each of the four *maneriae*, are F, G, a and ♮ – all on the little finger of the musical hand, as he observes. If the majority of the pitches in a given chant fall above the *clavis discretiva*, it should be considered authentic. If the majority fall below this pitch, the chant should be classified plagal. This seems perfectly reasonable as a tool to resolve doubts, but the *Summa musice* presumes that the skilled cantor-musicus will also be sensi-

---

[16] In endorsing the medieval belief in *musica mundana* the author breaks with his customary philosophical guide, Aristotle, who scorned this notion. On the natural–artificial distinction see C. Bower, 'Natural and Artificial Music: the Origins and Development of an Aesthetic Concept', *Musica Disciplina*, 25 (1971), pp. 17–33; G. Pietzsch, *Die Klassifikation der Musik von Boethius bis Ugolino von Orvieto* (Halle an der Saale, 1929).

tive to the *tropus*, a melodic 'turn' that expresses decisively the modality of a chant. This can come either at the beginning or at the end. In the latter position he relates it to the (added) *cauda*, 'a certain melodic movement which is customarily made when a chant is finished to distinguish its mode and to commend its tenor'.[17] The author of the *Summa* wishes to discourage the use of a *cauda* at the day hours and at Compline either with the single antiphon *super psalmos* or with the antiphon to the *Nunc dimittis*.[18] The purpose is quite clear: to restrict the *cauda* to moments of special liturgical solemnity, particularly the Gospel canticles of Lauds and Vespers.

Although the *Summa musice* cites many chants, it contains only a single musical example: the *seculorum amen* formula for psalmody in the second mode. In itself this is rather inconsequential, but the translation calls it 'the beginning of the second tenor' (p. 109), a misinterpretation of the text, which ought to be understood: 'secundum principium tenoris [modi] secundi' (1836–7). The translation makes little sense: only the *tonus peregrinus*, which the *Summa musice* attaches to the eighth mode, has a different tenor in the second half of the psalm tone.

The treatment of notation is not only brief but slightly abstruse, a situation due in part to the fanciful etymologies provided by the author. As Page observes, not all of the statements correspond to what we know of the neumes (quilisma, the distinction between plica and clivis). The *metrum* seems to distinguish between the performance of an ordinary podatus and its liquescent form (epiphonus): 'Pes notulis binis vult sursum tendere crescens;/ Deficit illa tamen quam signat acuta liquescens' (549–50). This seems to contrast the podatus with its liquescent form (epiphonus) and recommend that the second note of a liquescent neume should receive a lighter treatment.[19]

[17] 1850–2, p. 109. There is no basis in the Latin for Page's addition of 'which follows'. The *cauda* occurs typically at the last statement of an antiphon after all the psalm verses to be associated with it have been sung. For a generous selection of examples in each of the modes see T. Bailey, *The Intonation Formulas of Western Chant* (Toronto, 1974), pp. 60–77 and 16–17. Page provides an accurate translation of the closing passage of this chapter (19), hence I cannot understand his complaint that 'the Latin text of this last paragraph is contorted and elliptical'.

[18] This indicates that the author is a secular cleric: the monastic office has no antiphon with the psalms of Compline.

[19] The translation 'the *pes*, growing, wishes to stretch upwards with two marks; the high one, liquifying, abandons what it represents' does not suggest this nuance, but I cannot

Christopher Page has attempted to provide a literal translation for the *Summa musice*, eschewing thereby the elegant prose that typifies his other writings. This is undoubtedly the proper direction for a technical manual that not infrequently slips into arcane turns of phrase. Such an approach offers the reader the best opportunity to make close comparisons between the words of the author and the translator's interpretation of the same. Page's task was especially difficult in the *metra* which follow each prose chapter: the constraints of hexameter verse encode the teaching in complex, often elliptical formulations. Again and again, Page extracts plausible meanings from difficult passages that at first seem to defy explication. If there is an expression which does not please the critical reader, in most cases he or she can quickly arrive at an acceptable alternative, since Page has already done most of the labour of establishing the correct context. Inevitably, a number of problems remain to be solved, but the provision of a translation will surely advance the study of this important text.

This does not mean, however, that the reader can rely solely on the English translation. It is surprising that, having overcome prodigious difficulties elsewhere, the translator in not a few places chooses decidedly questionable interpretations of the Latin text. Bucephalus, identified as one of the horses of Alexander the Great, 'dances to music amidst the enemy' (p. 57). This apparently benign behaviour in a steed trained for battle rests on a misreading of the Latin 'insuper et Bucephal ad cantum saltat in hostes' (294). The verb 'saltare' in medieval Latin meant to assault or to attack, and the accusative case implies action towards a place or object ('amidst the enemy' would have been 'in hostibus'). A few lines later, another oversight in translation contradicts the author's intended meaning. Page renders 'magnos cantores sese tamen esse fatentur' (373) as 'yet they [singers who have not mastered even the relatively brief chants of Pope Gregory] show themselves to be expert singers'. Surely the author wished to imply that these inferior singers merely profess ('fatentur') themselves to be great.

The successful translation and interpretation of a medieval music treatise demands not only a thorough knowledge of the technical matters expounded by the author but also an understanding

entirely agree with the translator that this is 'a difficult line whose meaning is far from clear' (p. 67, n. 60).

of the way they are approached. Many treatises have yet another dimension, for the medieval author brings to his task a theological and liturgical culture inseparable from his mode of thought. In addition, the *Summa musice* also makes more than passing reference to the philosophical currents of its time. Regrettably, the English translation with its associated commentary and source citations does not always communicate or interpret accurately the thought of the author in these matters. This shortcoming robs the treatise of a significant dimension both for the modern reader whose Latin is limited and even for the Latinist who might not have at his fingertips all the theological, liturgical and philosophical learning that careful editorial work should bring to the task of interpreting a medieval document of this type.

The editor's introduction posts an early warning that, theologically speaking, all might not be well. Page cites an antiphon considered by the *Summa musice* to have a joyful message ('materia leta'): 'Surrexit pastor bonus qui posuit animam suam pro ovibus suis et pro grege mori dignatus est.' His translation ('The good shepherd arose [from the dead] who laid down his life for his sheep and was deemed worthy to die for his flock', p. 26) poses theological difficulties. The phrase 'dignatus est', found in this context in collects as well as in the present antiphon, must be translated 'deigned', and not 'was deemed worthy', if the text is to be consistent with traditional Christian orthodoxy. It was Christ himself who offered his life: he was not subjected to any judgment that deemed him 'worthy' to do so.[20] In the *metrum* which summarises the first chapter of the *Summa musice* there is a reference to an alleged threefold division of the treatise: 'Sic ternarius hoc tenet, occupat omne volumen,/Felici felix designans omine numen' (214–15). Page's translation of the second phrase ('the fortunate author representing the Godhead by a propitious token') appears startling, in so far as it seems that the author is comparing himself to the divinity. More sensibly, 'felix' should be construed with 'numen', and 'designans' with 'volumen'. This has the advantage of avoiding an unnecessary interpolation ('author') and of tying the ternary symbolism to the treatise itself.[21] I would translate: 'Thus the ternary number per-

---

[20] The other translated passage on this page ('Propter insuperabilem . . .') could have been more elegantly rendered by reversing the first two phrases.

[21] Another set of ternary parallels (2441–6) between musical instruments ('in vasalibus

vades the entire work, representing by an auspicious sign the blessed deity.'

Several passages in the final chapter seem to have suffered because of inattention to the wider references implied by the author's language. For instance, the English translation refers to 'the four first [sic] Evangelists' (p. 129). The Latin text draws a comparison between the four lines of the musical staff and 'in ecclesia quaternarius [numerus] precipuorum est evangeliorum, per que operationes fidelium ad beatitudinem diriguntur' (2464–5). The reference is obviously to the Gospels (*evangelia*) themselves, not to their authors (*evangelistae*). A neuter plural antecedent is, moreover, required by 'per que'. A liturgical frame of reference seems to be absent also in Page's translation of a remark about a certain kind of parallel between clerical ordination and the latitude permissible in the ranges of authentic and plagal chants. The author says that a bishop may ordain 'in quatuor temporibus', but is not obliged to do so. Translating this phrase 'on four occasions' obscures an allusion to the Ember Days, known as the *quatuor tempora*, the times during the year when sacred orders were traditionally conferred.[22] A few lines later in the same chapter (2485), a misunderstanding of the verb 'predicare', used in conjunction with the eight Beatitudes, leads to the translation 'granted by the Lord', instead of the more obvious 'preached'.[23] A probably accidental misreading of the Latin text ('redemptam' for 'redimitam') would have been avoided if the spirituality of religious life and the history of the religious orders in the thirteenth century had been kept in mind. The statement 'whence you see the Contemplative Life to be the Life of the Church and equally see it *redeemed* through the Active

---

vel in foraminalibus instrumentis vel in chordalibus') and the virtues of faith, hope and charity which implies that string instruments are the most excellent because they are identified with the greatest of all virtues, love, is obscured when the order of the instruments is transposed in the translation (strings, winds, percussion).

[22] 1611–14, p. 102. The Ember Days fall in December, during the first week of Lent, during Pentecost week and in September. The Saturday vigil at the end of the week was the normal day for ordination to major and minor orders – the usual term for these orders and preferable to Page's 'both the greater and the lesser Holy Orders'.

[23] Cf. the motto of the Order of Preachers (Dominicans): 'Laudare, benedicere, praedicare'. The Dominicans are mentioned elsewhere in the chapter, but only the note on p. 132 explains that the translation: 'the fifth [order] of the preachers' means the Dominicans. Does the line 'pede Franciscus nudo nodisque gravatur' (2618) include 'a surprisingly facetious reference to the knotted girdle of the Franciscans' (p. 134, n. 140) or an allusion to the grief caused to Francis by some of his followers?

Life' (p. 133) takes a decidedly controversial position on the relationship between the life of contemplation and the apostolate. The author (probably a secular cleric) is far more circumspect in expressing his opinion, stating that the contemplative life is *crowned* ('redimitam') by the active life.

This final chapter of the *Summa musice* refers the number nine to the number of psalms, lessons and responsories found 'frequentius et generalius' in the secular Office, and the author contrasts this with the monks 'qui pristinam consuetudinem in maiorem convertunt' (2497–8). By rendering this as 'who have altered the ancient custom *for the most part*' (p. 130, my italics) the translation misses the point of the comparison: a reference to monastic Matins which increased – at least from the author's perspective – the number of psalms, lessons and responsories from nine to twelve.[24] Because of its many allusions to non-musical matters, this chapter contains more potentially dangerous pitfalls than the remainder of the treatise. Still, it is difficult to understand how the author's gloss on the commandment 'Thou shalt not commit adultery' could be translated: 'that is to say you should have no carnal knowledge of any woman – be it in the flesh or in thought – unless she be the proper one' (p. 131). No translator's footnote clarifies the identity of this 'proper' woman, but the Latin calls her 'mulierem . . . legitimam' (2514–15) – that is, a husband's lawful spouse.

The author of the *Summa musice* imparts an aura of literary and philosophical learning to his discourse by introducing occasional illustrative quotations from Latin poets and Aristotle, identified as so often in the Middle Ages as 'the philosopher'. Page has tracked down most of these, sometimes having to correct the erroneous attributions of the *Summa*'s author. Ovid and Virgil are represented, but Horace is the author's favourite, almost always specifically named when a line of his poetry appears.[25] Page has also

[24] Ralph of Tongres (d. 1403) blamed the 'Teutonici' for slacking off from the Church's earlier custom of twelve psalms at Matins, and he admired Gregory VII (1073–85) for taking a stand against their practice. *Liber de officiis ecclesiasticis*, 9, ed. C. Mohlberg, *Radulph de Rivo, der letzte Vertreter des altrömischen Ritus*, 2 vols. (Louvain and Münster, 1911–15), II, pp. 15–18. Is this apparent endorsement of a nine-psalm norm yet another indication of the treatise's German origin?

[25] Inadvertently, one Horatian hexameter, set off in the text by italics, is unidentified in the source references and incorrectly identified in the notes to the English translation. 'Non cuivis homini contigit adire Corinthum' comes not from the so-called *Ars poetica* (Ep. 2.3) but from Ep. 1.17.36. The *Summa* quotes it, moreover, not for the purpose of

218

pointed out apparent reminiscences of other classical poets not directly named as well as passages modelled on an elementary schoolroom text, the *Disticha Catonis*.

These literary quotations are introduced as confirming *auctoritates* to reinforce the author's conclusions. In the preface to the treatise he renounces higher modes of philosophical investigation, because they are beyond the comprehension of the children ('puerorum') who are his intended audience. His discussion of music will not focus on 'quid habeat pro subiecto, et que sit propria passio subiecti eiusdem' (20–2), but he implies that he could undertake a discussion on this level if he chose to do so.[26] Nevertheless, some philosophical learning is woven directly into the argument, usually as principles that confirm the author's positions. The treatise does not display a knowledge of Aristotelian philosophy greater than one would expect from a graduate of the university arts curriculum, but it incorporates well-known passages from the philosopher's works into its own arguments. To reinforce his view that a deaf person cannot know anything of music he reminds us 'ut dicit Aristoteles, cecus non syllogizat de coloribus'.[27] The author of the *Summa* proudly calls attention to his Aristotelian citations, but without specifying the works from which they are borrowed.

Although Page has searched the medieval Latin translations of Aristotle, he does not always cite the sources closest to the wording of the *Summa* and hence those presumably familiar to its author. Aristotle is summoned by the author to explain why the musical hand is an appropriate learning aid: it addresses the senses – sight and hearing – which are most 'teachable' (*disciplinares*). Page quotes the *Parva naturalia* of Aristotle as the source of this principle, but the beginning of the *Metaphysics* offers a far closer parallel to the concept as presented in the *Summa*.[28] In order to demonstrate that

'alluding to the fame of Corinth as a place of sophistication and luxury' (p. 128, n. 133) but as a reminder that not all can attain the supreme spiritual goal: the contemplative life exemplified by the biblical Martha.

[26] Among the chant treatises of this time only those of Johannes de Grocheo, writing for *iuvenes*, and Engelbert of Admont are imbued with Aristotelian philosophy and logical method. See J. Dyer, 'Chant Theory and Philosophy in the Late Thirteenth Century', *Cantus Planus: Fourth Meeting – Pécs, Hungary, 3–8 September 1988* (Budapest, 1992), pp. 99–118.

[27] 883. Cf. Aristotle, *Physica (translatio vaticana)*, i.1, ed. A. Mansion, Aristoteles Latinus vii/2 (Bruges and Paris, 1957), p. 24. As Page noticed (p. 79, n. 78), Aristotle claims exactly the opposite.

[28] See *Metaphysica*, ed. G. Vuillemin-Diem, Aristoteles Latinus xxv/1–1a (Leiden, 1970),

the mode of a piece which moves through more than one mode must be determined by its conclusion, the author alludes to the Aristotelian doctrine of causality: 'Finis est optimum in re, et item, Finis est cuius gratia' (1776–7). Both of these phrases refer to the final cause, the purpose for which something is done. Page cites a passage from the *Nichomachean Ethics* as the source of this allusion, but the verbal form of the passage in the *Summa* points more directly to Aristotle's best-known statements of the principle in the *Physics* (2.2) and the *Metaphysics* (1.3).[29] While the translation of (1) 'the final purpose is the best in a thing' in the passage above is consistent with this context, I would change (2) 'whose beauty is the final purpose' (p. 107) to 'the end is [that] for the sake of which'.

Ultimately, the accuracy and clarity with which technical matters are rendered into English are the standards by which any translation of a medieval treatise on music theory must be judged. The present translation of the *Summa musice* is generally reliable in this respect, reflecting quite well the presentation of both familiar concepts and the doctrines proper to this treatise. The translation of the prose section flows more easily than does the translation of the *metra*, in part because of the highly compressed, abstruse language of the hexameter couplets.

One of the principal obligations that the translator must impose upon himself is consistency in the rendering of technical vocabulary. Normally, variety of diction commends itself, but the author's train of thought cannot be followed if the translation does not reflect his terminology in every detail. Page makes judicious choices by allowing some words to remain in their Latin forms and by citing others in parenthesis when he feels the reader ought to have immediate information about the original terminology.

In two cases, however, a more rigorous control should have been exercised in following exactly the usage of the *Summa*. Of the two

---

p. 5. Engelbert of Admont cites the same passage in a different context: *De musica* 4.3; Gerbert, *Scriptores*, ii, p. 339b.

[29] 'Natura autem finis est et *cuius causa fit*; quorum enim continui motus existentis est aliquis finis motus, hoc ultimum est et *cuius causa fit*; unde et poeta derisorie apposuit dicere: "habet finem cuius quidem causa factus est"; vult enim *non omne esse ultimum finem, sed optimum.' Physica (translatio vetus)*, ed. F. Bossier and J. Brams, Aristoteles Latinus vii/1 (Leiden and New York, 1990), p. 53 (italics added). Cf. *Metaphysica* 1.3: 'the purpose and the good'. There is a later echo of this distinction when the author explains the *cauda* in chant by reference to the tail of an animal: 'et quia cauda finis est animalis, et finis ex re nomen habere videatur' (1852–3).

terms, *clavis* and *articulus*, the first is by far the more important, since the *Summa musice* develops the meaning of *clavis* more extensively than any other theoretical work of the Middle Ages; it is in fact one of the most original aspects of the entire treatise.[30] An initial clarification of four related terms will be helpful for this necessarily abbreviated discussion of *clavis*. In the usage of the treatise *littera* means one of the seven letter names (A–G); *nota/notula* signifies one of the hexachord degrees symbolised by a solmisation syllable. *Clavis* is the conjunction of letter and hexachord degree, identified by a letter name, but by no means identical with it. The *articulus* is the physical location of the *clavis* combination on the hand. Careful study of chapters 8–18, where *clavis* recurs frequently as an essential element of the author's system, offers convincing proof that this hierarchy is essentially correct. *Clavis* has other meanings as well: the *Summa* uses it sometimes in the sense of 'clef'.

The treatment of *clavis* in the *Summa* is likewise consistent with the use of the concept in thirteenth-century chant theory. According to a treatise that claims to transmit the teaching of Johannes de Garlandia 'gamma.ut in regula vel in linea habet unam clavem et unam vocem: G est clavis, ut est vox'.[31] The *Summa musice* takes this configuration for granted when it first introduces the term *clavis* in the discussion of the hand:

Dicti doctores decemnovem sedes notarum locaverunt in ipsis [joints of the fingers], unicuique nomen proprium assignantes compositum ex littera, que est nomen clavis, et nomine vel nominibus note vel notularum quam vel quas insinuat ipsa clavis. ... In pulpa itaque sive in fronte pollicis locaverunt sedem notabilem, id est note convenientem, et eam gammut Γ *ut* appellabant, quod dicitur compositum a Γ, quod est littera Greca que apud Latinos dicitur G quod est *clavis* illius articuli, et a nomine cuiusdam note que dicitur *ut*, que domestica est illi *clavi* (699–702; 707–12).

---

[30] Some clarification could have been provided by F. Reckow's article 'Clavis' in the *Handwörterbuch der musikalischen Terminologie*, a work not cited in the bibliography. Whether or not this aspect of the *Summa* is consistent with a date *c.* 1200 must await further study.

[31] *Introductio musice secundum Johannem de Garlandia*, ed. E. de Coussemaker, *Scriptorum de musica medii aevi nova series*, 4 vols. (Paris, 1864–7), I, p. 159a. Lambertus lists the letters from A to G, 'que etiam claves vocantur, quia sicut per clavem reseratur sera, ita per has litteras reseratur musice melodia'. *Tractatus de musica* (Coussemaker, *Scriptorum*, I, p. 254a). The *clavis* served as the focal point for mutation from one hexachord to another: 'mutatio est sub una clavi et eadem unisona transitio vocis in vocem' (Jerome of Moravia, *Tractatus de musica*, 12; ed. S. Cserba (Regensburg, 1935), p. 49). Earlier in the chapter Jerome called the *claves* 'litterarum combinationes'.

This clearly defines the composite nature of the *clavis*, composed of the letter name by which it is identified and the solmisation syllable or syllables proper to it. The remainder of the quotation ('in pulpa') initiates the careful description of each *clavis* in the system. Given my interpretation of this passage, I would translate 'domestica' as 'resident' rather than as 'handmaiden' (p. 73). In his commentary Page says that he will 'generally translate *littera* as "letter" and *clavis* as "note"'. While this solution is not entirely satisfactory, at the next two occurrences of the term (italicised in the passage quoted above) it is translated 'letter'. This equivalent is very frequently the one chosen in the translation, thus imposing a single English term on two concepts kept distinct in the Latin.

As might be surmised, difficulties arise when both *littera* and *clavis* occur in the same sentence, each with its own proper meaning. In the discussion of intervals the author explains that the two notes that form an octave will have different locations on the hand, but that 'unaqueque littera initialis articuli, que est clavis illius, habet aliam litteram sibi consimilem' (977–9). This is translated (correctly, I think) as 'the initial letter of any connective, that is to say its *clavis*, has another letter similar to it'. (Later in the sentence, however, *clavis* again becomes 'letter'.) In some contexts similar to this one (1125–36, 1141–6) neither 'letter' nor 'note' would make much sense and the translation adopts what I believe to be the only proper solution: the special term *clavis* itself. The word can also appear in a context in which 'letter' would produce a strained translation. For example, instrumental musicians, according to the author, place a semitone between F and G or between G and a, 'et clavem istam clavem falsam appellant'.[32] This lack of precision in the translation of this concept does not do justice to the author's carefully nuanced explanations, nor does it facilitate comparisons with other treatises that employ the *clavis* mechanism. Were text and translation not in separate sections of this volume the task of ascertaining the relationship between the two on points like this one would have been far easier.

Clavis should sometimes be understood as 'clef', as in these couplets from the *metrum* of chapter 8:

---

[32] 1430–1. I would translate 'and they call that *clavis* a false *clavis*' instead of 'they call this the "false" *clavis*' (p. 96). Cf. also 1447 and p. 97.

Linea vel spatium currit quasi pagina tota
Ut clavis docuit que non est clave remota.
Queritur in palma cur linea non variatur;
Pagina sepe tamen, cum scribitur, hoc patiatur (847–50).

Although the translator considers this a 'contorted passage', intended to have a 'riddling quality', it becomes less so, if it is understood that the clef is said to determine the pitch value of a staff line and that the pitch represented by the line changes if the clef does. The last couplet makes a comparison between the invariability of the musical hand and staff lines whose values change according to the clef.[33]

On a matter of lesser significance than the above, I was distracted by the translation 'connective' as the equivalent of *articulus*, a term frequently used in the context of the musical hand. While 'phalange' is the appropriate anatomical term, 'joint' (as used in the culinary arts, for instance) seems preferable to me. The author's methodical description of the hand (ch. 8) assigns the *claves* to individual segments of the finger (*pulpa, sinus, gremium*) and to the base (*radix*) of the finger, not to the point where the phalanges join one another.

While the publication of the *Summa musice* in a modern edition draws attention to an area of chant theory commonly neglected, the present translation, commentary and accompanying material have a number of shortcomings. The footnotes are often enlightening, particularly when the treatise delves into areas that fall within Page's sphere of interests, and the translation has indubitable merits in solving many puzzling aspects of a difficult text. It can also be very misleading, however, forcing the reader to make constant reference to the Latin original, a procedure made needlessly difficult by the format of the book. This valuable document deserves reissue with a consistently trustworthy translation (ideally on facing pages), commentary and editorial helps which draw out the full range of its teaching.

Joseph Dyer
University of Massachusetts at Boston

---

[33] *Summa musice*, pp. 77–8; cf. lines 1167–9 and 1181–4. I am aware that my interpretation would be more secure were 'pagina tota' accusative, a metrical impossibility at this point in the line.

Ellen Rosand, *Opera in Seventeenth-Century Venice: the Creation of a Genre.* Berkeley, Los Angeles and Oxford, University of California Press, 1991, xxvi+684 pp.

Title and subtitle define the high ambition that shapes Ellen Rosand's work. It is ambitious not in its manner – thorough-going rather than flamboyant – but in the conclusion it seeks to establish. Opera as a genre starts here: so the subtitle asserts, without a shadow of a question mark; and what starts it is not 'Venetian Opera', which might imply a local variant, but *Opera in Seventeenth-Century Venice*.

Opera in Venice (in practice between 1637 and 1678 rather than over the century as a whole) was, Rosand contends, *the* opera: 'What happened to opera in Venice during the seventeenth century was fundamental to the art itself: there and then, opera as we know it assumed its definitive identity – as a mixed theatrical spectacle available to a socially diversified, and paying, audience, a public art.' Rosand does not look at the possible competing claims of, for example, the Roman works on sacred subjects by Landi, Marazzoli and others, or the Paris *comédies-ballets* and early operas of Lully, except by implication when she points out that only in Venice in her chosen period could 'regular demand, dependable financial backing, and a broad and predictable audience' sustain a corpus of over 150 operas by twenty composers and about forty librettists, put on in nineteen theatres. The rapid establishment of a produc-tion routine, in other words, as well as of an agreed aesthetics, define the new genre more than does the achievement of any one work. If there is a key work it is not one of Monteverdi's operas but the Cavalli–Cicognini *Giasone*, which she sees as both embody-ing many traits common to the genre and marking a point of bal-ance in its evolution; the most obvious legacy of that evolution is the predominance of the prima donna.

Rosand's book, the culmination of twenty years' research, has also been given by its publisher a markedly ambitious format: 684 large-type pages, of which 211 are music examples, 39 extracts from Italian-language documents, and 13 bibliography, the whole weighing 3lb 10 oz. In every way it asks and deserves to be taken seriously as the definitive statement about early opera.

A paradox the book does not quite address is that the corpus of work it analyses and celebrates is largely unavailable to the modern audience. Compare the revival of Renaissance polyphony from Dufay to Victoria (actually a series of revivals stretching back to the early nineteenth century, if not earlier): a minority audience has all along been able to experience the genre by listening to or, better, taking part in *a cappella* singing or instrumental playing in small groups; nowadays it has the further resource of recordings, often put out in modest editions soon deleted. Rosand does say that 'given a chance to speak for themselves . . . seventeenth-century operas appear less archaic . . . than, until recently, we have been led to believe'. But the 'chance to speak' cannot depend on the Dolmetsch-like efforts of a few: it needs the expensive resources of opera houses.

In the revival of the past thirty years or so, have any of Rosand's 150-plus operas (other than those of Monteverdi) established themselves as works still fully alive in the theatre? The answer is a matter for critical judgment. I happen to think that, in the experience of audiences, even Cavalli has so far remained 'archaic'; others no doubt think differently. But if the works of Cavalli, Sacrati, Cesti, Sartorio and Boretti fail to achieve modern theatrical life as Monteverdi's surviving operas have, Rosand's study, however successful, will do no more than focus the academic endeavours of students able to read scores.

Her own approach is academic in a double sense: not only does she display a traditionally academic thoroughness in analysis and classification; she rightly takes a great deal of notice of the academic affiliations of early opera itself, in particular of early librettists' membership of the Accademia degli Incogniti, and of the ways in which the philosophical libertinism of that body influenced their practice and their debates. The book is impressively saturated in detailed knowledge of the surviving corpus of work (more often librettos with their cognate apologias and correspondence than complete scores). In comparison, opera as a performing art is somewhat neglected. We do not hear much about the technical development of singing, though it is part of the author's thesis that the singer's art gradually swamped the literary side of opera as the centre of interest. The whole visual side with its appeal to the sense of the 'marvellous' gets a serious look in only apropos of the five-year career of the Teatro Novissimo, an emanation of the Incogniti which launched the great scene designer Giacomo Torelli. This in turn has implications for the decline Rosand sees as having set in in the 1670s, which is in the first place a decline of the libretto as the controlling matrix of opera.

Here is another paradox: Rosand insists that 'opera has survived because it is essentially a popular art'; it matters to her case that opera in Venice was 'a business' and the audience for it a 'full spectrum' of Venetian society. There is a tension between the academicism of the early librettists, sometimes fairly esoteric, and the alleged breadth of the audience; it is not fully eased by the use of expressions like 'the Incogniti publicity machine', which seem anachronistic.

How broad is broad? How popular is popular? Clearly, the paying audience for opera in Venice from 1637 was broader and more popular than the audience invited to opera performances in cardinals' palaces in Rome. But Rosand's contention that the noble builders of Venice opera houses were in the first place interested in profit (with prestige a secondary consideration) seems unproven. What evidence there is suggests that they hoped not to make a loss – a significant difference, if what is at issue is the coming of a commercial outlook. About the social make-up of the audience we know little except that it included many upper-class persons (Venetian nobles and foreign tourists); the *volgo* in the stalls' can scarcely have been a 'full spectrum' given prices of admission that remained high until the price war of 1674–80 – partly outside Rosand's period, and treated by her as a symptom of decline.

To establish the commercial nature of opera production Rosand points, as others have, to the much reduced instrumental forces called for by Monteverdi's Venetian operas compared with his Mantuan *Orfeo*. Scenery and machines were no doubt also cheaper than in a court theatre (or at the extravagant Novissimo), but by how much? An answer might tell us a good deal about audiences' priorities. In general, Rosand may have relied too much on the celebrated papers of Marco Faustini, the only known collection of a seventeenth-century impresario's business correspondence. They do show, already in being at a remarkably early date (the 1650s–60s), the 'tripartite cooperative organisation' of proprietor, impresario and artist familiar as the norm in nineteenth-century Italy.

On the other hand, the view that 'the artists, who originally participated in the running of the theater . . . eventually became
employees of the impresario' may need to be qualified in the light
of further archival research. There is ample evidence that opera
management by an artists' cooperative was common in Venice
Ascension Fair seasons between 1730 and 1760.[1] This evidence,
dug out of notarial archives (a process not unlike looking for a
needle in a haystack), may well be found for earlier and later
periods, and show the Faustini model of organisation as one among
several.

Rosand's saturation in her 150-plus operas and in the surrounding literary evidence, admirable as it is, does not quite save
her from the usual pitfall of this approach, namely the assumption
that the status and value of opera rises and falls with whatever we
understand as the artistic integrity of its text. To begin with, as
she deals with the 1630s and 1640s, all is well, because that
assumption was the one normally made and acted upon at the
time. The librettist (reckoned to be an amateur) was the author,
the composer was an artisan, and even singers at times 'reassur-
ingly' complained if they were given their scenes piecemeal: they
too saw the integrity of the dramatic text as central. Change was
not quite linear, for Monteverdi and to some extent Cavalli were
part 'creators' even of the literary text, while later composers made
less difference. The real motor of change as Rosand sees it was
the increasing geographical separation of librettist, composer and
singer up to the start of rehearsals: 'paradoxically, the separation
of the singers from the actual creation of the work eventually
resulted in an increase in their final impact on it – or at least the
visibility of their impact'.

So far so good. Problems arise when Rosand comes close to
endorsing later academic – Arcadian – claims that the multiplica-
tion of arias, already detectable in Cicognini's *Giasone* of 1649, and
in full spate by the 1660s, was an abuse of the form. She is too
sophisticated to swallow whole the claims of literati (to be repeated
at intervals throughout the eighteenth century) that opera was
going to the dogs because singers' shenanigans were swamping
the genre's literary integrity. Thus she writes that the Arcadians

---

[1] See J. Rosselli, *Singers of Italian Opera: the History of a Profession* (Cambridge, 1992), pp. 88–9.

'eventually succeeded in promoting a restoration of literary standards to the "decadent" genre', the quotation marks around 'decadent' avoiding a direct commitment; she shrewdly points out that
the acceptance by the 1660s of the term *dramma per musica* as the
norm showed librettists themselves admitting that their texts were
not self-sufficient.

Yet she holds up Sartorio's *Orfeo* of 1673 – the mythical hero
turned into a conventional jealous husband at the heart of an
erotic-sensational plot – as exemplifying 'the erosion of operatic
decorum', and the rise of plagiarism (sometimes of whole arias) as
'symptomatic of the decline of the genre' because it showed up a
loss of musico-dramatic specificity. Are we sure that musico-
dramatic specificity was what audiences looked for in opera performances? According to Berlioz (in 1830) it was the last thing on
Italian operagoers' minds; maybe 1680 was not very different. By
concentrating as much as she has on texts, at the expense of the
element of performance, Rosand has in effect left the notion of
'decline', based on a literary judgment, as the only possible interpretation of what happened to opera in Venice from the 1670s,
qualify it though she may here and there.

Texts are what we have; performance tends to evaporate. In her
dealings with texts Rosand is remarkably, at times exhaustively
informative, for instance about the many allusions to the history,
the pre-eminence, or just the local gossip and in-jokes of Venice.
(She may however exaggerate the decline of the habit from the
1670s, supposedly a token of the europeanisation of the genre: flat-
tering allusions to the Venetian foundation myth were inserted by
Metastasio into *Ezio* (1728) and by Solera into *Attila* (1846), both
for performance in Venice; there are probably other, less well-
known examples, for if one thing is clear about the history of Italian
opera it is audiences' tolerance, indeed appetite for *topoi* only
gradually adapted over time).

She particularly fastens on the long debate about verisimilitude
in opera, which went on throughout the period and well beyond
her terminal date. We may think it at first sight puzzling that
writers and composers worried so much about the verisimilitude
of making people sing formal songs or arias on stage when they
seem to have been ready to admit without much argument the
exchange of sung dialogue (or verse); but they did.

The art of equivocation cultivated by the Incogniti, Rosand

brings out, helped them to find ingenious excuses not only for these operatic procedures but for others which breached the so-called Aristotelian unities. Even then it was for many years important to justify formal arias as actual songs, or as utterances by characters out of the ordinary (gods, nymphs, madmen, shepherds) or too 'low' for their utterance to matter (comic servants) or in appropriate states (sleep, dreaming, soliloquy, in the end a more general 'emotional overflow'). The debate was elaborate and prolonged, and Rosand shows convincingly that Cavalli, for one, at times avoided for the sake of verisimilitude cues for arias dropped by his librettist. Even when faced with a strophic text he would set part of it as recitative and take to closed forms only where the words provided strong motivation of the kind just outlined: 'there is often more "music" in the recitative than in the arias'. It might be as well, all the same, not to rule out of these debates an element of coquetry or play.

Rosand spends much time on the taxonomy of arias – comic, 'trumpet', affect-driven, love duets, sleep scenes, invocations and mad scenes, most of them with obvious descendants in the practice of later opera – and on the gradual progress of the aria towards the *da capo* model. The use of *sdrucciolo* (dactylic) line-endings in invocations 'apparently appealed to something quite fundamental in human experience', in German as well as in Italian; 'the domination of the rhythm gives the sense that the character is being ruled by an urgent force over which he or she has no control'. English is not very helpful here: dactylic endings mark something as little ominous as Hood's 'Take her up tenderly,/fashioned so slenderly'; the *sdrucciolo* ending of a (very short) line in Italian may be identified with the sinister or awe-inspiring chiefly because it promotes a jagged musical setting.

A separate chapter deals with the lament, for which Arianna's in Monteverdi's opera of 1608 gave the 'paradigm for close to half a century', while his 'Lamento della Ninfa' supplied the cliché of the descending minor tetrachord ostinato and the combination of form and unpredictability within a strophic context. Rosand has found a delightful episode that might be called Pirandellian if it were not characteristically baroque in its play with illusion: a singer used an operatic lament to denounce and curse her successful rival in love.

And then? Oddly for a book on 'the creation of a genre',

Rosand's no more inquires into the development of opera after 1678 than it does into putative rival schools before that date. In 1679 the young Alessandro Scarlatti's operas began to be performed, mainly in Rome and Naples; of his eventual total output (between sixty and seventy) only two were written for Venice. His and other composers' works current on the influential 'ducal circuit' (Parma, Modena, Mantua, Pratolino, Florence, Livorno) either side of 1700 were only in varying degrees rooted in the Venetian system of opera production. Venice, it is true, remained the busiest centre of operatic creative activity in Italy down to 1797, and one of the three most important down to 1860. We are presumably to take it that because opera in Venice between 1637 and 1678 was an activity dense, continuous and self-aware the descent of all later opera from it obviously follows. Such an assumption depends in part on one's acceptance of the still vital, non-'archaic' character of the operas then produced; in part on a genetic conception of the history of art forms (with, possibly, Darwinian overtones of the survival of the fittest) which not everyone will think the most illuminating.

John Rosselli
Cambridge

JOHN M. WARD, *Music for Elizabethan Lutes*. 2 vols., Oxford, Clarendon Press, 1992, vol. I (text), xiii+158 pp.; vol. II (music), xi+173 pp.

For over forty years John Ward has been publishing articles of great importance for the study of secular music in Tudor and Stuart England. As every grateful reader knows, they belong to a genre of their own. Ward's method is to take some manuscript or printed source, or a particular repertory, and explore its nature and purpose not merely in general terms but by following up the provenance, context, concordances and cognates of every piece, any one of which may become the root of a fresh tree of knowledge sprouting its own profusion of shoots, suckers and runners. By the end an unexpected piece of musical history, often with the most varied implications, will have been built up, while for the patient student the footnotes amount to a work of reference in themselves.

A collected edition of Ward's articles with a comprehensive index, although a formidable undertaking, would be of untold value.

The new study, the largest that Ward has published, is essentially an assemblage of smaller ones on the familiar pattern, and in certain respects an understanding of its evolution is important to the reader. An account of this appears in the preliminaries, rather surprisingly as part of the acknowledgments; it is easily missed if interest has been kindled by an initial glance at the list of chapter headings. The present reviewer, with more enthusiasm than caution, plunged straight into the main text at page 1 and in due course suffered the consequences. The prospect offered is clear enough. Opening and closing chapters on Philip van Wilder, 'luter' to Henry VIII and Edward VI, and John Johnson, luter to Queen Elizabeth, are bridged by a roughly chronological series of studies of the manuscripts containing the intervening lute repertory. There follow seven appendices, the commentary to the 154 music examples in the second volume (most of them complete pieces), the bibliography and index.

For some thirty years van Wilder was held in the highest esteem by his royal employers. Ward gives an account of his life which supplements without superseding his article in *The New Grove Dictionary*, discusses the few pieces with ascriptions that might be intended to indicate his authorship, and concludes that only one is likely to be his. Even though no English lute manuscripts of his time survive it is strange that more of his music is not found in later copies; perhaps he preferred not to write it down for fear of its falling into the wrong playing or transcribing hands. At all events the chances of history have diminished his perceptible impact to that of one of the long succession of immigrant musicians who must have introduced the continental songs and dances found in the earliest sources. These are not the work of professionals but compilations made by amateurs.

The first four belong to the late 1550s or the 1560s: London, British Library, MSS Stowe 389 (the Raphe Bowle manuscript) and Royal Appendix 58; Washington, Folger Shakespeare Library, MS V.a.159 (sometimes misleadingly called the Giles Lodge manuscript); and Yale University Library, James Marshall and Marie-Louise Osborn Collection, Music MS 13 (the Osborn commonplace-book, often known as the Braye manuscript). Ward adopts the same procedure for each: after provenance, make-up, scribal features and so on he discusses subjects of particular interest raised by the contents and appends an annotated complete inventory. Where a piece appears in the music examples there may be further information in the commentary. The examples themselves do not follow the order in the manuscripts, but are drawn from a far wider range of sources and proceed in step with the discussions that they serve to illustrate. Quite often a piece may be relevant to more than one topic, or to different aspects of the same topic which arise in connection with different manuscripts, so that not all related examples can be grouped in one place and the reader is kept dodging from one end of the music volume to the other. That is no great hardship, but something much more disconcerting happens when the Osborn manuscript is reached. Here references to music examples dry up altogether, at least for items in the manuscript itself. They are not to be found in the text, nor the footnotes, nor the inventory. The transcriptions will be discovered only by chance, perhaps by way of the index, grouped exceptionally in one block and in manuscript order as Examples 74–125, and placed beyond examples relevant to manuscripts discussed later in the text. True, there is a cross-head before Example 74, but nothing encourages a consecutive reading of the examples that might bring it to notice. The first thing that anyone lucky enough to own a copy of the book needs to do is to write the example numbers against the 52 numbers in the inventory of the manuscript, and the inventory numbers against the examples and the commentary on them. Only then can this section of the text be read.

How did the confusion arise? The answer appears in the acknowledgments. Originally Ward planned to publish an edition of the Osborn book on its own:

During the time spent brooding on an edition, it became obvious that the importance of the Osborn commonplace-book . . . would best be shown if the pieces were placed in context. Thus what began as a smallish anthology of mid-century music for the lute, gittern, and guitar has become a much larger one and the introductory essay a short history of music for plucked stringed instruments (the cittern apart) from the accession of Elizabeth I in 1558 to the last decade of the sixteenth century.

In fact the book would have been, and to some extent still is, a companion piece to Ward's invaluable edition of the Dublin Virginal Manuscript, which similarly includes a great number of additional transcriptions from outside the source, providing context and in many cases making available important material not printed elsewhere. The two editions also resemble one another in their propensity to keep growing, but whereas the Dublin one has expanded through three published versions the Osborn edition has undergone its partial metamorphosis into a 'short history' in private.

In the event it is not only the Osborn manuscript that is transcribed complete: though scattered, the whole contents of the Folger book accompany it, along with nearly everything from the two British Library manuscripts and a few odd pieces rounded up from minor sources of the same period. Thus almost the whole lute, gittern and guitar repertories recorded in English sources up to about 1570 are included. Beyond this point Ward is obliged to be much more selective, both in his choice of manuscripts for discussion and the number of examples he can give. The Willoughby manuscript (Nottingham, University Library, MS Mi LM 16, sometimes called the Lord Middleton lute book after its present owner) represents the continuing amateur tradition in the 1570s and 1580s. Ward remarks that it was a long time in the making, and suggests it was begun about 1570. That seems a little early for two reasons: one of the first pieces is an early work of John Johnson, whose date of birth Ward himself places tentatively at about the time when Bowle was copying his book (1558), and only a few pages later there is a 'Pauyon philips' that Ward does not print but advances persuasive arguments for assigning to Peter Philips, who was not born until 1560 or 1561. However, the point does not greatly affect the date of the music copied. Of about the same period is Edinburgh, University Library, MS Dc.5.125, the last manuscript to be fully described. It differs from most others in being largely the work of professionals, the most prominent of whom seems to have been an Italian in English employment. These last two manuscripts, together with the Marsh book, of which a much briefer but very useful account is worked in, provide the immediate background to the music of John Johnson, the first of the important English lute composers.

The wealth of varied information hung upon this framework is not easily summarised. Every scrap of documentation about the instruments, their importation, cost, maintenance and tunings, and the methods of playing them is garnered, with speculation about how the techniques required by particular gittern or guitar pieces may indicate for which instrument they were primarily intended. The hand of each scribe and his repertory are scrutinised in an attempt to decipher his nationality, his amateur or professional status, his musical preferences or those of his patron, the meaning of any special markings he may employ, and the extent to which a sketchy or apparently incomplete tablature may have provided all that was necessary for much more accomplished music-making.

One of the most important elements in the book derives from Ward's perennial fascination with the tunes, grounds and harmonic patterns that shade into one another in the tangled international network of popular music, and as ever he calls on an extraordinarily comprehensive knowledge of the sources in tracing their relationships. His method is not to try to define the musical characteristics associated with particular titles too narrowly, but the more instructive one of gathering together concordances and cognates from English sources in much broader families, showing how stock formulae were affected by aural transmission and musical practice. Perhaps some of these families become a little over-extended: a journey from Walsingham that ends up in Searching for Lambs could eventually round up a virtually limitless flock, and the list of medleys might almost have included itself. But it is, of course, their exhaustiveness that gives these compilations their immense value. Whether or not they are linked to discussions in the text their preferred position in the book takes the form of footnotes to the inventory of John Johnson's works that forms one of the appendices. Where Johnson provides no suitable peg they are fitted into manuscript inventories or the commentaries to music examples. This arrangement causes difficulties of various kinds, which two examples will serve to illustrate.

In the inventory of Johnson's works, pavans on the two *passamezzo* basses are placed separately from the galliards, and consequently the very extensive lists of other settings are similarly split; in the process, settings of the *passamezzo moderno* in neither pavan nor galliard form have been omitted altogether. The second example concerns a dance – one that the reader is led. The list of *passamezzo antico* settings that excludes galliards contains some eighty settings in English sources. Although it includes other variant forms of the bass the *romanesca* is not mentioned: having a name of its own it has its own list which with perseverance may be tracked down in the commentary to Example 91. Here the variant of the bass known as 'Tinternel' or the 'Short Alman' is represented only by a reference to a vocal version (Example 11). In fact Johnson made two settings, and back in his inventory there is a highly informative footnote about 'Tinternel', with Ward's own gist of the bass and discant and a similar gist of 'Ruggiero' for comparison. Yet even here no mention is made of Examples 67b and c, which give slightly different and equally valid gists of the same two patterns, though a chain of references might eventually lead to them, and on the way to a third gist of 'Tinternel' connected with the vocal version. In cases like this readers have no reason to suspect at any given point that there is more to discover; otherwise a search in the two indices, intelligently and knowledgeably made by Tim Crawford, would cut most of the corners, though not quite all. In addition it must be said that reading is frequently hindered by wrong cross-references, duplication of information in different places with minor variations, and other muddles (compare, for instance, the linked examples 86, 110, 129 and 143 with their commentaries).

The amateur lute anthologies of the mid-century include, as Ward emphasises, few pieces of intrinsic value, but they shed light beyond the limited field that first meets the eye. One important recurrent theme, raised by numerous arrangements, is that of song; it is dealt with primarily in the discussions of the Bowle and Osborn manuscripts (the latter including a special section with an inventory on the songs in British Library, Add. MS 4900), and three appendices, devoted respectively to music known to have been associated with verses in Tottel's *Miscellany* of 1557, the tunes in the lost Wynn copy of it, and settings of Wyatt and Surrey, one of whose poems is allotted the equivalent of a further appendix in the commentary to Example 104. Ward distinguishes two kinds of ballad setting. Tunes in what he calls court ballad style, which are associated with verse from Tottel's collection and poetry by Surrey (but scarcely with Wyatt's, which he believes to have been rarely sung), were apparently often devised for a particular poem. They call little attention to themselves, being in the nature of 'word carriers' or *modi da cantar*: some of Henry VIII's songs belong to the same tradition. By contrast the city or street ballads of the broadsheets were framed to already popular tunes with a life of their own.

This distinction cannot, of course, be pushed too far: both kinds of tune might take the form of discants to stock harmonic patterns, and the court melodies could, like those for broadside ballads or metrical psalms, serve for more than one set of verses, something that their rather uniform character encouraged. By the 1570s these recitation schemes had been ousted by the livelier popular tunes, and by the more distinctive melodies of the consort song. With the help of arrangements of consort songs and even of extracts from church polyphony the lute song advanced towards the more developed form of its best achievements. But singers of both lute and consort songs still needed to preserve the old skill of fitting any irregularity in a succession of verses into the unvarying melodic pattern put before them. On other kinds of vocal music, however, the lute manuscripts are silent. They offer no help in bridging the gap between the more complex Henrician court songs and the relatively simple part-songs represented in the Mulliner book (British Library, Add. MS 30513), nor the one that separates the latter from those published by Byrd in 1589.

Among the single-strain genres that tend to fade from view after the 1560s are not only song arrangements but a wide variety of dances and the like, many with obscure titles. These offer a challenge to Ward that he tackles with boundless curiosity and energy. To take a single example, two versions of the tune known in Britain as 'John come kiss me now', one on each of the *passamezzo* grounds but both entitled 'The Antick', launch an essay of extraordinary scope (as the commentary to Example 105) covering the tune, the uses of the words 'antick' and 'buffons' and the dances or dance-like activities associated with them, and lists of innumerable pieces under these titles in English and foreign sources with details of their melodies and basses; two side issues, the 'Matachins' and 'Le Forze d'Ercole', are pursued further two numbers later in the commentary. Such unpretentious pieces as these were naturally favoured by amateurs, and it is significant that the Osborn scribe, clearly a more proficient player than his fellows in the 1560s, already included more dances in several strains and even pieces by Francesco da Milano and Narvaez. Both these composers reappear in the Willoughby book, where the dances are restricted to pavans, galliards and almans but graced with written-out decorated repeats, as was to become usual.

By the 1570s, of course, Italian lute music had long been in circulation. From 1555 to 1578 the only designated luter at court was Anthony de Countie, a Milanese about whom Ward provides a substantial amount of biographical information. No music by him is known, except possibly an 'Anthony Pauyn' (which, as is pointed out, might equally well be by one of the Anthony Bassanos), one of a small number of obviously Italian dance pieces that bring a new harmonic richness to the repertory. A sample of what local Italians had to offer is provided by the large contribution to the Edinburgh manuscript of a professional Italian scribe who may also have been a composer; it consists entirely of fantasias, intabulations of vocal music and galliards. Ward is scathing about his contributions in the first two categories, but remarks that 'Elizabethan lutenist-composers, probably for social as much as artistic reasons, neither intabulated vocal music nor cultivated the fantasia and related forms'. He does not specify the social pressures involved, but if he himself can see the weaknesses of the potential models (as Byrd, in slightly different contexts, made it clear in musical terms that he did) it is hard to see why lutenists should be denied all power of independent thought or action.

At all events, for whatever reason they showed other preferences, one of their number being de Countie's successor as royal luter, John Johnson, whose work Ward sees as the culmination of this phase of English lute music. They took enthusiastically to the pavan and galliard, composing freely as well as on standard harmonic schemes. One of the attractions here may have been the variation element entailed in the repeats, for, as Ward emphasises, the English predilection for variations goes back a long way, especially in the form of discants on short grounds known as hornpipes and dumps: a hornpipe for lute is mentioned as early as 1474. Although founded in an international improvising technique, written examples from England differ markedly in their formal processes from their continental counterparts, whether they employ indigenous or international basses. The English used instrumental virtuosity to articulate the structure, in a long piece such as the

237

'Dump philli' by grouping variations into contrasting sections, in others by gràdually quickening movement before a final return to the quieter manner of the opening. Ward demonstrates the point tellingly by comparing the Duke of Somerset's Dump with similar pieces by Capirola and Neusidler, and an English setting of 'Conde claros' with one by Morlaye. The same procedures are, of course, a feature of the well-known Aston Hornpipe and My Lady Carey's Dump for keyboard, and they were greatly developed by Byrd. What the lute books bring home is how deeply ingrained they were in English practice as a means of providing a lengthy textless piece with strong continuity and a sense of beginning, middle and end. It was a good legacy, capable of extension to quite different modes of composition and instrumental textures.

Nearly half of Johnson's surviving output consists of grounds, treated for the most part in the discant tradition. The style fell out of favour with the next generation of lutenists, but Ward, while finding Johnson's examples uneven in quality, has high praise for the best. Unfortunately he has room to print only one of them, and only two other complete pieces. Although he adds some more fragmentary or schematic music examples to clarify his discussions, some of the latter go into considerable detail and seem to presuppose that readers will have a complete text before them. And in fact that is clearly what he intends, for under his name in the bibliography appear two publications too hopefully dated 1991, one of which is a complete edition of Johnson's lute music. The other, a volume of Elizabethan tablatures in facsimile, also supplements the present book, which can thus be seen to take its place as yet one more instalment, albeit an exceptionally rich one, in Ward's perpetual work in progress. Long may it continue.

Oliver Neighbour
London

BLAKE WILSON, *Music and Merchants: the Laudesi Companies of Republican Florence*. Oxford, Clarendon Press, 1992, xv+298 pp.

Lay religious confraternities have for the last few decades become an important subject of investigation by Italian historians. Perhaps the best-known example to the English-speaking world is Brian

Pullan's *Rich and Poor in Renaissance Venice*. Over the past twenty years this classic book, together with the numerous studies of Dominican confraternities by Father G. G. Meersseman, has inspired both social and ecclesiastical historians of the Anglo-Saxon and Italian academic communities.[1] Conference proceedings and monographs have now appeared about confraternities in many parts of Italy, but the most favoured centres remain Florence and Venice, where they provide grist for the mill of Renaissance scholarship.[2] The very nature of Renaissance studies has led more recently to the emergence of studies of confraternities by historians from other disciplines. For example, the monographs by Patricia Fortini Brown and Samuel Edgerton have examined confraternal patronage of art, while an increasing number of articles have appeared on particular confraternity commissions.[3] Historians of literature have quarried fraternity records for evidence of the vernacular religious poetry, the *lauda*, and the sacred drama mounted for public festivals.[4] Musicologists have also for some time been interested in the music of late medieval and Renaissance confraternities, whether it is in the context of the more general surveys of Nino Pirrotta and Giulio Cattin or the detailed studies of Cyrilla Barr and Frank D'Accone of late medieval Florence.[5]

[1]   B. Pullan, *Rich and Poor in Renaissance Venice: the Social Institutions of a Catholic State to 1620* (Oxford, 1971); G. G. Meersseman, *Ordo fraternitatis: confraternite e pietà dei laici nel medioevo* (Rome, 1977); R. F. E. Weissman, *Ritual Brotherhood in Renaissance Florence* (New York and London, 1982); J. Henderson, 'Piety and Charity in Late Medieval Florence' (Ph.D. dissertation, University of London, 1983), and now under the same title (Oxford, 1993); R. Mackenney, *Tradesman and Traders: the World of the Guilds in Venice and Europe, c. 1250– c. 1650* (London, 1987).

[2]   L. Fiorani, ed., 'Le confraternite romane: esperienza religiosa, società, committenza artistica', *Ricerche Storiche per la Storia di Roma*, 5 (1984); *Le mouvement confraternel au moyen-âge: France, Italie, Suisse*, Collection de l'École Française de Rome 97 (Rome, 1987); T. V. Verdon and J. Henderson, eds., *Christianity and the Renaissance* (Syracuse, NY, 1990), part 2.

[3]   P. Fortini Brown, *Venetian Narrative Painting in the Age of Carpaccio* (New Haven and London, 1988); S. Edgerton, *Pictures and Punishment: Art and Criminal Procedure during the Florentine Renaissance* (Ithaca and London, 1985).

[4]   See the classic A. d'Ancona, *Origini del teatro italiano* (Turin, 1891 edn), but more recently N. Newbigin, ed., *Nuovo corpus di sacre rappresentazioni fiorentini del Quattrocento* (Bologna, 1983), and C. Barr, 'Music and Spectacle in Confraternity Drama of Fifteenth-Century Florence: the Reconstruction of a Theatrical Event', in *Christianity and the Renaissance*, ed. Verdon and Henderson, pp. 376–404.

[5]   N. Pirrotta, *Music and Culture in Italy from the Middle Ages to the Baroque* (Cambridge, 1984), and G. Cattin, *Music of the Middle Ages* (Cambridge, 1986); C. Barr, *The Monophonic Lauda and the Lay Religious Confraternities of Tuscany and Umbria in the Late Middle Ages* (Kalamazoo, MI, 1988); F. D'Accone, 'Alcune note sulle compagnie fiorentine dei laudesi durante il Quattrocento', *Rivista Italiana di Musicologia*, 10 (1967), pp. 38–76, and

It is, then, within the context of the existing work of historians of art, religion and society on the one hand, and of music on the other, that we must place Blake Wilson's *Music and Merchants*. In this six-chapter book, Wilson examines the musical activities of the *laudesi* companies in relation to their devotional-liturgical history, and then assesses their contribution to the musical life of Trecento and Quattrocento Florence. The first and last chapters seek to place the *laudesi* companies within the wider social, religious and political context. Inevitably Wilson relies extensively here on other historians and adds little which is significantly new to our knowledge of the subject. Indeed by adopting unquestioningly one of the standard clichés of the historiography of the friars – that the Franciscans and Dominicans justified wealth[6] – the author provides himself with the title and theme of his book, namely that it was the 'merchant culture' of late medieval Florence which imbued confraternities with their distinctive character. This is an unfortunate phrase because of its restrictive nature and although justified in a footnote (p. 2 n. 5) does give a misleading impression. For confraternities, as Ronald Weissman has shown, attracted a wide range of members from throughout the guild community, a catchment area which was extended gradually from the second half of the fifteenth century to include the *sottoposti*, who had traditionally been regarded as too potentially seditious to be involved.[7] It is when Wilson moves from the wider political or economic context towards concentrating on the lauds produced by the companies themselves that he is at his strongest. In chapter 1, for example, he discusses the thematic link between lauds and sermons, showing how influential were the friars in providing the devotional style of the *laudesi* companies.

The four central chapters of this book deal instead with the internal activities of these groups. The first (chapter 2: 'Lauda-

---

'Le compagnie dei laudesi durante l'Ars Nova', *L'Ars nova italiana del Trecento* (Certaldo, 1970), pp. 253–80.

[6] B. Rosenwein and L. K. Little, 'Social Meaning in the Monastic and Mendicant Spiritualities', *Past and Present*, 63 (1974), pp. 4–32; L. K. Little, *Religious Poverty and the Profit Economy in Medieval Europe* (London, 1978); and on the Florentine context: L. R. Lesnick, 'Dominican Preaching and the Creation of a Capitalist Ideology in Late-Medieval Florence', *Memorie Domenicane*, new ser., 8–9 (1977–8), pp. 199–247. See more recently for some salutary remarks on this theme: D. D'Avray, *The Preaching of the Friars: Sermons diffused from Paris before 1300* (Oxford, 1985), pp. 217–19.

[7] Weissman, *Ritual Brotherhood*, pp. 37, 163–4.

Singing and the Laudesi Company') sets out the origins and structure of the companies and goes on to outline their main types of
services. Although much of this is already well known,[8] an interesting contribution is the discussion of the Lenten period. Wilson
shows how the evening services became penitential in character,
encouraged by 'phenomenal preaching activity' every evening in
the case of the largest companies of S. Zanobi at the cathedral and
Orsanmichele. At the same time their musical life intensified with
the hiring of professional singers to sing the Passion and Lament
of the Virgin. Long poems on the Passion in the form of sonnets
and *canzoni* were composed by poets such as Antonio Pucci, well
known for their composition of more secular lyrics. It would also
have been interesting to know if the nature of this penitential activity changed over time, whether, as in the case of the flagellant
companies, it became more emphasised under the influence of the
Observant movement of the late Trecento and Quattrocento.

Chapters 3 and 5 break away from the organisation of the other
sections. Instead of the more general discussion of chapters 1 and
2, we are treated to a short history of each major *laudesi* company
in the city, which, in common with chapter 5, reads more like a
catalogue and would have been best summarised in chronological
form, referring the reader to an appendix containing more detailed
histories. Instead we are provided with a blow-by-blow account of
when each company is recorded as having first sung *laudi*, when
it first employed professional singers and musicians, and when
polyphonic performance was first introduced. Chapter 5, which
adopts the Trexlerian title of 'Ritual Space and Imagination',
examines each company's relationship with its altarpiece and identifies the location of its chapel. Despite the catalogue presentation,
both chapters do provide interesting information along the way.
Chapter 3 discusses the extraordinary musical life of the largest and
most affluent confraternity, that of the Madonna at Orsanmichele,
including the company's involvement with the wider ecclesiastical
and communal context: the employment of the commune's pipers
and trumpeters at major civic festivals, such as that of St Anne,
and of the papal singers in 1413. Moreover, we also learn about
two other subjects: what might be dubbed the 'professionalisation'

[8]   Cf. the articles of D'Accone mentioned above and Henderson, *Piety and Charity*, ch. 3.

of the musical life of these voluntary groups, and the abandonment of ferial services in the fifteenth century, when they concentrated more of their resources on their festivals and commemorative services, both underwritten increasingly by bequests.

Chapter 4, which is the most original section, develops this theme further by outlining the development of performance practice and discusses some of the major singers and instrumentalists employed by Florentine *laudesi* companies. Four main periods are identified. First, there is the poorly documented late Duecento, when amateur members sang monophonic lauds. This, together with the second period, the Trecento to the early Quattrocento, is portrayed as the golden age of monophony. Evidence is drawn mainly from *Laudari* and payments to singers. The beautifully illuminated and notated *Laudari*, which were in effect the lay equivalent of the clergy's service books, have survived for a handful of Florentine companies, the most famous of which are those belonging to the *laudesi* of S. Egidio and S. Spirito. Account books have also provided an invaluable source for Wilson, as they did for Frank D'Accone and Cyrilla Barr before him. He has shown that the majority of *laudesi* groups employed two or three singers, although the two largest, that of S. Zanobi in the cathedral and Orsanmichele, went in for larger choirs as well as instrumentalists, including players of the lute and rebec. Orsanmichele emerges at this time as particularly significant as the centre of a public cult of not just the Virgin Mary but also St Anne, who, following the banishment of the tyrannical Duke of Athens in 1343, had become the special advocate of Florence. The company was unusual in having an organ in its oratory, and the best-known of its organists was the composer Francesco Landini.

In this discussion emphasis is placed on the secular rather than ecclesiastical roots of monophonic lauds, especially through their reliance on the popular form of the ballata. The late Trecento was already seeing the beginning of the change which came to dominate the performance practices of the majority of *laudesi* companies in the Quattrocento: the move away from monophonic to polyphonic performance with the employment of a growing number of singers, and in this third period, *c.* 1415–70, the *lauda* came to reflect the more general movements in the worlds of both music and poetry. The mid Quattrocento is seen as the most prolific period for the production of lauds, especially through the influence of the poet Feo Belcari. In particular Wilson hypothesises that Belcari may have been the link between the Venetian *lauda* tradition associated closely with Giustiniani's more florid style and the developing performance practices of Florentine lauds, although it is surely wrong to refer to the Venetian Scuole Grandi as '*laudesi* companies' (p. 167). Belcari was, in fact, a key figure in the Florentine confraternal world because he was a member of a large number of companies and also of the Medici circle.[9] Indeed it would have been interesting if Wilson had teased out further the exact connections between the Medici, confraternities and the musical life of mid to late Quattrocento Florence, especially under Lorenzo, who himself joined many of the more prominent confraternities and was a composer of *laudi* and *canti carnascialeschi* and the author of *sacre rappresentazioni* performed by religious companies.

The final period discussed in this book, *c.* 1470–1570, saw the extension of two important trends: the employment of more musicians and the development of larger polyphonic choirs of *sovrani* and *tenoristi*. In this way Florentine *laudesi* companies provided the musical environment within which local composers, such as Bernardo Pisano and Francesco de Layolle, would have received training. Once again the close relationship between secular and sacred traditions is emphasised, especially in the post-Savonarolan period, when poets such as Castellano Castellani helped to reinforce the links between the *laudesi* repertory and the carnival songs. It was within the contest of this creative relationship that we see the emergence of the newer three-and four-part style. It might also be pointed out that it was precisely this period which saw the emergence of the patrician carnivalesque fraternities of the Diamante and Broncone as well as the circulation of parodies of fraternity statutes by such prominent writers as Niccolò Machiavelli.[10] The wider background to these changes in the late Quattrocento and Cinquecento are further explored in the concluding chapter, when, as Ronald Weissman has shown, confraternities went initially through a period of crisis, reflecting the demographic and

[9]   See D. Kent, 'The Buonomini di S. Martino: Charity for the "glory of god, the honour of the city, and the commemoration of myself"', in *Cosimo 'il Vecchio' de' Medici, 1389–1464*, ed. F. Ames-Lewis (Oxford, 1992), pp. 49–67.
[10] See Henderson, *Piety and Charity*, ch. 10.

political problems of the period 1490 to 1530. But confraternities then came under the influence of the centralising tendencies of the church (and the Medici grand dukes), reflected in the shift away from the employment of lay to clerical singers, just as they came to be based more squarely on the parish with the Counter-Reformation emphasis on the parochial devotions of the Quarantore and the Rosary.[11]

This is a book with an eccentric structure, which does, however, contain useful elements, particularly the discussion of the wider literary and musical context for the lauds produced by Florentine devotional companies. New information is also undoubtedly added concerning the identity and employment of singers and instrument-alists by *laudesi* companies. The fifty-two-page appendix also adds additional information and documentation concerning a variety of topics, though in the process reinforcing the impression of the book as a catalogue: extracts from *laudesi* company documents cited in the text, a list of the types of available documentation, a profile of the singers as listed in the 1427 Catasto, a list of the companies' documents, and a series of musical examples.

John Henderson
Wolfson College, Cambridge

[11] Weissman, *Ritual Brotherhood*, ch. 6; C. F. Black, *Italian Confraternities in the Sixteenth Century* (Cambridge, 1989).